THE ART OF CONJECTURE

The Art of Conjecture

Bertrand de Jouvenel

Translated from the French by Nikita Lary

BASIC BOOKS, INC., PUBLISHERS

New York

© 1967 by Basic Books, Inc.
Library of Congress Catalog Card Number: 67–12649
Manufactured in the United States of America
Designed by Sophie Adler

Originally published in French for *Futuribles* by Éditions du
Rocher under the title *L'Art de la conjecture*.

HELENÆ
*stet sicut arbor super
flumina dierum*

Preface

It has become customary that commissions of experts meet to reply to questions like the following: what will be the population of the country, or even of our planet,[1] in 10, 15 or 25 years, or indeed at the end of the century? What will be its composition in age categories, its regional distribution, its concentration of urban agglomerations? In what proportion will production have increased, what modifications will its composition and utilizations have undergone? How will the consumption of energy have been augmented, and in what forms? And equally for raw materials: where will these natural resources be obtained, and with what changes in the channels of trade?[2]

Such questions are habitually classified under the headings of demographic and economic forecasts.[3] They naturally give rise to others, commonly called social forecasts. Thus one will examine the explosion of the cities caused by the swelling of the manpower supply, their extension and the specialization of administrative, commercial, industrial and residential zones, the growing volume of the daily flow of transportation resulting from the separation of place of domicile and work. One will look for what changes in the structure of the job market will be entailed in the assumed progress in production and what corresponding changes may be expected in the structure of job qualifications, itself tied to progress in education. One will wonder to what new rhythm the discipline of work will be reduced and in what proportions the different forms of reduction will take place: shortening of the work week, lengthening of annual vacations, beginning work at a more advanced age, longer life after retirement; one will wonder what use will be made of this leisure time, important for the amount of consumption, but determinant especially of the quality of civilization. These are already trite topics of social prevision.

But how can we envision great social transformations—and particularly rapid ones in technologically backward countries—without considering problems of arrangements placed before the public authorities, difficulties created for them by awakened hopes which often wish to be served by means the least apt to satisfy them, tensions born of impatience and obstinacy, antagonisms coming more from passions than from self-interest. And how can we avoid examining the transformations and shatterings of political forms?

To instigate or stimulate efforts of social and especially political forecasting is the purpose of *Futuribles,* a research organization formed in Paris, thanks to the aid of the Ford Foundation, by a small group presenting a wide range of nationalities and specialities, brought together by a common conviction that the social sciences should orient themselves toward the future. In some five years, over one hundred and twenty contributions have been published, obtained from authors of fifteen different countries.[4] A liaison has been established across territorial frontiers and those of intellectual disciplines, between minds which consider reflection about the future as a social duty. This liaison seems to us destined to become organic. Prognostications emitted from time to time, here and there, of one thing and another, by well-meaning individuals or well-chosen committees, clearly constitute only one stage of transition toward a continual commerce of visions of the future, fostered by contributions of the most diverse specialities, improved by mutual criticism.

But what is the mode of formation of these visions of the future? The activity of forecasting proceeds: that is a fact. How does it proceed? That is a problem, and my whole subject.

Why have I chosen this subject? I did not choose it, it imposed itself upon me. Destutt de Tracy said very well: "It is the constant march of the human mind. First it acts, then it reflects on what it has done, and by so doing learns to do it still better."[5] It is the practice of forecasting that leads us to its analysis whence its theory may arise. If it is natural and necessary, as I shall indicate, for us to have visions of the future, we owe them to an exercise of imagination which is secret, but which we can and should seek out. Otherwise, we would only be able to set one opinion of the future over against another: of their origins and meaning remaining hidden, only the event could decide among these opinions. But if we want henceforth to decide that one of them appears better founded, we must know how each one is founded, on what suppositions its thought is grounded, and by what courses it has arrived at its conclusions. One may then discuss "reasoned conjectures."

The present work bears on the customs of the mind in its commerce with the future. It is part of our general concern to link together efforts of prediction. On the one hand, we at *Futuribles* thought it useful to point out various work which has a bearing on different aspects of the future;[6] on the other hand, it seemed necessary to provoke discussions about the intellectual maneuvers used in predicting. To this end, seminars have been held, the first in Geneva in June 1962,[7] the second in Paris in July 1963[8] (the one at Geneva was organized with the assistance of the Congress of Cultural Freedom, to which I should like to offer my thanks). It was to put into motion the discussion at these two conferences that this work was presented, in two successive versions. The present is the third.

The greatest satisfaction that I might obtain from this work would be if it got rid of the prejudices against a useful activity, which is nothing but the development of a quite natural activity—prejudices for which a justification is found every time, which is too often, that a conjecture is disguised as a prophecy.

NOTES

1. Cf. United Nations, *The Future Growth of World Population*, New York, 1958.

2. Cf. *President's Report on Raw Materials* (known as the Paley Report), 5 vols., Washington, 1952.

3. François Hetman has systematically assembled an armful of such forecasts in his *Etude SEDEIS,* number 859, suppl. 1, of July 10, 1963, under the title *Croissance démographique et économique: examen des prévisions à long terme.*

4. These essays were published in French as supplements to the *Bulletin SEDEIS* (205, boulevard Saint-Germain, Paris, 7°). A first volume, bringing together some of the essays in an English version, was published by Droz, at Geneva.

5. Destutt de Tracy, *Eléments d'idéologie,* first part (original edition, 1804), pp. 19–20 of the 1817 edition.

6. See "Les Futuribles, à travers livres et revues" (by François Hetman) which appear periodically in the series *Futuribles* of the *Bulletin SEDEIS.*

7. See the analysis of the Geneva discussions by Michel Massenet, *Futuribles,* number 52. The reflections of the same author on methodology constitute the *Futuribles,* number 60 (*Introduction à une sociologie de la prévision*) and number 66 (*Les méthodes de prévision en sciences sociales*).

8. See on this subject the introductory exposé by Pierre Massé: "De l'incertitude économique à l'incertitude politique," *Futuribles,* number 69; the report presented by Daniel Bell, analyzing the processes used by various authors of *Futuribles* essays: "Douze modes de prévision en sciences sociales," *Futuribles,* number 62, since published as "Twelve Modes of Prediction—A Preliminary Sorting of Approaches in the Social Sciences," *Daedalus,* volume 93, number 3 (1964), pp. 845–880; and the report by Saul Friedländer: "La prévision en relations internationales," *Futuribles,* numbers 70, 71, 72.

Contents

INTRODUCTION

1

On the Nature
of the Future

In Latin the ways of speaking about the past and the future present an asymmetry that is illuminating and useful: past events or situations are *facta* and future ones are *futura*. These past and future participles come from different verbs—*facere* (to do or to make) and *esse* (to be). *Facere* is used only to describe past events or situations: they alone are "done," accomplished, completed, shaped. *Esse* is used for future events or situations. Everything that has not yet come about is opposed, in Latin, to what is. We can see this same opposition in the contraries *perfectum* and *infectum*. Something that is not an accomplished fact is designated much more clearly in Latin by the expression *infectum* (non-fact). An *infectum* becomes fact only if and when the event or situation occurs.

It seems to me that the Latin expressions help to contrast what is accomplished or achieved and has taken unalterable form with that which is in progress, still fluid, and capable of ending or being completed in various different ways.

There is a difference between the nature of the past and that of the future. It should hardly be necessary to emphasize that I am referring here to the difference that is perceived by the mind of an active human being.

With regard to the past, man can exert his will only in vain; his liberty is void, his power nonexistent. I could say: "I want to be a former student of the École Polytechnique"—but this is utterly absurd. The fact is that I did not go to the École Polytechnique, and nothing can change this fact. Imagine that I am a tyrant and that my authority is sufficient to have the school records changed so that they show me as a member of the class of 1922. This would merely record a falsehood, not a fact. The fact that I did not go to the École Polytechnique cannot be changed. The fundamental impossibility of changing the past accounts for those very important moral sentiments—regret and remorse.

But if the past is the domain of facts over which I have no power, it is also the domain of knowable facts. If I claim to be a graduate of the École Polytechnique, evidence is easily assembled to prove me a liar. It is not always so easy to determine whether alleged facts are true or false, but we always consider that they are in principle verifiable. The impatience and irritation we feel when faced with conflicting testimony bearing on the same fact are signs of our deep conviction that this *factum* is knowable. And in such a situation we do not hesitate to say that one of the witnesses who presented testimony must have been lying or mistaken, even though we may not know which one was actually at fault.

Now let us suppose that I say: "I will go to Australia." Put into the past tense, my assertion would be a falsehood: it is not true that I have gone to Australia. But by using the future tense I have placed my assertion outside the domain of recorded, attested, and verifiable *facta;* I have projected my assertion beyond the domain of the true and the false, and this "beyond" constitutes another domain, where I can place images that do not correspond to any historical reality. An image of this kind is not a mere fantasy if I have the will and feel I have the capacity to bring about at some later time a state of affairs that corresponds to the image. The image represents a possibility because of my power to validate it in this way, and represents a *project* because of my will to do so.

Can an assertion of this kind be true or false? As a statement of intention it can, but it cannot as a statement of fact. I am telling an untruth if, when speaking, I have no intention of going to Australia; I am telling the truth if I have such an intention. (We shall see that the truth or falsity of statements of intention can be weighed—it is a matter of degree—and in this respect statements of intention differ from statements of fact, which are simply true or false.) On the other hand, my presence in Australia is not a *factum*, and so the question of the truth or falsity of a statement of fact does not arise.

Now let us put ourselves in the position of someone who is waiting for me to visit him in Australia. For this Australian my arrival is a *futurum* attended by a measure of uncertainty until I actually come. If he attaches some definite probability to the event, the judgment by which he does so is a personal one. What he arrives at is a "subjective probability." Thus if two Australian friends of mine discuss this future event with one another, each may attach a very different degree of likelihood to the same *futurum*.

For man in his role as an active agent the future is a field of liberty and power, but for man in his role as a cognizant being the future is a field of uncertainty. It is a field of liberty because I am free to conceive that something which does not now exist will exist in the future; it is a field of power because I have some power to validate my conception (though, naturally, not all conceptions indiscriminately!). And indeed the future is our only field of power, for we can act only on the future. Our awareness of this capacity to act suggests the notion of "a domain in which one can act."

On the other hand, the future is a field of uncertainty. What will be cannot be attested to and verified in the same way as an accomplished fact. When I say: "I saw Peter on my way here," I am testifying, but when I say: "I shall see Peter on my way back," I am making a supposition. If we are faced with two conflicting opinions regarding a past event, we try to determine which one is true; if we are faced with two conflicting opinions regarding a future event, we try to determine which one is more plausible. For, in the latter case, we have no way of arriving at certainty.

It seems, then, that the expression "knowledge of the future" is a contradiction in terms. Strictly speaking, only *facta* can be known; we can have positive knowledge only of the past.

On the other hand, the only "useful knowledge" we have relates to the future. A man wishing to display his practical turn of mind readily says: "I am only interested in facts," although quite the opposite is the case. If his aim is to get to New York, the time at which a plane left yesterday is of small concern to him; what interests him is the takeoff time this evening (a *futurum*). Similarly, if he wants to see somebody in New York, the fact that this person was in his office yesterday hardly matters to him; what interests him is whether this person will be in his office tomorrow. Our man lives in a world of *futura* rather than a world of *facta*.

The real fact collector is at the opposite pole from the man of action. One erudite scholar might spend years establishing the facts about the assassination of Louis, duc d'Orléans, in 1407, while another might devote his time to tracing Napoleon's itinerary day by day. Here are *facta* that could have no effect on our judgments concerning the future and on our present decisions.

For this reason these *facta* do not concern our practical man. If he is interested in certain *facta,* it is only because he uses them in presuming a *futurum.* For example, he may be worried about the departure time of his plane. Tell him that this flight has left on time for a long succession of days, and he will be reassured. He regards these *facta* as a guarantee of the *futurum,* which is all that matters to him. Now let us suppose that this man contemplates buying a business that holds no interest for him except as an investment. If the accounts show that sales have increased steadily every year, he will derive from these figures a strong presumption that this steady increase will be maintained in future sales.

The case of the business concern differs from that of the airplane in two immediately apparent ways: first, a much larger stretch of time is considered; next, and more particularly, the investor counts on the continuance of the same change, whereas the traveler counts on a simple repetition of the same phenomenon.

In both cases, however, the only use of the known *facta* is as *raw material out of which the mind makes estimates of futura.* The unceasing transformation of *facta* into *futura* by summary processes in the mind is part of our daily life, and thus the undertaking of conscious and systematic forecasting is simply an attempt to effect improvements in a natural activity of the mind.

2

A Need of Our Species

The scrupulous student of fact brands assertions about the future as intellectual "adventurism": they are, he claims, the business of charlatans, into whose company the sober-minded scholar should not venture. Another, sterner critic admits that we must, perforce, divert some of our attention from intelligible essences to things as they happen to be, but proscribes speculation about their future aspects as too great a diversion. A third complains that our appreciation of the present moment is impaired when we cast our mind to the uncertainties ahead. In turn, a moralist warns against a concern with the future, lest the clear and immediate prescriptions of duty be supplanted by selfish calculations.

No doubt these objections have some foundation; but the representation of future changes is nonetheless a necessary factor in our activity. Because of our natural responsibilities as men, we need foresight—a view stretching, more or less deep and wide, into time. We are curious about the future because we have cares (or cures, in the now-obsolete meaning of the Latin *curae*).

One of the striking features of the biological world, in all its diversity, is that the perpetuation of a species becomes a more and more intricate problem the higher the species ranks on the ladder of beings. For simple organisms, the role of the adult is confined to the abundant emission of germ cells. Carried by water, air, or the blood of a parasitized organism, a sufficient proportion of the cells encounter the right conditions and grow up autonomously. Superior animals lack this capacity for autonomous development: they are born helpless and dependent—more so if they are called to a greater perfection—and their period of maturation is long in proportion to the excellence of the species.

Thus the efforts that parents must devote to rearing their offspring increase in intensity and duration right up the ladder of beings. And since physicists have introduced us to the notion of entropy—a tendency toward the dissolution of forms—we should not find it strange that more care is needed to ensure the complete development of a more highly structured, and therefore more improbable, organism. Without the development of the moral virtue of devotion to offspring, there would be no perpetuation of highly organized animals. For better protection of the young, a coalition of parents is required: this coalition can be dissolved if the first group of offspring reaches maturity before a second group is born. The coalition needs to be permanent if the time between births is shorter than the period of maturation. Thus, among our remote ancestors, there must have been a state of "sociality," which preceded and prepared our own "humanity." If moral attitudes—not only of devotion to children, but also of parental solidarity—had not developed, we would not have assumed the form of men. But these affective dispositions would have been ineffectual without the intellectual virtue of foresight.

Many human groups must have perished through improvidence, and without any doubt, the men who have increased, multiplied, and peopled the earth are the prudent ones.[1]

Custom—a Guarantee of Foreseeability

Empirical psychologists represent the learning process as the progressive storing of procedures associated with favorable results. This is sufficient to explain why anthropological findings indicate that life in primitive societies is so largely ruled by custom. In a perilous world it is a fine achievement for a man if he lives to an uncommon old age, and having manifested their own prudence, the elders are now qualified to teach others the skills of prudence. What they inculcate are the well-tried procedures whose use should be continued. They pass on the recipes ("tradition" properly means "passing on") and recommend "routines"— the trodden paths.

Routines help to save us efforts of foresight: if I have an operational recipe, guaranteed to yield certain results, all I need do is follow the instructions faithfully. Who would be so foolish as to waste time trying out ways of cooking an egg or solving a quadratic equation? It is scarcely necessary to point out that the vast majority of our actions—at present, just as in the distant past—conform to recipes. Accordingly, it should not be difficult for us to imagine a society tied even more closely to recipes. At school, when we failed to do a sum, the teacher would say that we had not done it the right way, meaning the way we had been shown; similarly, we can assume that, in the past, failure and misfortune were readily attributed to departures from or breaches of the "right" practices.

Since we cannot live except in a social group, nothing matters more to us than our relations with other men, and nothing is more important to foresee than the way other men will behave. The more their conduct is governed by custom and conforms to routines, the easier it is to foresee. A social order based on custom provides the individual with optimal guarantees that his human environment is foreseeable. It is hardly surprising that the maintenance of a familiar social order has always been regarded as a Common Good whose preservation was essential.

Hence, aberrations of conduct were condemned, and change was feared and regarded as a corruption. The idea of the security afforded by the routine and familiar was so deeply ingrained that even extreme reformers appealed to this notion, saying they asked for no more than a return to the "good old ways." Thus, in calling for the redistribution of land holdings, Tiberius Sempronius Gracchus claimed, with some foundation, that his reform was designed to bring back a society of peasants who owned their own land and lived off their own crops. A rather fanciful theme dominated the long press campaign that helped to prepare the French Revolution: the advocacy of a return to the Frankish custom of the *champ de mars* or the *champ de mai*—assemblies of warriors at which decisions were taken concerning affairs of state. All this pseudo-archeology went to mobilize something that had never been, in the service of a leap into the unknown. And surely everyone knows that the Reformation, for all its radical innovations, was conceived and presented as a restoration of the practices of the early Church. The idea of "moving with the times" would have seemed abhorrent to the reformers, who wished, on the contrary, to "correct the abuses introduced over the centuries." The examples I have adduced are sufficiently striking and it seems unnecessary to cite any more. They all bear witness to the power of that which has already been seen, tried, and experienced.

What a contrast with the spirit of our times! When de Gaulle wished to condemn the French regime in Algeria, he found no stronger way of branding it than *Algérie de papa.* Compare this with the references of the Romans to the "ways of our fathers" (*mos maiorum*). The attachment to the past which was once a sign of virtue and wisdom is now a sign of vice and folly: nowadays our positive value is change. This intellectual revolution is without precedent, and we owe to this new attitude an extraordinary progress in all the practical arts, which are no longer fettered by procedures handed down from generation to generation. But about human relations, our uncertainty is now greater than it had been in the past.

Foresight Becomes More Necessary

Our positive knowledge of our social environment consists of knowledge of the present state of affairs (or, more precisely, it is a composite image of more or less recent past states of affairs). It would remain valid in its entirety, and for always, if nothing ever changed, but this is impossible. However, the fewer changes we anticipate, the more we can continue to rely on our knowledge for the future. If society tends on the whole to conserve the present state of affairs, our present knowledge has a high chance of being valid in the future. On the other hand, the future validity of our knowledge becomes increasingly doubtful as the mood of society inclines toward change and the changes promise to be more rapid.

We are in the position of a tourist who is planning a journey with the help of a guidebook that is already out of date. Under these conditions, it would be imprudent to trust the guidebook blindly, and we would be better off if we had the intellectual courage to figure out where it is wrong and how it needs to be revised. As foreseeability is less and less granted to us and guaranteed by an unchanging social system, we must put more and more effort into foresight. A saving of effort is possible in a society whose life is governed by routines, whereas the exertion of foresight must increase in a society in movement.

NOTE

1. The connection between the formation of larger social groups and the successful struggle against mortality is discussed by Ludwik Krzywicki, *Primitive Society and Its Vital Statistics* (Warsaw, 1934).

3

Terminology

In modern French, the word *prévision* has come to mean forecast or foresight, rather than foreknowledge or prescience. Maupertuis[1] was the first writer to make use of the word in its present acceptation, and his usage provoked a dispute worth recalling, for it may help us to understand the nature of forecasting and foresight more clearly. Ever since his expedition to Lapland, in the course of which he had substantiated his views on the shape of the earth by measuring the arc of Tornea, Maupertuis enjoyed a reputation throughout Europe. In 1752, while president of the Academy of Berlin, he published his *Letters,* which contain the ideas of interest to us here. There would be little point in going into the various reasons[2] for which Voltaire attacked Maupertuis in a series of cruel pamphlets, derided him and, some say, hastened his death. But it is not without significance that Maupertuis was defended by Euler and died in the arms of Bernoulli, both of whom remained faithful to him. This gives the Voltaire-Maupertuis affair the air of an episode in the war of the "two cultures," literary and scientific.

The Memory-Prevision Symmetry

Maupertuis writes:

Our mind—that being whose chief property is to perceive itself and what is presented to it—has, in addition, two other faculties, *memory* and *prevision* [*prévision*]. The one is a retracing of the past, the other an anticipation of the future. The greatest difference between the mind of man and that of an animal lies in these two faculties.[3]

In proposing the memory-prevision symmetry, Maupertuis emphasized that both our memories and our previsions are very imperfect, and suggested, on the other hand, that our anticipations are perfectible, just like our knowledge of the past. And one should add that Maupertuis foresaw the future correctly with his prevision of an improvement in our knowledge of the past.

Maupertuis asserts that, individually, men have better memories than animals. This we may readily grant, and also that the progress of a society is accompanied by a tremendous improvement in its collective memory. A primitive people's only "public libraries" are its old men, whereas a civilized nation has large archives. We ourselves see that facts are recorded in increasing volume every year—so much so that to dredge out matter bearing on a given question from the sea of recorded fact we need the help of machines. Not simply an expansion in our current records of the recent past is under way, but also a progressive discovery of the distant past. We know the history of the earth and the early days of man far better than that at the time of Maupertuis.

An Error of Montesquieu

A specific example will indicate the progress our knowledge of the past has made since the eighteenth century. Two and a half centuries ago Montesquieu asked: "Why is the world so little populated in comparison with former times?"[4] He added:

After performing the most exact calculation possible in this sort of matter, I have found that there is scarcely one tenth as many people on the earth as in ancient times. What is surprising is that the population of the earth decreases every day, and if this continues, in another ten centuries the earth will be nothing but a desert.[5]

This question so preoccupied Montesquieu that in his next ten letters he offered different explanations for his discovery, and thus worked out a sort of "sociology of depopulation," whose tone anticipates *L'Esprit des lois* and clashes with the rest of the book.[6]

Montesquieu was wrong about the trend of his age: it was a faulty knowledge of the past—his own recent past—which led him to say: "The population of the earth decreases every day." And in our age, we could not make such a mistake about developments in our own recent past. We have, moreover, better estimates of the population in "ancient times": what Montesquieu had in mind was plainly Greco-Roman civilization, and at present it is believed that the population of Europe at the death of Augustus was definitely smaller than in the days of Montesquieu, rather than ten times greater.[7]

If, then, we have made such progress in our knowledge of the past that even a schoolboy could point to Montesquieu's error, should we not recognize "*in the knowledge of the past, an art born of human industry*"? —as Maupertuis said.[8] And should we not concur with Maupertuis and hope that progress will also be made in what he calls "the opposite art, that of foreseeing the future"?[9]

Voltaire's Criticism

Voltaire believes that Maupertuis is talking nonsense when he establishes a symmetry between the future and the past:

> He asserts that it is as easy to see the future as the past; that predictions are of the same nature as memory; that anybody can prophesy; that this depends only on an extra degree of activity of the spirit, and that it is only necessary to "exalt" the soul thereunto.[10]

And again:

> But the Inquisitor will not laugh when he is informed that every man may become a prophet; for the author finds no more difficulty in seeing the future than the past. He avers that the arguments in favor of judicial astrology are as strong as those against it. He then assures us that the perceptions of the past, the present, and the future differ only in the greater or less activity of the soul. He hopes that a little more heat and "exaltation" in the fancy may serve to point out the future, as the memory shews the past.[11]

If we allow for Maupertuis' incaution and for Voltaire's exploitation of it for the purpose of caricature, we can see what lends substance to Voltaire's criticism: namely, the symmetry that Maupertuis set up between the past and the future. There is a "sociological" symmetry in the sense that a society with a better knowledge of its past is also more preoccupied with its future and the resources of memory are used in anticipatory speculations. But the symmetry is false if understood in the sense that the future is knowable in the same way as the past—and indeed, I began by asserting a fundamental difference in kind between the past and the future.

How does this difference vanish in the eye of God, and how can we reconcile God's omniscience with man's free will? These are some of the most difficult of all metaphysical questions. Molina's attempt to answer them from a standpoint favorable to free will[12] unleashed the anger of the Jansenists, and the resulting quarrel between Jesuits and Jansenists shook the Church during the second half of the seventeenth and the first half of the eighteenth century. This story does not concern us here, but the language we use has metaphysical implications, of which we should be aware.

In his first attack on Maupertuis, Voltaire pretends that the work he is criticizing was written by a young forger posing as the president of the Academy, and derides him in this manner:

> In the first place, it may not be improper to inform this young author that foresight [*prévoyance*] in man is not called Foreknowledge [*prévision*]; that the word Foreknowledge is sacred to God alone, and denotes the power by which he looks into futurity. He should be acquainted with the meaning of words before he starts to write.[13]

Certainly, it is necessary for us to attribute unambiguous meanings to the words we employ in the present undertaking. In attacking Maupertuis, Voltaire was indubitably right with regard to the historical meaning of the French word *prévision*. If we open a dictionary contemporary with these authors, we find:

> PRÉVISION : Terme de théologie. Il se dit de Dieu, et signifie *connaissance de ce qui adviendra.*
> PRÉVOYANCE : Action de l'esprit qui considère *ce qui peut arriver.*[14]

The contrast is very strong. On the one hand, we have true knowledge, immediate and certain, of the future. On the other, we have—and let us weigh the words carefully—an action of the human mind: there is an effort or *work* tending to make us know "what may happen" (*ce qui peut arriver*) rather than "what will happen" (*ce qui adviendra*). The result of this work is a *fan of possible futures,* or of futures which seem likely to us. But when we have completed this work to the best of our ability, we cannot say with certainty which of the seemingly possible futures will actually come about, nor even whether the future which will actually come about is contained in our fan of possible futures.

Thus, according to this old usage, *prévoyance* describes a mere effort of the mind, whereas *prévision* describes a complete and assured possession of the future. And to be sure, when we speak nowadays of *prévision* in French (and "prevision" or "foresight" in English), we in no sense intend to imply that we have a "knowledge of vision," such that all things in future time are offered to us in the manner of "objects present to us."[15]

When we foresee or forecast the future, we form *opinions about the future.* When we speak of "a forecast," we simply mean an opinion about the future (but a carefully formed one). When we speak of "forecasting," we mean the intellectual activity of forming such opinions (serious and considered ones, but with an uncertain verification). This needs to be stated clearly and emphatically, particularly since aspirations the forecaster does not, and should not, have are often attributed to him.

Futurology?

More than anyone else economists have made forecasting into an important industry. They commonly use the term "prediction,"[16] which presents no drawbacks so long as it is correctly understood. My colleague N. "predicts" that the sale of automobiles will increase next year by so many thousand units: this means that after mature consideration of all the relevant factors he could find, he thinks this figure more likely than any other. But the strength of the term is suggestive, and there is a danger of misapprehension: the word seems to provide a completely certain verdict.

Any such misapprehension on the part of the forecaster's audience is, I think, very dangerous. The persiflage that sometimes greets the forecaster's work may madden him, but he must fear skepticism far less than credulity. In all ages men have gathered about fortunetellers, and when these persons achieve a recognized position and are able to back their pronouncements with figures, they will attract a rash of customers who accept their words as "what science says." The forecaster who takes care to give his best opinion does not want to make others believe that there is a "science of the future" able to set forth with assurance what will be. He is apprehensive of letting this misunderstanding arise. And it is to prevent this illusion that I reject the term "futurology."[17] This word would be very convenient for designating the whole of our forecasting activities, except that it would suggest that the results of these activities are scientific—which they are not, for as I have already said the future is not a domain of objects passively presented to our knowledge.

Why Conjecture?

The reason why the word "conjecture" appears in the title of this book is precisely that it is opposed to the term "knowledge." In the famous *Ars Conjectandi,* Jacques Bernoulli stresses the distinction: "With regard to things which are certain and indubitable, we speak of *knowing* or *understanding;* with regard to other things, of *conjecturing,* that is to say, *opining.*"[18] But since I have mentioned this great man, I should add that he defines the "art of conjecture"[19] in a sense very different from the one which is used here. Our problem would amount to distributing probabilities among different possible futures only if the whole set of possible futures were presented to our knowledge. However, the supposition that the possible futures are "given" to us in this way is very far from the truth. On the contrary, they have to be constructed by "pro-ference": the action by which the imagination derives possible futures out of present states, which are known more or less well. The intellectual construction of a likely future is a work of art, in the full sense of the term, and this is what "conjecture" means here. In this "composition" of the mind, we should make use of all the relevant causal relations that we can find; their respective roles and their connections with one another will depend on a hypothetical model, and their "triggering" will depend on intervening facts, which have to be presupposed. The conjecture will be more or less well-reasoned.[20] What is of vital importance for the progress of this art of conjecture is that an assertion about the future should be accompanied by the intellectual scaffolding which supports it: this "construct" must be transparent and articulated, and subjected to criticism. Using the word "conjecture" in this sense, I very much prefer it to "forecast," "foresight," and "prediction," but as these terms have become part of the language, I shall continue to use them. However, when we come to consider the predictions of eminent writers (chapters 8 and 9), I shall attempt to reconstitute the intellectual procedure that they have omitted to set forth.

Why Futuribles?

The term "futuribles" is the label of an intellectual undertaking. It was chosen because it designates what seems to be the object of thought when the mind is directed toward the future: our thought is unable to grasp with certainty the *futura*, the things which will be; instead, it considers the possible futures. But this notion of the "possible" must be made a trifle more rigorous.

There are many future states of affairs which we have no reason to regard as impossible; it follows, in accordance with the law of contradiction, that we should regard them as possible. But a future state of affairs enters into the class of "futuribles" only if its mode of production from the present state of affairs is plausible and imaginable. For example, aviation was seen as a possible already in ancient times, but it became a futurible only when certain new facts made its development conceivable. One of the strengths of this example is that when the flying machine first became a serious prospect, it could be imagined as "lighter than air" or "heavier than air," and in the latter case, with either moving wings or rigid wings. There was a plurality of futuribles and in general this is the case. Perhaps I shall be allowed the following metaphor: a futurible is a descendant of the present, a descendant to which we attach a genealogy.

A futurible is a *futurum* that appears to the mind as a possible descendant from the present state of affairs. Let us make use of an image. A boat has traveled down the Mississippi—the past. It approaches the delta—the set of future outcomes at present pictured by the mind, that is to say, the *currently valid futuribles*. Let A stand for the set of futuribles that I perceive at time T_0. I make another examination at a later time T_1, when I perceive another set, B, of currently valid futuribles. Clearly, some of the futuribles that appeared in set *A* will not be included in *B*. If we examine the futuribles at successive times and find that nothing takes place except a series of eliminations, it is clear that we arrive, by degrees, at a certitude. This is what happens when we set ourselves a question concerning a fixed date and a well-defined object of thought. But this is no longer so if our question about the future is vaguer. In this case, some of the previously contemplated futuribles are eliminated from each successive present, but at the same time new futuribles appear. And, logically, it is necessary for new futuribles to appear, because otherwise the mere succession of time would procure increasing certainty for us, and, though our certainty about particular things does increase, it would be absurd to assume that this holds true for things in general. If at some instant of time we were able to give an exhaustive listing of all the futuribles, it would follow by hypothesis that no new futuribles could ever be added to this set, and that, on the contrary, at later instants of time the set could only lose members. Thus the assumption that an exhaustive enumeration of the futuribles can be given leads to the untenable consequence that there is a progressive reduction of uncertainty in general. We must conclude, therefore, that there is no time at which we can enumerate the futuribles exhaustively.

Consequently, the futuribles should be thought of as those descendants from the present state that now seem to us possible. A futurible needs to be provided with a date of origin. We shall see later that it is also important to attach a due-date or expiration date to it. It is necessary to emphasize that the mind is by no means inclined to contemplate a large variety of possible futures, and tends rather to attach itself to the futurible that appears to be intellectually the most probable or affectively the most desirable. Man is fortunate when the desirable and the probable coincide! The case is often otherwise, and thus we find ourselves trying to bend the course of events in a way which will bring the probable closer to the desirable. And this is the real reason why we study the future.

NOTES

1. Pierre-Louis Moreau de Maupertuis, born in Saint-Malo in 1698, died in Basel in 1759, member and pensionnaire of the Académie des Sciences, Paris, in 1731 and of the Académie Française in 1743, president of the Academy of Berlin in 1744.

2. In particular, Maupertuis' nasty quarrel with his colleague König.

3. Maupertuis, *Lettres* (original edition, 1752), Letter II, in *Oeuvres complètes* (1768 edn.), II, 212.

4. *Lettres persanes* (1721), Letter CXII.

5. *Ibid.*

6. Letters CXIII to CXXII. The importance he attached to this question appears in these ten consecutive letters, which display a homogeneity quite uncharacteristic of the book as a whole.

7. We must pay tribute to David Hume for his refutation of Montesquieu's opinion in the essay *On the Populousness of Ancient Nations.* Hume's conclusion is amusing: a reference to a passage in which Diodorus Siculus makes the same complaint as Montesquieu.

8. Maupertuis, *Lettres*, Letter XVIII, in *Oeuvres complètes*, II, 333.

9. *Ibid.*

10. The letter from Voltaire to König, November 17, 1752.

11. Voltaire, *Diatribe du docteur Akakia, médecin du pape*, a work falsely dated from Rome, 1753, in *The Works of M. de Voltaire*, trans. T. Smollett, T. Francklin, and others (4th edn,; Dublin, 1772), XIV, 289.

12. Molina, a Spanish Jesuit, expressed his opinion on the matter we are discussing in a work published in 1588: *Concordia liberi arbitrii cum gratiae donis, divina praescientia providentia praedestinatione et reprobatione.* A convenient edition was published in Paris in 1876.

13. *Diatribe du docteur Akakia,* in *op. cit.,* p. 287.

14. Richelet, *Dictionnaire* (1759 edn.).

15. The classical meaning of "prevision" is so strong that even for God it designates the contemplation of things that will be, to the exclusion of things that could be. A passage from St. Thomas illustrates this:

> Yet some distinction should be noted among the things that are not actual. Though some of them are not actual now, nevertheless they have been or will be actual, and all these are said to be known by the knowledge of vision. For since God's act of understanding, which is his being, is measured by eternity which is without succession and comprehends all time, the instantaneous glance of God falls on all things in any period of time as on things present to him. But there are other things in the power of God or the creature which are not, nor have been, nor ever will be; these he is said to know by the knowledge of simple intelligence, not of vision, for vision implies a real object apart from the viewer.

(*Summa Theologica,* Ia, q. XIV, art. 9, in St. Thomas Aquinas, *Philosophical Texts,* trans. Thomas Gilby, Oxford University Press.)

16. Thus, throughout his very fine book, *Economic Forecasts and Policy* (Amsterdam, 1961), H. Theil speaks of "predictions," a "prediction" being defined as "a statement concerning unknown, in particular future, events."

17. The term "futurology" was proposed by Ossip K. Flecktheim in 1949, with the explanation—disturbing, I think—that it describes a "new science." See "Futurology: the New Science?" *Forum*, III, 206–9; and "Futurology: the Science of Probability," *Midwest Journal*, II (Winter 1949), 18–19. If it could be clearly understood to designate a concern not a science, the word would be suitable.

18. *Ars Conjectandi* was published after the death of the author by his nephew Nicholas (Basel, 1713). In spite of its fame, it was never reprinted. Both this quotation and the next are taken from the second chapter of the *Pars Quarta, tradens usum et applicationem praecedentis doctrinae in civilibus, moralibus, et oeconomicis.*

19. "We define," says Bernoulli, "the art of conjecture, or stochastic art, as the art of evaluating as exactly as possible the probabilities of things, so that in our judgments and actions we can always base ourselves on what has been found to be the best, the most appropriate, the most certain, the best advised; this is the only object of the wisdom of the philosopher and the prudence of the statesman."

20. The expression "reasoned conjecture" is an old one. It was used in the eighteenth century by J. L. Favier (1711–84), who in his time had an immense reputation as an expert on foreign policy. His principal work, famous long before it was made public by the seizure of the papers of Louis XVI, was entitled *Conjectures raisonnées sur la situation actuelle de la France dans le système présent de l'Europe, et réciproquement sur la position respective de l'Europe à l'égard de la France, enfin sur les nouvelles combinaisons qui doivent ou peuvent résulter de ces différents rapports, aussi dans le système de l'Europe.* This work, which was commissioned by the Comte de Broglie to be presented to Louis XV, is dated April 16, 1773. It was published by P. L. Ségur in 1801, in a work in three volumes (mostly taken up by Favier's memoir) entitled *Politique de tous les cabinets de l'Europe sous les règnes de Louis XV et Louis XVI.*

Part I

PERSONAL DESTINY

4

The Project

We know from personal experience that images are formed in our mind. That the multiple excitations of our sensory system[1] should be transmuted into an organized image is something much stranger than the storing and recollection of these images by our memory, and is not explained by science. It is natural to call images referring to the present or the past "representations," for they "represent" *facta,* in however subjective a manner. But the name "representations" is also commonly extended to images that do not represent any reality past or present, fabrications of the mind whose formation is much more mysterious than that of representations properly so called.[2]

These fictions[3] are of major importance in our life. Although we discard the vast majority as fantasies,[4] we value a small number of them, and these can serve as the cause of future realities.[5] There is no volition without object, and the object of a volition is that a fiction of the mind become a "fact." This *fact* is the goal of action (in the sense of "action" defined below). When we retain a fiction as something to be enacted, it serves as the source of systematic action. This fiction—a non-fact— can be situated only in the future, which is necessary as a receptacle for a fiction accompanied by an injunction to become real. The image summons a future reality: *fictio quaerens veritatem.*

In this chapter we shall rapidly discuss four points: 1. without representations, there would be no actions, only reactions; 2. sustained, systematic action aims at the validation of a representation projected into the future; 3. other things being equal, an assertion about the future must be weighed according to the strength of the intention; 4. a man who acts with sustained intention to carry out a project is a creator of the future.

A Representation and an Action

All living matter is "excitable": when it comes into contact with something, it responds by characteristic movements. The capacity for reacting is not the exclusive property of plants and animals, and we find it even in mere fragments of live tissue. As we apply stimuli to more highly organized forms of living matter, the phenomenon becomes increasingly complicated and sophisticated. It is, however, an illusion to suppose that action properly so called is reducible to such reactions.

Consider Mucius, surnamed Scaevola,[6] who deliberately held his right hand over live coals to let it be consumed. We all know that the natural reaction of a hand (and all living matter) is to withdraw from a flame. To prevent this, an effort opposing the reaction is required, and what we have here is, properly speaking, an action. It is by no means true that everyone could perform the same action as Mucius; and, clearly, Mucius would not have acted like this on just any day or with just any fire: he did so on an occasion when, in his eyes, this gesture was meaningful.

In general, I consider that any behavior which is not a necessary consequence of the external pressures acting on a man should be called an "action." We may discuss whether the struggles of a child when he sees the nurse preparing an injection needle constitute an action or an "anticipated reaction." But to speak of an "anticipated reaction," we must admit that a representation of the future event forms in the child's mind and that this representation, rather than sensation, is the cause of the child's movements. And it seems to me that the necessary intervention of this representation makes the child's movements into an action, though only of the lowest order, such as we find in animals. When American Indians tortured a captive at the stake, I think they participated in a tragedy, looking for a conflict of representations in its protagonist—the representation of what he was about to suffer made the coward groan even before the ordeal, whereas the representation of the heroic attitude kept the brave sufferer from groaning right to the end.

An action is an agent's own to the extent that the representation is properly his own. We do not hold a man responsible for behavior under the influence of representations suggested by hypnosis. On the contrary, we consider that his responsibility is engaged to the highest degree when he acts in response to an image he himself has formed.

Images are formed in our mind and inspire us; we know this from daily experience. It is absurd to look for explanations of human conduct which disregard this essential phenomenon. Our actions properly so called[7] seek to validate appealing images and invalidate repugnant ones. But where do we store these images? For example, I "see myself" visiting China, yet I know I have never been there and am not in China now. There is no room for the image in the past or the present, but there is room for it in the future. Time future is the domain able to receive as "possibles" those representations which elsewhere would be "false." And from the future in which we now place them, these possibles "beckon" to us to make them real.

Jhering expressed the point quite aptly: if nothing happens without sufficient reason, the sufficient reason of human action is expressed in terms of *ut* rather than *quia;* man acts, not "because . . . ," but "in order to. . . ." Action is explained by its final cause, its goal:[8] "In this sense we may say that in volition the practical motive lies in the future."

We are to understand by this that the future is the domain into which a man has projected, and in which he now contemplates, the possible he wishes to make real, the image that is and will be, as long as it subsists in the mind, the determining reason for his actions.

Design, Project, Intention

Here we shall be dealing with an image: the word "design" comes from the Latin for "image," *signum,* and has two meanings in English, an image that is drawn with a pencil and an image that is formed in the mind. In French the word *dessein* retained these two meanings until the eighteenth century, when the variant *dessin* was adopted for a drawing. Félibien wrote, before this distinction was introduced: "*Dessein* is a generic term; it is used for the outward expression, or visible image, of thoughts in the mind, as well as for what has been framed beforehand in the imagination."[9]

We shall be dealing, moreover, with the casting forward of an image:

the word "project" comes from *pro-jacio*. Cournot once said: "Languages . . . first express spatial relations, and then with their help, temporal relations; *antea* and *postea,* which refer to time, have as roots *ante* and *post,* which express positions in space."[10] I project, that is to say, I cast something forward into time. What do I cast? My imagination, which jumps to a time not yet accomplished and builds something there, a *signum;* and this "construct" beckons and exercises a present attraction on me. Thus actions coming before this imagined future are determined by it and prepare it rationally.

I am tempted to compare the projection of the image "over there" to the rock climber's fling of a rope "up there": in each case, the throwing comes first and enables the actor to move toward the "hitching point." But there is a difference. The fixed point of the climber exists objectively and provides physical aid, whereas a project exists only subjectively and provides only moral stimulus.

Since I have ventured this metaphor, I shall also use it to compare an intention to the taut rope with which the rock climber hauls himself to his goal. His chances of carrying out his project depend on the strength of his intention: *in-tendere* means "to tend," "to stretch," "to strive *toward* a goal."

Assertions about the Future

An assertion about the future is a perfectly ordinary occurrence. In the bus, I overhear a stranger saying: "I will be in Saint-Tropez in August." He "sees himself" in Saint-Tropez, although he is now in Paris, as I could testify; couched in the present tense his assertion would be an obvious untruth. But the future is available, allowing him to assert something that is not now the case, but is a future possibility. In August, an observer will be able to determine whether the assertion has been proven.

An assertion about the future is not indicative of a fact, but of an intention. It might be very important for Secundus to know whether our stranger, Primus, will really be in Saint-Tropez next August. Secundus first appraises the objective possibility (very weak, if the chances are that Primus will be called up by the army before August). He then considers the strength of the intention: will Primus do all that is needed to carry out his project? If so, Secundus will say that the intention was strong, and if not, that it was weak and inconstant.

We often disagree about the nature of our projects, but in so many different ways that we can find no convenient basis for comparing different people. On the contrary, intention provides a convenient basis for comparison. It is easy to observe that Primus usually pursues a design vigorously and steadfastly, whereas Secundus does not. We see Primus' strength of intention as a character trait lending to his projects a solidity quite lacking in those of Secundus. Because Secundus does not mobilize his energy; he fails to realize his projects, and thus they are scarcely more than daydreams.

The quality of intention we have just indicated—intensity—is of great importance. But we can also speak of the quality of intention in a different sense, namely, with reference to moral direction. Until now, we have treated intention as a way of being related to a given goal or target. However, it is also very plausible to see intention as a more general way of being, a direction in which a person continually bends his energies, a course in which his different projects constitute successive stages. Instead of each project engendering an intention, the general intention engenders each individual project. The advantage of this presentation is that it helps to bring out the following point—man is not active because he has projects, but has projects because he is active. And certainly it is part of the nature of any organism to expend energy. In this we must recognize the original phenomenon that gives rise to project-formation mediated by representations.

Ego, Creator of the Future

It is fundamental that Ego know himself as a cause. It has even been claimed that self-consciousness comes from the experience of causing[11]—an experience from which the very notion of cause is acquired.[12] Ego knows he has forces at his disposal, forces he can mobilize by conscious effort in order to carry out a project. That it depends on me to adopt a project or not and apply to it a larger or smaller portion of my forces is something I am intimately convinced of, and so is each man in particular. To discuss whether we are all victims of illusion is of no practical interest, for in our individual attitudes and our mutual relations we all behave as though we accept these truths.

We should note that for an observer facts come in a chronological sequence that is both truthful and misleading. It is true that I arrived in New York only after taking the plane for New York, but it is also true that I took this plane only after forming the project to visit New York. My presence in New York (a *factum*) is established, and it is the result of actions that are also established, but these actions are the consequence of my imagining myself in New York. In the order of desire or intention, the end, according to St. Thomas, comes before that which is done toward the end.[13] Our understanding of human affairs would be badly limited or even deformed if we confined ourselves to the order of facts, and ignored the order of intentions.[14]

Knowing myself as a cause, I contemplate various effects: Situated where? In the future. We have already described this process of forming constructs placed in the future. If my efforts are sufficient, I shall find my construct "standing" tangible and actualized when the right time comes. But I cannot be certain of this. I am certain only of my design and my intention. I want to transform this certitude into a definite reality. I shall do everything in my power to make my particular design a certainty in fact. The verb *certare* means "to struggle" and, in law, "to try to obtain a decision."[15] What could be more revealing? Thus, in the clearest of all languages, I can compose a sentence that sums everything up: *Certo ut certum fiat in re quod certum in mente.* The last *certum* denotes the well-defined character of the image on which my mind is quite decided; the previous *certum* denotes the result I seek—for things to be in fact like my image. But, to obtain this, an effort is required, a struggle denoted by *certo*.

NOTES

1. The structure and working of the sensory system are of a complexity unsuspected in the days of sensualist psychology. This point has been well put by John M. Stroud:

> "Wild slashes with Occam's razor notwithstanding, man is apparently complicated enough to be practical—and this appears to be a confoundedly high degree of complication."

("The Fine Structure of Psychological Time," in Henry Quastler, ed., *Information Theory in Psychology* [Glencoe, Ill.: The Free Press, 1955]).

2. The formation of these images seems to belie the rule *Nihil in intellectu quod non prius erit in sensu.*

3. This word seems appropriate, as the past participle of *fingo* designates what is imagined and, literally, shaped. It is significant that the potter, *figulus*, molds the clay into a shape that he first sees in his mind.

4. We dismiss the fictions of our dreams, and indulge ourselves in fictions spun in daydreams only as a game, or through weakness. It is worth noting that a child acts out the fictions which come to his mind, and if we know what the fiction is, we can explain and even anticipate his gestures. His act is a sort of shadow of the behavior we shall discuss—the voluntary action of an adult.

5. An image conceived by the mind is the progenitor of a *factum* if the image is elected by the will and the *factum* is then brought into being through action (this action is the servant of the image and a creator of the future). We can understand why, through a quite improper extension, the ancients regarded dream-fictions as premonitions of reality, for in both cases the image precedes the event! Yes, but if the event follows the image (and this is by no means always so) in the image-goal case, it is only because of the motive power of the image: the image gives rise to a sufficient effort. There is no analogous reason for an event to come after a dream-fiction. But this error is a sort of obscure tribute to the role a fiction is *able* to play.

6. "The Left-Handed One."

7. I shall not repeat the phrase "action properly so called," and shall simply say "action."

8. Rudolf von Jhering, *Zweck im Recht.* Published in English as *Law as a Means to an End* (New York: The Macmillan Co., 1914). See Chap. 1, "The Law of Purpose."

9. Translated from the quotation in Richelet, *Dictionnaire* (1759 edn.), I, 738.

10. Cournot, *De l'enchaînement des idées fondamentales* (1911), p. 25.

11. This is asserted by Maine de Biran:

"The 'I' begins to exist for itself only in the exercise of free activity, or in conscious effort that gives rise to a particular sensation, *sui generis,* related to this effort in the manner of an effect to its cause. The 'I' lies wholly and indivisibly in this relation of the acting cause to the resulting effect. The cause senses or perceives itself in the effort, which is itself sensed or perceived in consciousness only through the muscular sensations it produces. The 'I' which is present to itself in effort is the true and unique subject to which all other immediate products of this same free activity are attributed."

(*Prolégomènes psychologiques,* in *Oeuvres,* ed. Victor Cousin [4 vols.; Paris, 1841], III, 305.) Or more simply: "The 'I' senses itself as a force, an energy, a power to act." (*Sur les Réflexions de Maupertuis,* in *Oeuvres,* II, 304.) And again: "The feeling of the 'I' is identified with the feeling of a free force which knows itself through consciousness of its own acts." (*Ibid.*, IV, 47.) Or: "Free action is the first and necessary condition of apperception, or knowledge of one-self." (*Ibid.*, IV, 340.) Finally: "The 'I' exists only in conscious effort." (*Ibid.*, IV, 374.)

12. "How would we know that there are causes if we did not know primitively, or did not immediately perceive, that we are causes; that is to say, if the 'I' were not a cause for itself, and the perception of its primitive causality were not the same as the apperception of its existence?" (Maine de Biran, *Réponses*, in *Oeuvres*, IV, 369.)

13. *Ordo petitionum non respondit ordini executione, sed ordini desiderii sive intentionis, in quo prius est finis quam ea quae sunt ad finem.* (*Summa Theologica* IIa, IIae, q. LXXXIII, art. 9.)

14. Leibniz writes: "This reminds me of a fine passage in the *Phaedo* of Socrates, which conforms marvelously with my sentiments on this point. . . . Its relevance here has made me want to translate it:

". . . I was surprised to see that he [Anaxagorus] had made no use of this governing intelligence which he had put forward . . . in which he did as the man who having said that Socrates does things intelligently, and afterwards going on to explain in particular the causes of his actions, would say that he is seated here because he has a body composed of bones, skin, and sinews, that the bones are solid but they have gaps or joints, that the sinews can be tightened and relaxed, and that is why the body is flexible and finally why I am sitting here. Or if, wishing to account for this present discourse, he were to have recourse to the air, the organs of speech and hearing, and similar things, forgetting meanwhile the true causes, namely that the Athenians have believed that they would do better to condemn me rather than to acquit me, and that I myself have believed that I did better to stay sitting here than to flee. For by my faith, but for this, these sinews and bones would have been with the Beotians and Megarians long since, if I had not found that it is more just and nobler on my part to suffer the penalty which my country wishes to impose on me than to live elsewhere vagabond and exiled. That is why it is unreasonable to call these bones and sinews and their movements causes. It is true that he who should say that I could not do all this without bones and sinews would be right, but the true cause is something else, and this is only a condition without which the cause would not be a cause."

(Leibniz, *Discourse on Metaphysics,* trans. P. G. Lucas and L. Grint [Manchester: Manchester University Press, 1961], p. 20.)

15. Ernout and Meillet, *Dictionnaire étymologique de la langue latine.*

5

The Conditional

I have formed a representation that does not correspond to observable reality and placed it in a domain suited to receive it; now my activity tends toward the validation of what my imagination has constructed. For the event to comply with my design, the moral force of my intention must hold and push me on the road to the goal. But the road must really lead to the goal; and this implies that the appropriate road has been discerned (an intellectual operation). Hobbes put it like this: "For the thoughts are to the desires as scouts, and spies to range abroad, and find the way to the things desired."[1]

The image that I have formed and placed somewhere in "time to come" is like a beacon beckoning me. I could march straight to my goal: this is the heroic attitude represented in legends by the young knight who, from afar, sees a princess in a vision and sets off, confident his dream will keep him on the right road and his courage will meet any obstacle. He does not worry beforehand about encountering dragons or having to cross bridges no wider than "the edge of a sword." In the saint we find an even more pronounced expression of this attitude—he only needs to be faithful, and is quite happy if he can persist on the path revealed by God, whatever his worldly success or failure; God alone must smooth the way, if He so chooses.

Coming down to a more common attitude, we find man preoccupied with the choice of the best road, the road presenting the least obstacles (or, in other words, obstacles he has the best chance of overcoming).

[33]

But as soon as we raise the problem of the best road, the future intervenes as an "object of knowledge." A simple example will illustrate this. A medical expedition must provide urgent relief to a devastated region—the problem is quickly solved by finding the shortest route on a map. But this solution rests on a postulate, namely that the map, which portrays a past state of affairs, is still valid at the time of the operation, in the immediate future.

Let us further suppose that the emergency is due to a flood. The shortest road into the region runs across a bridge threatened by rising water; the leader of the expedition has learned that yesterday it was possible to cross the bridge. But will his vehicles be able to cross it when they reach it tomorrow? He does not know; he thinks it possible that the bridge will be open, but also possible that it will not—and in this case the convoy will have to turn back and much valuable time will be lost. Thus the choice of a road is affected by uncertainty about a future factor. Except for this uncertainty, the leader of the expedition would unhesitatingly have taken the shortest route indicated by the map, but instead he now deliberates. Will he gamble on the bridge being open or will he choose what appears to be the safest solution, a longer road where no factors of uncertainty have been indicated?

"Casuels"

Problems of decision arise when future uncertainties are taken into consideration. Let us consider a trivial example. In April, Primus forms the project of buying a house belonging to Secundus, for he knows that, in October, Tertius should repay him a sum of money sufficient to cover the down payment. Suppose Primus believes it certain that Secundus will not sell the house to anyone else and that Tertius will discharge his debt on time. The choice between buying now and buying in October is a simple weighing of definite advantages against definite drawbacks: enjoyment of the property this summer versus the payment of interest on the money borrowed pending Tertius' settlement of his debt.

But Primus doubts that Secundus will hold the house for him until October—a reason for buying immediately. And he also doubts that Tertius will discharge his debt—a reason for delaying the purchase. As soon as Primus recognizes that for him the actions of Secundus and Tertius are uncertain, the degrees of likelihood he attaches to their actions become important factors in his decision.

The greater he thinks the likelihood of Secundus finding another buyer and the lesser he thinks the likelihood of Tertius breaking his word, the greater will be his haste to buy. Obversely, as the likelihoods are reversed, his haste to buy will diminish.

Now what is Primus doing when he takes into account the possible actions of Secundus and Tertius? He is scanning the future for mobile elements that are independent of his will: these mobile elements are seen by him as future contingents, or, as I prefer to say, *casuels*.

It is particularly important to note that the events Primus picks out as uncertain—his *casuels*—are not the only *casuels* liable to affect the results of his action, rather they are the only ones he identifies and takes into account. Even though he buys the house and Tertius pays up, he can still be prevented from moving in—if, for example, he is stationed abroad. The event was unforeseen, but surely not entirely unforeseeable? "Primus should have considered this possibility," we might say. But if we were to take that position, where should Primus stop in his evaluation of possibilities? No decisions would ever be made if we did not limit the number of uncertain factors to be taken into consideration.

The Path on the Map

An individual who forms and pursues a project is generally inclined to postulate the stability of the universe. Suppose that Ego's project is to be (or have his son be) in such and such a situation in a certain year in the future. Suppose, moreover, that this situation now exists objectively: it is a "post" or "station." Clearly, Ego's project is limited to transporting himself (or his son, or some other person who is close and dear) from the position he presently occupies to another presently existing position— the desired one, which he does not now occupy.

Here Ego's design is a simple and clearly defined change of position, in a social space that he regards as a "datum"; it is a displacement to be effected in time and is perfectly analogous to a journey in space. A presently known "map of society" indicates which path to follow. A youth with the goal of going to the École Polytechnique has no doubt about what steps to take; his path is marked out as clearly as a slalom course. Thus his project will fail only if he misses a "gate" or is beaten by other competitors. There is no uncertainty about the "course"; the only uncertainty concerns the performance of the student (that depends on him) and how his performance will compare with that of others.

For the time being let us picture society as a vast complex of exactly defined situations, connected by well-known ways of advancement. Anybody wanting to go from A to B has no doubt about the way to take. The only thing that could prevent one from reaching B is a congestion arising because more travelers press along path AB than there are empty spaces in B. In other words, there is an imbalance between the supply of position B and the demand for them—a phenomenon unavoidably present in any society.

Many human projects have the simple character just described. They can fail only because there is congestion, only because too many desire-arrows are aimed at the same target. However, the inconvenience and disappointment that some must suffer when there is too great a pressure in the same direction are of much less interest to us than the disturbance of Ego's efforts brought about when Alter's path crosses Ego's. Here it is no longer a question of desire-arrows all traveling in the same direction, though in too great numbers to all reach the target, but rather of trajectories interfering in such a way that one or both of the projects must fail. The collision of two cars at an intersection provides a trivial illustration. There is no enmity between the two drivers, no fundamental incompatibility between their projects, and yet each driver in pursuing his own project puts a *casuel* in the way of the other, one that can prove fatal at that.

We say that Primus' project failed because of a mishap if its realization was checked by an action of Secundus not specifically directed against him. The untoward event is fortuitous, an "accident"—this word properly means "fortuitous encounter," and because fortuitous, therefore unforeseeable. "Unforeseeable" is used here in the strict sense of the word; any man knows that life is filled with accidents, but it is impossible for him to imagine in a specific manner all the different accidents that could occur, and if he attempted to do it, he would go mad. It would be prudent for Primus to take special precautions with regard to Secundus if he knows that Secundus has proclaimed the intention of killing him. But with regard to the unknown driver who may one day kill him in an accident, it is obvious that Primus can only adopt precautions of a very general nature.

He cannot foresee each individual action that "is not concerned with him"—in the true sense of the phrase—and is not directed at him; he must attempt to foresee such actions as a rough over-all approximation if their global effect changes the circumstances of his own action. Consider yet another trivial example. Primus lives in Fontainebleau and drives every day to his office in Paris. If he has to be there by a fixed time, he would be imprudent not to leave earlier on Mondays and earlier still on the morning after a holiday, when the situation confronting him is, for his purpose, equivalent to an extension of the distance; at these times the traffic, its swollen volume acting as an obstruction, is forced to move more slowly.

This deformation of the map is episodic and periodic. It can be foreseen because the phenomenon is a recurrent one and also because there is a sufficient reason for it. With the perspective gained from this type of deformation, we can turn to a theme of much greater interest—historical deformation. It is, for instance, a historical deformation that, in traveling time, the distance from Paris to New York should now be as short as the distance from Paris to Brive.

The Deformation of the Social Surface

This theme is of primary importance. The deformation of the social surface should be understood in a metaphorical and quite general sense. Such a deformation occurs if, for example, Primus builds up his savings bit by bit, thinking that they will afford him a certain standard of living in his old age, and then inflation partly wipes them out. We can picture this as a contraction of the steps Primus had taken toward his goal, or as a *recession* of his goal; thus there is a *deformation*. Or consider a parliamentary candidate who "cultivates" the electors of a constituency in a time of limited suffrage and suddenly finds that his goal has become more remote due to the introduction of universal suffrage. Or imagine that a young man embarks on a career leading to the governorship of a colony and then sees the colonies disappear. His goal has been obliterated.

A man's actions are situated in a *field of operations* that the mind is naturally inclined to treat as a stable *datum.* In other words, a man uses a "Map of the Present," which, he assumes, remains valid throughout the period of his interest. If his project is to reach a certain situation or place, he can locate this target on the Map of the Present, and on this point he can place a marker indicating his projected date of arrival. His path is now defined, even though it may comprise alternatives if he allows for the intervention of *casuels*. But these *casuels* are events of the same order as the man's own actions. Of a quite different order are the landslides and upheavals that can occur. A project can be "very well calculated" with respect to *casuels,* yet fail owing to a social deformation.

A qualification is called for here: there is one project and one only that a man can maintain whatever the circumstances—his project to strive toward moral perfection. This truth is an old one, but that is no reason why it should be forgotten.

Let us return to projects that are subject to circumstances. Clearly, a man generally bases his calculations on the Map of the Present; the luminous spot that attracts him is situated both in his *personal future* and in a *social present;* he plots his path on the basis of a given map of society. In general, it is not natural, nor even possible, for a man to conceive what deformations the map will undergo. Now these deformations are precisely the object of our attention.

How do these deformations arise? It would be simpler to define when they do not arise. The social surface is nothing but the contour or outline of a host of moving bodies—like the outline of a swarm of bees or a school of fish. To the extent that the same repetitive patterns and mutual relations are maintained in the behavior of different people, the social surface is stable. When I say "I have a flight which will get me to New York in time for the conference," I quite rightly speak of my way of arriving in New York in good time as something that I "have"—a way resting on the behavior of all sorts of unknown people at Orly, Kennedy Airport, and on the plane, on all of whom I am counting. A strike at Orly will remind me that my certitude about the configuration of the social surface is a postulate relating to the behavior of other men.

Nothing is absolutely solid in society. A lifelong wish has been fulfilled and Primus has been appointed prime minister. But is he really prime minister if the government he has joined is jeered by the populace and forsaken by the police? Wandering through his office, Primus repeats to himself a vain title now empty of all substance because its substance is made up of the attitudes people usually assume toward its bearer. Any power, whether social or political, is maintained by people's attitudes; any project, short or long, shallow or profound, is founded on their attitudes and behavior.

Now each of us is capable of changing his attitude and behavior. By a false analogy with the movements of the molecules of a gas, one might think that the movements of the individual members of a society do not affect the whole—but nothing could be further from the truth. The gaseous state is a total absence of form; this formlessness arises from and is maintained by random movements, but no definite form could be conserved in the same way. Chance might produce it, but it could not maintain it.

The problem of form has not ceased to exercise the mind of man, and two key notions always emerge—program and pressure. The easiest case to understand is a stage play; in each performance, we find the same form: each actor faithfully executes his role and is enclosed in it by the cues of the other players. Metaphorically speaking, the cells of an organism function in the same way; each one is endowed with a complete genetic program but is pushed into a special job. And, in a sense, the emphasis now placed on the genetic code carried by cells vindicates Maupertuis' hypothesis[2] of a special memory imprinted on them.

Concerning the individuals of a society, we cannot doubt that they have received a code of behavior from their family and from society, that they are subject to pressure from their fellow men, and that they are pushed into particular roles. But we also know that they are able to form and pursue projects. And each project is the germ of a shoot which may or may not be propitious for the maintenance of the general form of the society.

Lesage once made use of a Lame Demon who unroofed houses to reveal what was going on inside. Let us suppose that this *diable boîteux* could reveal people's minds in the same way, enabling us to surprise the projects each member of a society forms in his inner self. We could then apprehend, at their origin, those shoots which as they grow will deform the familiar social surface and produce swellings, fractures, and cracks.

What will these changes be? How can they be foreseen? Here lies the subject that preoccupies us.

NOTES

1. Thomas Hobbes, *Leviathan,* Part I, Chap. 8.
2. Maupertuis, *Essai sur la formation des corps organisés* (Berlin, 1754).

6

The Future as an

Object of Knowledge

Man is a being who desires and who acts. He needs the future—into this domain he projects the image toward which his will directs his actions, the image representing his wish. But he conceives of the future as something other than a receptacle of the images he undertakes to transform into realities. Man is also a being who knows or strives to know; and he thinks of the future as a domain inhabited by future realities, or *futura*, of which he tries to form adequate images.

The expression "That will be" can be used with very different meanings. Sometimes, when it is doing the work of "That shall be," it indicates a strong involvement of the speaker's desires ("I want this to happen, and will make it happen"). At other times, when it is doing its own work, it is a simple judgment of fact ("I see this coming, whether I like it or not"). In the former case, we would speak of a project; in the latter, of foresight. The statement "I see this coming" corresponds to the attitude of a spectator who tries to identify future events, which, in his conception, come toward him, growing more and more recognizable as they draw nearer. On the contrary, a man with a project strides toward the goal he has chosen.

I want to examine here what degree and mode of knowledge we have, or think we have, of things to come, or *futura*. My purpose is, may I repeat, essentially descriptive. What I shall look at is the way our mind treats the future.

Futura Subjective Certa

It is all very well to say that the future is unknown. The fact remains that we treat many aspects of it as known, and if we did not we could never form any projects. Even a perfectly simple project such as attending a conference involves our feeling assured the conference will take place. The acquisition of a railway timetable is evidence that we trust to a present statement of future events. Notes of future events stud the pages of a memorandum book. When we speak of incertitude, we often do nothing more than insert a question mark somewhere in a string of assertions. Thus a novelist with the project of winning the Prix Goncourt may doubt that he will be its recipient but not that the prize will be awarded; and if the first point naturally matters to him, it appears to us merely as an uncertain facet of an assured event.

A man's project is situated within a framework of subjective certainties that he uses in order to take his bearings. The subjective certainties are the features of the future that he treats as known (*foreknown*) and does not question, on which he bases his calculations, and in relation to which he regulates his course of action. Let me give a specific illustration. (A great tragedy has occurred since this was written, and if I retain the following passage, I hope nobody will see in it a sign of insensibility to the loss of so noble a figure, *amor ac deliciae generis humani.*)

Suppose that in 1962 a Democratic politician toys with the project of succeeding John F. Kennedy to the Presidency. The relevant aspects of the future held certain by him are as follows: 1. as far as man can see, there will continue to be a President of the United States; 2. Presidential elections will take place on the second Tuesday of November in 1964 and 1968; 3. except for a physical accident, John F. Kennedy will be the Democratic candidate in 1964 (a President is always renominated by his party at the end of his first term of office); 4. Kennedy cannot run as a candidate in 1968 (because of the constitutional amendment prohibiting a third term of office); 5. the Democratic candidate of 1968 will be nominated by the party convention to be held around July of that year.

Our politician thus clearly sees that a necessary (but not sufficient) condition of his occupying the White House is for him to obtain an absolute majority of the votes cast at the Democratic National Convention of 1968. But we see no less clearly that his project rests on assumptions which he regards as certainties and which appear as *solid* elements in his representation of the future.

When I speak of "certainty" in this book, it should always be understood that the certainty is somebody's and that it may be falsified by events. This conforms to present usage, from which we should depart as little as possible. A man is certain about a future thing when he does not doubt it in any way. This does not mean that a denial of this thing is logically absurd or historically impossible. There is evidently no logical absurdity in imagining that American Presidential elections will not be held in 1968, whereas there would be in supposing that the number 13 could be thrown with two dice. Nor, as I shall bring out below, is there a historical impossibility. What constitutes the certainty in the sense that I am taking it here is that a given person does not contemplate that things could be otherwise. Since we are examining the way our mind thinks the future, I am fully justified in thus speaking of certainty in this sense of subjective certainty. Later we shall see whether there are any grounds for speaking of objective certainty, and if so, it will be designated as such; but in the absence of a qualifying adjective, I shall always mean subjective certainty.

Structural Certainties

The certainties of our American politician are really aspects of an order that is held by him to be certain. In all cases where our future certainties are features inherent in an order in which we have confidence, I shall speak of *structural certainties*.

We have a rich store of structural certainties about the natural order —when I see the sun setting, I expect it to appear again; when I see winter coming, I expect it will be followed by spring. These are simple examples. In all ages and lands, a profound instinct has led men to set up a social order affording them analogous assurances. Certaonties provided by the natural order and by the social order resemble one another in that they are all aspects of an order. If we are confident that the sun will rise, it is not because this expectation has never been deceived within the collective memory of mankind, but because that occurrence is an aspect of the clockwork of the heavens. Similarly, if Americans are confident that Presidential elections will be held on the first Tuesday after the first Monday in November 1968, it is not because of an observed recurrence, but because the elections are an aspect of the constitutional order.

Nonetheless, there is a major difference: the natural order is a *datum*, whereas the constitutional order is a construct. The constitutional order is modifiable and can, moreover, collapse.

Americans do not doubt that the President now in office will be succeeded by another President selected by a well-known procedure. Nor did the French doubt in 1785 that on his death Louis XVI would be immediately followed by another king of France designated according to the well-known rule of succession through the male line. But this certainty was belied by the event. Though a long and uninterrupted series of applications of the same rule fosters our conviction that this rule will continue to be valid, this example from the history of France attests that a long chain of past recurrences affords no objective guarantee for the future. This point bears emphasizing, for in some fields something held to be probable on a priori grounds is later held to be proved if it is confirmed by a long series of tests. Not so in history; here our conviction is strengthened without its objective foundation being verified. And, indeed, in a case such as we are considering, we must ask two questions—the immediately settled one as to whether a given rule belongs to the established order, and the infinitely more difficult one as to whether this order will be maintained.

The French example we have given provides an interesting historical lesson. The old monarchy, under which the head of state was selected in accordance with an unchanging rule, collapsed one hundred and seventy years ago. Except during the sixty-four years of the Third Republic, there have been only two cases where a head of state was chosen by the same rule as his predecessor: Charles X succeeded Louis XVIII in accordance with the ancient monarchical rule, and René Coty succeeded Vincent Auriol in accordance with the constitution of the Fourth Republic. In all other cases, the new head of state was installed, or installed himself, by virtue of a new rule. And this is worth noting, for it suggests that a structural certainty which collapses is not easily replaced by another.

Contractual Assurances

Let us repeat it again: a man's project is founded on many assurances which he thinks he has about the future; some—the ones I have called *structural*—depend on the established order in which he moves, while others depend on people's undertakings to do something (for example, a contract or a promise). When I take a train in order to keep an appointment in town, I am confident that it will take me to a station close to the designated meeting place—and this certainty is structural. I am also confident that my partner will be there at the appointed time. But though the train could have a breakdown, it is far more likely that my partner will forget our appointment. Thus it would be a great license to speak of certainty here. True, in practice I neglect the likelihood of being let down, and accordingly I could speak of a "moral certainty," following an ancient usage.[1] The expression is a recognized one, but inconvenient, and it would be more suitable to refer to a *sufficient certainty,* that is, a certainty sufficient for me to leave the contrary event out of consideration. But is this not still too strong and would it not be better to speak of assurance? For certainty implies that I in no way envisage the absence of my partner, and that is more than I can say and would prevent me from speaking of a greater or smaller confidence in his promise to meet me.

In all ages, keeping one's word has been considered to be of major importance. The reasons for this are easy to see—we need holds on the future, and we are provided with such a hold when somebody promises something to us ("I know he will be there; I have his word for it"). In that extreme form of action—war—no operation can be carried out unless men are in the specified positions at the specified times. In business, a "firm which does not honor its commitments" causes others to collapse. Indeed, the word "honor," which I have just used, is inseparable from the ideas of commitment and expectation. A man of honor behaves in the way expected of him and as he has committed himself to do. Consequently, for a partner or neighbor, his honor is a guarantee of the future; so much so that if his sense of honor grows weak and people doubt that he is bound by his word, they try to strengthen the assurance he gives them by making him take a solemn oath or by inducting conjurers. A promise or oath in the presence of witnesses and with the handing over of a security occupies a large place in the ancient customs of all peoples.[2]

And how could it be otherwise? Montaigne once said that a liar undermines society.[3] But we must add that a man who promises some future action and convinces us he will carry it out thereby drives a pile into a marshland: we go forward, confident of finding piles here and there; this is of great value, and for our expectation to be deceived is correspondingly grave.

In fact, the more one thinks about man's efforts to introduce something known and steadfast—something reliable—into the shifting ground of the future, the more important these efforts appear to be. They may be interpreted as an offensive collectively waged on the future and designed to partly tame it. As a consequence, the future is known not through the guesswork of the mind, but through social efforts, more or less conscious, to cast "jetties" out from an established order and into the uncertainty ahead. The network of reciprocal commitments traps the future and moderates its mobility. All this tends to reduce the uncertainty.

We have said enough about particular projects formed by an individual and about the knowledge of the future assumed in their formation; now we must ask ourselves whether men have always behaved as if society were animated by an obscure general wish to give itself a sufficiently known future. But this idea suggests another. Our modern civilization has repudiated the sacredness of institutions and commitments, and therewith the means of achieving a known future. As we have loosened our guaranteed holds on the future, so have we facilitated change and made the future unknown. Clearly, we have far fewer certainties about the future of our civilization than the Chinese once had about the future of theirs. The great problem of our age is that we want things to change more rapidly, and at the same time we want to have a better knowledge of things to come. I do not say a reconciliation of these desires is impossible, but it does raise a problem.

NOTES

1. See, for example, Jacques Bernoulli, *Ars Conjectandi*, Part IV, p. 217.

2. In primitive times a security was not designed to serve as a possible means of compensation, and in this respect it differed from the present system of mortgaging property in order to back up a promise. The pledge was a simple ring or among certain primitive peoples a mere stone—a token of purely moral worth; to brand the promise-breaker with infamy, it was sufficient to produce his pledge.

3. "Our understanding of one another being conducted through speech, he who counterfeits his speech betrays public society. It is our only tool for communicating our wishes and thoughts; it is the interpreter of our soul. If it fails us, we no longer cleave together, and we know one another no more; if it deceives us, it breaks off our commerce and dissolves all the ties of our polity." (Montaigne, *Essais*, II, Chap. XVIII.)

7

The Principle
of Uncertainty

As shown in the preceding chapter, we think certain aspects of the future are known, because we rely on "dikes" built to contain its uncertainty. But the more we trust these "dikes," the less they provoke our curiosity. And when people speak about knowledge of the future they are not usually concerned with the aspects they believe to be trustworthy: what they would like to guess is the novelty ahead. We cannot, however, discuss the nature of this undertaking until we consider the "being" of the future.

To start with, I wish to consider the expression "The Discovery of the Future"—the title of a lecture given by H. G. Wells sixty years ago on the difference in the mind's relations to the past and to the future.[1] In this lecture Wells made this important assertion:

I believe that the deliberate direction of historical study and of economic and social study toward the future and an increasing reference, a deliberate and courageous reference, to the future in moral and religious discussion, would be enormously stimulating and enormously profitable to our intellectual life.

Wells's recommendations create no difficulty, but the title he chose does raise a problem. We speak of "discovery" when a present, hidden object is brought to light. We would say without hesitation that we have discovered a distant object, when it is perceived by us through a pair of fieldglasses; that we have discovered a minute form, when it is revealed to us by a microscope. In both cases we feel convinced that the object existed before we became aware of it. The continent we call America existed before Christopher Columbus landed in the Caribbean. And thus the expression "discovery of the future" implies that the future already "exists" in some manner.

Is this notion acceptable?

The Future Regarded as Pre-existent

If I think of the future as pre-existent—something existing before it appears—I regard it as something which is by nature visible, though invisible to me because my sight is too feeble. Having ample opportunity to observe that others know things that I ignore, I will willingly admit that cleverer men than I can see things in advance.

Such seems to have been the prevailing attitude of man toward things to come; man has always assumed that they could be foretold. It is significant that every language contains an archaic word for the man (or woman) who has the faculty of foresight (*mantis, vates, kahin,* etc.). If soothsayers play an important part in epics about the dim past of each civilization, the reason cannot lie in a mere coincidence of poetic imagination. Even within historical times, official recognition is sometimes accorded to divination—as for instance in the age of Cicero.[2] And though divination may now be no more than a trade, it has no lack of adepts, as can be seen in the popular press.

We should not be surprised that man's interest in foretellers has survived the falsification of countless predictions. What man regards as possible, he sometimes believes to be very difficult; as long as he is sure that a target is really there, he can still hope that a better marksman will hit it, despite all the bullets which have gone astray.

The considerations impelling us to regard the future as objectively certain seem very strong. To start with, let us consider astronomy, the most ancient of all sciences and one which has long fascinated mankind. An ordinary man has advance knowledge of when he will see the full moon; similarly, the specialist knows what complex configuration of the heavens will be observed on a certain date in the future; and men could say as much—about the more easily observable stars—in the days when the heavenly bodies were still thought to move on a celestial sphere. The foreseeability of the map of the heavens has made a deep impression on man. Since ancient times he has had an obstinate belief in a correspondence between movements in the heavens and changes on earth, in a correlation between stellar *conjunctions* and *conjunctures* of human events.

I will not enlarge on the persistent prestige of astrology, but wish to point out that in Descartes's time the office of royal professor in mathematics went to an ardent astrologer, Jean-Baptiste Morin,[3] who, according to Bayle, played a very important role thanks to his predictions.[4] Morin was, at the same time, enough of a scientist to draw Descartes into a discussion of the theory of light. But even though the prestige of astrology fed on superstition about the influence of stars, it also rested on a more solid intellectual foundation: the conviction that every occurrence in the universe is due to the working of a vast mechanism and that the heavens—the most easily observable part of this mechanism—can tell us about happenings elsewhere because of a simple correspondence between the parts. By taking one step more and letting the notion of a parallel correspondence drop, we can arrive at the belief that conjunctures of human affairs take place in the same mode, with the same necessity, as stellar conjunctions.

Thus we end up with a belief that nobody criticizes as superstition and to which many think there is no reasonable alternative.

On the Objective Certainty of the Future

There have always been important thinkers who maintained that the future course of human affairs is *objectively certain*. Jacques Bernoulli put it like this:

> All things past, present, or future that exist or are done under the sun are always perfectly certain, both in themselves and objectively. Things present or past are established facts; since, by mere fact that they are or have been, they cannot not be or not have been: but it cannot be doubted that the same holds for future things. . . .[5]

How are we to understand this objective certainty? Perhaps it is a simple consequence of the law of contradiction? Thus, it is true that a certain sea battle took place yesterday, and therefore it is not true that the sea battle did not take place. But similarly would we say of a sea battle to take place tomorrow that it is now certain it will take place then, or will not take place then? Aristotle, from whom I have borrowed this example, clearly distinguished between the necessity (logical) of the disjunction and the lack of necessity (historical) of either of the branches.[6]

None of us would hesitate to say about some specific future event: "It is possible the event will take place and also possible it will not." And we would not even think to add: "For that matter, it is logically necessary that the event will or will not take place," for we do not see in this statement any source of knowledge. But Diodorus of Megara once wished to deprive us of the notion of "possibles."

For him, a possible can only be something that is or will be true; what is to be hereafter comes about necessarily; what will not be, cannot be.[7] Cicero upheld this opinion and illustrated it in a letter in which he was concerned with the possibility of a visit from his friend Varro: "You must know that about things possible I agree with Diodorus. If you are about to come, you must know that your coming is necessary; if you are not, your coming is impossible."[8] He discusses the opinion of Diodorus at greater length in another passage where the notion of a "possible" is yet again ruled out—nothing but the necessary could come about in the past and everything that can happen either is now or will be. The notion of truth is introduced: for things future, just as for things past, truth cannot change into falsehood (*nec magis commutari ex veris in falsa posse, quae futura sunt quam ea quae facta sunt*). Finally, if immutability is manifest in things past (*in factis*), this property pertains no less to things future (*in futuris*) even though their immutability is less manifest.[9]

Uncertainty—Of Things or of the Mind?

According to the doctrine of Diodorus, I am wrong whenever I say of a future event: "There are several possibilities"; there is only one possibility, the one which will be actualized. Suppose that we ask an American political expert to tell us who will be President of the United States in 1969 and he answers us by drawing up a list of "possibles." This reply, it follows from Diodorus, betrays the expert's ignorance—just as if I were to answer the question: "Who was king of France in 1569?" by giving a list of names between which I hesitate, instead of simply saying "Charles IX." In short, there is nothing uncertain about the future but only ignorance in the surmiser.

We can justify this doctrine only by so interpreting it as to do away with all its interest. Thus, suppose that during Spinoza's lifetime I foretell his death in The Hague; this comes to pass; and so, after the event, it turns out that I foretold the truth—in making my prediction, I was speaking the truth. But this truth appears to us as something fortuitous rather than necessary. Whereas Diodorus would want to claim very much more: his doctrine is in accord with the Stoic hypothesis of an all-embracing mechanism. The doctrine recurs in similar philosophies, as for instance Spinoza's, which is criticized by Bayle in the following terms:

> Spinozists are confronted with a great difficulty in that according to their doctrine it was just as impossible in all time for Spinoza not to die in The Hague as it is for two and two to equal six. They are well aware that this is a necessary consequence of their doctrine, and a consequence which repels, frightens, and arouses opposition because of its absurdity, its diametrical opposition to common sense.[10]

Cassandra and Oedipus

If a particular event is necessary, it is in itself capable of being foretold. But consider the consequences. Suppose that Cassandra had specified that Troy would fall when a wooden horse was brought within its walls. The Trojans, had they believed her, would have left the horse outside the city, and her prediction would have been falsified. But then a supposedly "necessary" event would not have taken place, and a logical contradiction is implied.

According to Cicero, the Stoics believed in the necessity of the future and the possibility of divination.[11] At first sight, the two seem perfectly compatible: if the future is fixed, it is knowable. The Stoics said that the gods, acting out of benevolence, helped man to know this necessary future. But, if we fore-know the future, we can change it, and it is no longer known. And, if we cannot change the future, prior knowledge ceases to be a good. Had Priam always known of the catastrophe by which his days would end, how cheerless his life would have been![12]

The myth of Oedipus seems specially designed to show that man is powerless to change a future of which he has foreknowledge. The oracle said that the son born to Laius would murder his father and wed his mother; Laius' subsequent action of leaving the child to die of exposure was precisely what led to the fulfillment of the prophecy. This tragedy evokes profound terror but has no demonstrative value. A precise prediction can be belied. If Henry IV of France had known that Ravaillac planned to kill him, he would have imprisoned the would-be assassin and the so-called "necessary" event would not have taken place.

A principle of uncertainty characterizes the particular events which most directly interest us, inasmuch as any knowledge we acquire of them can incite us to an action which will contradict this knowledge.

The Dominating Future and the Masterable Future

The reader is no doubt impatient with my long discussion of the particular event. "Of course," says he, "the particular event is unpredictable. The main outline of the future is all that interests us." I agree. All the same, by discussing the particular event, we have brought out the interplay of knowledge and power: the "knowledge" of a future event often spurs man to act so as to contradict that "knowledge." This is an important point, because man's power to act varies in extent and because there are different levels of power.

For a given person, who is at once knower and agent, the future is divided into *dominating* and *masterable* parts. The masterable future is what I can make other than it now presents itself. Consider this trivial example: I foresee that I will be soaked by rain, but I can contradict this prediction simply by putting on a raincoat. Here "it will rain" describes a dominating future over which I have no power.

I come now to what is, I think, the crucial point: in human affairs the future is often dominating as far as I am concerned, but is masterable by a more powerful agent, an agent from a different level. Suppose that I am the head of a business and that I see an economic recession coming: all that I can do is to adjust my actions so that my business will suffer as little as possible; I can, for instance, reduce my inventory. For me, the recession is a dominating future, but not so for the government, which has ways of preventing it. The government controls monetary and fiscal policy, public-works spending, and so forth, and thus it can master my dominating future.

We have not wasted any time by acquainting ourselves with an uncertainty principle which arises from our power to prevent now foreseen future happenings.

For the uncertainty principle, which holds on the smallest scale for individual man, also holds on a bigger scale for a higher-level agent.[18]

The Interplay of Knowledge and Power

Let me consider by way of example a phenomenon which I take to heart. During the last fifteen years there has been a considerable increase of noxious fumes in the atmosphere of Paris. The average inhabitant has become quite conscious of this nuisance: he expects its further progress, and this to him is a dominating future—there is nothing he can do to change it and his only possible alternative is to move out of town.

The individual town-dweller, while expressing his feeling that the atmosphere has worsened and his opinion that it will worsen further, feels no urge to give a quantitative expression to past and future change. But some sort of "pollution index" can be constructed by the aggregation of various measurements, and such an index will be needed by a committee of citizens formed to demand corrective action. The future course of that index will then be plotted by direct extrapolation of past increases, or by a somewhat less crude procedure, based on extrapolation of underlying factors. In any case, what one thus gets is "a line of the future" representing what is "expected to happen."

This is often called a "prediction"; but, if that term is used, it should be accompanied by the adjective "conditional." The true meaning of this forecast is to express the belief that the future course will be such, unless something is done, done by an agent of a superior level with sufficient powers to deal with pollution as a future *to be mastered.*

I call a forecast of this kind a "primary forecast"—*primary* not because it is a fairly simple intellectual procedure, but because it represents a first stage in our dealing with the future course of a phenomenon; it is taken as the final stage only in the absence of any human agency capable of exerting a strong influence on the course. If there is an authority with such a capacity, then the primary forecast serves to challenge this authority: "This is our future, unless you take measures to amend it."

What measures? Some elimination of exhaust fumes will be obtained if traffic jams are eliminated, since idling engines are particularly poisonous. Far better results will be achieved if cars are fitted with devices turning the fumes back into the cylinders. But assuming that such a device cuts down the emission by a given percentage, the mere increase in the number of cars will in time nullify the gain. Finally one may contemplate some such radical measure as banning internal combustion engines[14] in towns and supplying energy to cars by fuel cells or other forms of storage. Obviously the authority has a choice of measures differing in efficiency, which it takes more or less time to bring into operation and which car users and manufacturers will regard as more or less annoying.

The partisans of each measure will claim that it will work wonders, its opponents that it is not energetic enough or that it is too radical. It is then of great interest to the authority to obtain definite answers to this question: "Supposing that we now adopted measure B, and taking into account that it cannot be immediately operative and that when it is operative, there will be another period before its effect is complete, what can we expect the future course of pollution to be?" Experts dislike plotting a new "line of the future" manifesting the effect of measure B; they prefer "interval prediction" ("no more than . . . and no less than . . .") to "point prediction" (the stating of definite values), but the authority tends to insist upon a definite "path," it being understood there is much leeway right and left.

It is in any case best for our present purpose to imagine that the authority is provided by its experts with a set of curves, one of which represents the "primary forecast," while each of the other curves pictures the more or less amended course of the phenomenon expected after the adoption of this or that corrective measure. The set of these curves constitute a fan of possible futures, of futuribles; it is not an exhaustive set: this or that "mix" of individual measures would produce another curve, and the discovery of a new process or the gaining of wider powers by the authority might introduce yet other possibilities.

The preparation of any of these curves is a "secondary forecast." While the primary forecast was a "prediction" *conditional* on the absence of any corrective action, each of the new curves is a "prediction" of the corrected course *conditional* on the taking of a certain definite action.

Obviously forecasts of this nature are of immense importance in decision-making. The making of such forecasts requires far more understanding of the phenomenon than is needed for a primary forecast. The efficiency of a factor to be injected can be evaluated only on the basis of known or presumed causal relationships.

Nonhistorical and Historical Predictions

The urge and indeed the necessity to deal more and more consciously with the future must lead to ever-wider use of primary forecasts (which are challenges) and of secondary forecasts (which are possibilities depending upon action). It is important to realize that neither a primary forecast nor a secondary forecast constitutes a *historical* prediction. The primary forecast is not an inevitable course of things; indeed our motive in formulating it is to provoke action apt to change it. A secondary forecast is meant to display what, to the expert's best estimate, can be brought about *if* the corresponding action is taken.

There is yet another form of forecast, which may be called "tertiary." Its author is aware of the primary forecast, of the proposals submitted to the authority, and of the secondary forecasts representing the expected outcomes of these proposals. Now he wants to "predict" what the course of pollution will in fact turn out to be. This implies a "prediction" bearing upon the behavior of the authority. For instance, a man may argue like this: "Knowing the temper of the authority, I assume that its choice of corrective measures will fall upon the least unpopular, which happens also to be the least promising. After some time, it will become clear that the nuisance is not being properly countered, and the authority will then respond to the outcry by taking a much stronger measure; but it will compensate for that show of strength by a weak and loose implementation." From suppositions of this nature our forecaster will derive his "line of the future," which this time has the character of a historic prediction (though only imperfectly, because he excludes exogenous factors).

It is immediately clear that this sort of forecast, which includes guesses concerning the choice and timing of unique moves by a few individuals, is most hazardous. Any confusion between "tertiary" forecasting and the other types must be carefully avoided.

NOTES

1. Delivered at the Royal Institution on January 24, 1902, and published by A. C. Fifield, London, 1913.

2. Cicero speaks of divination in great detail in *De Divinatione*.

3. For a very circumstantial account of Morin's life, with many intriguing details, see Bayle's *Dictionnaire* (4th edn.), III, 424–31.

4. Morin's large work, *Astrologica Gallica*, was posthumously published in 1661 thanks to the generosity of the queen of Poland, to whom he had once foretold a throne. Bayle portrays him as an intimate of Chavigny, the Secretary of State, who relied on his advice in choosing times for journeys and important undertakings.

5. "Omnia quae sub Sole sunt vel fiunt, praeterita presentia sive futura, in se et objective summam semper certitudinem habent. De praesentibus et praeteritis constat; quoniam eo ipso, quo sunt vel fuerunt, non possunt non esse vel fuisse: Nec de futuris ambigendum . . ." *Artis Conjectandi Pars Quarta, tradens usum et applicationem praecedentis Doctrinae in civilibus, Moralibus et Oeconomicis,* ed. Nicholaus Bernoulli (Basel, 1713), p. 210.

6. "Dico autem puta necesse quidem fore navale bellum vel non fore cras, non tamen fieri navale bellum cras necessarium neque non fieri; fieri tamen vel non fieri necessarium." Aristotle, *Peri Hermeneias,* trans. Guillaume de Moerbecke, in V. J. Isaac, *Le Peri Hermeneias en Occident de Boèce à saint Thomas* (Paris, 1953), p. 168.

7. "Ille enim id solum fieri posse dicit, quod aut sit verum, aut futurum sit verum: et quidquid futurum sit, id dicit fieri necesse esse, et, quidquid non sit futurum, id negat fieri posse. Cicero, *De Facto,* VII.

8. *Ad Familiares,* IX, Letter 4 from Tusculum (June 707).

9. "Placet igitur Diodoro, id solum fieri posse, quod aut verum sit, aut verum futurum sit. Qui locus attingit hanc quaestionem, nihil fieri, quod non necesse fuerit; et, quidquid fieri possit, id aut esse jam, aut futurum esse; nec magis commutari ex veris in falsa ea posse, quae futura sunt, quam ea, quae facta sunt; sed in factis immutabilitatem apparere; in futuris quibusdam, quia non apparent, ne inesse quidem videri." Cicero, *De Facto,* IX.

10. "Chrysippe," note S, in Bayle, *Dictionnaire* (4th edn.), I, 174.

11. *De Divinatione,* in particular I, xxxviii.

12. Atque ego ne utilem quidem arbitror esse nobis futurarum rerum scientiam. Quae enim vita fuisset Priamo, si ab adolescentia scisset, quos eventus senectutis esset habiturus?" *De Divinatione,* II, ix.

13. Thus one must not be carried away by an analogy with Heisenberg's uncertainty principle, which is valid only on the atomic scale.

14. I speak as though internal combustion engines were the only source of pollution: this is an arbitrary but convenient simplification.

Part II

OF PREDICTIONS

8

Predictions: I

To cull old predictions about important subjects from great or worthy writers was the first idea that came to me when I began this study.

The predictions are old; their future is our past. Consequently, we can compare them with actuality. It so happens that events contradicted most of the predictions I shall mention; but it would take a base mind to rejoice at the mistakes of men who are a credit to our species and a very commonplace one to conclude that prediction is a foolhardy enterprise. The spirit in which this little collection should be approached is very different.

"Proference"

Man draws assertions about the future out of his present knowledge. If the reader studies himself reading a newspaper, he will notice that he often formulates *futura* which seem to be "promised" by the facts in the articles. By an unconscious procedure, he "deduces" a future aspect from a present one: but the term "deduction" suggests a rigor of which the procedure is devoid. The action of going from present data to an assertion about the future is *sui generis;* it lacks a name, and so I propose to call it "proference"; this suggests the action of carrying forward and will serve us more or less adequately.

The purpose of the quotations gathered here is to illustrate the elementary modes of proference. The mind spontaneously uses certain tricks for transforming present knowledge into "pseudo-knowledge" of the future. We shall see them employed. Observation and introspection both confirm that the mind uses these devices. A little reflection will show that we have no reason for assuming an exact correspondence between the process of preference and the process of history. On the one hand, I derive my view of the future from my view of the present; on the other, the future state of affairs comes out the present state of affairs. The two processes are of a quite different order. To improve forecasting is to bring the intellectual process closer to the historical process.

We obviously need to acquaint ourselves with the modes of proference, and to start with, it is worth considering the elementary modes, as the more elaborate ones may well turn out to be combinations of the simple ones.

I have said that the predictions assembled below illustrate the simple modes of proference. And indeed, the predictions were not the result of a conscious effort to forecast the future, even though they were made by eminent thinkers. Some of the predictions—as, for instance, Rousseau's—were tossed into a text quite incidentally; others—as, for instance, Condorcet's—were used as postulates in a discussion dealing with something quite different. And since these forecasts were not "careful" ones, they prove nothing about the impossibility of making better ones. Somebody might object to my picking forecasts so little valued by their own authors. But I did not say the authors attached no value to them. Quite the reverse. If the predictions were not carefully "worked out," the reason was that they seemed perfectly evident to their authors. Thus Rousseau says "it is very easy to foresee that . . ."; Condorcet speaks of "the great probability that . . ."; and Maistre says "the odds are a thousand to one that . . ."

Those men thought their pronouncements were *evident.* Simple, naïve modes of proference, which make a particular future seem evident, sometimes go wrong. This is one of the lessons that will emerge from the examination we are about to conduct, and it is a most useful lesson, for nowadays forecasts often seem very powerful because of the mathematical tools employed in them, but are really based on perfectly naïve modes of proference.

Our scrutiny of past predictions will enable us to make an inventory of the mind's natural modes of proference. It would be a great mistake to think that these simple modes are scorned in systematic forecasting, although their use may be regulated.

Prolongation of a Tendency

We generally imagine the future scene in terms of differences relative to the scene we now know. We naturally tend to think that elements of the scene that have remained unchanged will continue unchanged. This can be put so as to correspond more closely to the psychological reality: it is natural for us *not to think* of changes in parts of the scene that by standing still have left us unaware of their mobility. We are alert to future change only in parts where previous changes have made us aware of mobility. If the unchanged parts of the scene are important, the future validity of the "Map of the Present" is by so much the greater.[1] The unconscious purpose of primitive institutions is, it seems, to provide an assurance of continued validity. We ourselves are far removed from such a "stationary state"; we are vividly aware that many things have changed, and admit that they, these same things, will go on changing. But in what way will they change? The simplest idea to suggest itself is that they will change in the same direction and even at the same rate as in the past. In a supposedly stationary state, we postulate that tomorrow will be the same as today; likewise, when we are aware of movement, we assume that tomorrow will differ from today *in the same way as* today differs from yesterday. In doing this, we simply apply the postulate of inertia to moving things instead of to stationary things.

This simple idea exerts a strong sway over our minds. The lifespan of man has become longer; it will become still longer. The number of work hours in the year has decreased; it will decrease yet further. The standard of living has risen; it will rise even more. Whatever the precise reasons given to justify each such assumption, they are brought in only to justify this immediate and spontaneous conviction—things will go on *that* way, for they have already gone *that* way. The sharper our awareness of a past movement, the stronger our conviction of its future continuation. A comparison of French and American forecasts of economic growth shows how persuasive past change is felt to be: American experts say that the standard of living in the United States will go up 50 per cent during the next twenty-five years, while French experts say theirs will go up 150 per cent.[2] Yet we can find no reason for this enormous difference except in the past rates of growth of the two countries. (In the case of the United States, it makes no difference whether the "past" used as a basis for the projection is a short past, extending back as far as the end of World War II, or a long past, stretching back into the nineteenth century. Whereas the French figure is based on the short past alone, the long past would lead to a lower figure than for the United States.)

Because prolongation of present tendencies plays such an important role in our anticipations, it is not surprising to find that this mode of proference was also important in former times. Thus, on the basis of the political evolution of the nineteenth century, Émile Faguet made this prediction for our own century:

> The chances are that from now on history will be less filled with vicis-situdes, less colorful, and less dramatic. The great conqueror, the great re-former, and the great statesman will become increasingly rare.[3]

He was convinced—fifteen years before World War I, eighteen before the advent of Lenin, and twenty-three before that of Mussolini—that nations would no longer be ruled, but would govern themselves in a "spirit of peaceful conservatism, economy, timidity, and preservation of the status quo." He was so confident of this progress that he even allowed himself to strike a note of regret for the disappearance of men of great ambition.

A century earlier, Condorcet committed the very same error. In 1784 he spoke about

> . . . the great probability that we have fewer great changes and fewer large revolutions to expect from the future than from the past. The progress of enlightenment in all the sciences throughout every part of Europe, the prevailing spirit of moderation and peace, the sort of disrepute into which Machiavellism is beginning to fall, seem to assure us that henceforth wars and revolutions will be less frequent.[4]

"Fewer large revolutions . . ." five years before the French Revolution; "less frequent wars . . ." eight years before Condorcet himself called the nation to a war which was to ravage Europe for twenty-three years; "the spirit of moderation and peace . . ." less than ten before he died a victim of the Reign of Terror.

Yet it is very natural to count on the persistence of a tendency. Look at what J.-P. Rabaut, a Protestant pastor, wrote (in 1791!):

Everything announces an age in which that madness of nations, war, will come to an end. The fury of the primitive hordes has already abated . . . wars are less wholehearted than among ignorant peoples; legions clash with one another with civility; heroes exchange greetings before slaying one another; soldiers from opposite camps visit one another before giving battle, just as men dine together before gaming. Neither nations nor even kings fight any longer, but armies and paid men. It is a game with limited stakes. War, once a frenzy, is now no more than a folly.[5]

Wars have become gentler, therefore they will be gentler yet! What happened was quite the reverse. Attacks in column formation—advocated half a century earlier by Folard,[6] and always rejected as too deadly by the generals of the *ancien régime*—were adopted by the generals of the Revolution, who were not restricted to "paid men" and were abundantly supplied with "cannon-fodder" now that the "nation was fighting." I use Rabaut's own terms to emphasize the reversal of the tendency in which he had so much trust.

The trouble with prolongation of a tendency is that the reversal of the tendency is not anticipated. This comment is not intended to condemn extrapolation,[7] but only to serve as a warning.

Analogy

No procedure comes more naturally to the mind than looking for analogies. All science begins with classification. We would never have learned anything if we had never thought: "This object resembles this other, and I expect it to manifest the same properties." Even the savage who kept his fire burning had to think: "This *too* is wood and it *too* will burn." The classification of objects involves a prediction of how they will behave in given circumstances, and hence the classification of objects is associated with the classification of situations. Just as two objects recognized as similar should behave in the same way, so two situations recognized as similar should evolve in the same way. Rather than two ideas, we have here two aspects of a single idea, which is essential to any advancement of our knowledge. Taxonomic knowledge implies prediction: I saw that the conjunction of *A* and *B* gave rise to event *C,* and if I recognize two new elements as identical to *A* and *B,* I expect their conjunction to give rise to an event identical to *C.* Such a prediction is implicit when a new case is assimilated (justifiably) to a previous one. For example, in France at the time of the Directory, people began to realize that revolutionary fervor had exhausted itself and that, with the failure of new institutions to foster security or command respect, the republic lacked a foundation on which to settle. They saw in this situation a resemblance to the events of the English revolution after the death of Oliver Cromwell and recalled the outcome of that situation in 1660—the restoration of Charles II by General Monk. Same situation—same outcome. This idea haunted the royalists, who thought they had a Monk in Pichegru. The *coup d'état* on the eighteenth of *Fructidor* of the year V removed their man, but it seemed to them that the unavailability of a particular man could not stop an "objectively necessary process" (although this term is an anachronism here, their thinking resembled that of "historical materialists" later on). And after the thirtieth of *Prairial* of the year VII, when it was the turn of Sieyès to look for a general, the royalists had no doubt that this general, whatever his own intentions, would eventually play the same role as Monk.

The republicans were no less aware of the analogy. But since they rejected the event it foreshadowed, they drew from the analogy a warning rather than a prediction. For instance, in his pamphlet *Des suites de la Contre-Révolution de 1660 en Angleterre,* Benjamin Constant tried to make the prospect of a restoration appear frightening by describing the punitive measures that followed the Restoration in England (his pamphlet appeared in 1799, not long before the *coup d'état* of Brumaire).

We see here the two uses to which an analogy lends itself: on the one hand, to predict what *must* happen; on the other, to foresee what *may* happen. I regard the latter course as the only advisable one in human affairs, although man tends to adopt the former course when the analogy foreshadows a pleasing event. Thus, a little more than a quarter of a century later, the French liberals were strongly inclined to assume that "history repeats itself": for the analogy between the restoration of the Bourbons and that of the Stuarts, between Charles X and James II, now pointed to an event they desired—the replacement of the Bourbon dynasty by the liberal dynasty of the Orléans. In 1830 the awaited event took place.

Analogy is more rational than extrapolation. To anticipate by extrapolation is to take things as they come—the intellectual effort involved is minimal, whereas a prediction by analogy presupposes that the mind has sufficiently delineated the present situation to find some analogues for it, judging the resemblance to be fundamental enough for the same sorts of events to follow as in the reference-situation. Consider this example. At the end of World War II an American economic forecaster sees certain analogies with the situation at the end of World War I: but are they sufficient to warrant the prediction of a depression like that of 1920?[8] And similarly, the French political forecaster of 1962 sees an analogy in the conflict between Parliament and the president of the Republic with the situation in 1877: but is the resemblance sufficient to make the same outcome likely?

In asking whether the resemblance is sufficient, we raise the question of determining factors. Unless two situations resemble each other in respects that are causally significant, we can hardly expect the same effects to follow. It is obvious that in spite of causally significant points of resemblance, two situations will differ in other respects, which may also be causally significant. What is important to emphasize is that the effort of analysis required in the analogical method is commendable and conducive to progress, even though practical conclusions may remain uncertain owing to the complexity of real situations.

The "Railway"

In the previous section I mentioned two instances in which situations in France were interpreted in the light of previous situations in England; the idea underlying both these analogies was that a short sequence of events would conform to the same pattern as an earlier one. An idea of a much more ambitious nature is that history is repetitive in its general course, and not merely in short runs. That is to say, the secular sequence of important events in one country is "signaled" by the secular sequence of such events in another country.

According to this conception, a nation is like a train traveling some distance behind another down the same track. The same railway station may lie in the "past" for the passengers in the first train, but in the "future" for the passengers in the second. The latter see the same scenes go by as their predecessors, and see them in the same order, and consequently can obtain prior knowledge of the scenes.

The idea is a queer one, and yet forecasters have made use of it. In particular, French minds were obsessed by it during the restoration of the Bourbons. By way of example, consider this passage written by Madame de Staël's son in 1825:

> When I let my thoughts run over the history of the two countries [France and England], I am struck by a remarkable parallelism; in one and the other I find series of almost similar events, and each phase of the history of England precedes the corresponding phase in France by a century and a half.
>
> In 1215, the English barons exacted from King John the Magna Carta, which the English still revere as the foundation of their liberties. One hundred forty-one years later, the Estates-General of 1356 took advantage of the captivity of John II of France to insist upon guarantees to the nation as the price for the subsidies they granted his son.
>
> After the War of the Roses, the nobility were mutilated and exhausted; Henry VII and Henry VIII availed themselves of the opportunity to institute despotism by encouraging the commons. One hundred fifty years later, the wars of the League over, Richelieu achieved a like but much more extensive success by pursuing a similar policy.
>
> The age of Elizabeth offers a striking analogy with that of Louis XIV. During both reigns, the greatness of the monarch (more real in the case of Elizabeth), the victories abroad, the splendor of the court, and the brilliant state of the letters—consoled the subjects for their lack of liberty.
>
> In 1640, the Long Parliament began the struggle of the English against Charles I. One hundred forty-nine years later, the Estates-General were summoned to Versailles.
>
> One hundred forty-four years lie between the death of Charles I and that of Louis XVI.
>
> Lastly, the restoration of Charles II came one hundred forty-four years before that of the Bourbons. And if we read the history of the two revolutions side by side, countless astonishing similarities in the order of events and ideas, and even in the smallest circumstances, strike the eye.[9]

Implicit in this passage is the prediction that the Bourbons will be dethroned a second and final time, giving way, as in England, to a Whig monarchy. This prediction was verified (1830 minus 1689 equals 141 years). But no less implicit is the prediction that the French liberal monarchy will endure a long time, just as in England. But this did not take place. The "railway" perspective gives no forewarning of the revolution of 1848 or of the *coup d'état* of December 2, 1851. Nor does it suggest the pattern of French history after 1848—an oscillation, now slow, now rapid—between a parliamentary republic and a personal power far less restricted than that of the old kings.

This way of contemplating the future has so little foundation in reason that it would not even deserve to be mentioned here if it did not frequently function as a hidden assumption in forecasts. Indeed, in our day such an assumption subtends many predictions about the "developing nations."

The United Nations graph on which different countries are ranked on a dollar scale according to their national per capita income is ideally designed to foster the "railway" outlook. This way of comparing countries makes us commit two serious errors: first, thinking that two countries at the same income level are in analogous situations; second, thinking that the present state of a country with a low income is analogous to a past state, more or less remote, of some other country with a high income. When, one may ask, was the American nation at the "stage" which is currently that of China? These errors can too easily give rise to the conviction that the "developing nations" will undergo the same evolution as the developed nations (hopefully at a faster rate), and will thus pass through the same stages.

NOTES

1. Thus it seems unlikely to Macbeth that Birnam wood will come to Dunsinane.

2. For the United States, see E. F. Dennison's report for the Committee on Economic Development, and for France, the preliminary work for the twenty-five-year plan.

3. *Que sera le XXᵉ siècle?*, an essay published in *Questions politiques* (Paris: Armand Colin, 1899) and reprinted in *Futuribles*, No. 232.

4. *Mémoire sur le calcul des probabilités*, read by the Marquis de Condorcet at the Académie Royale des Sciences, August 4, 1784, Part III, p. 675, of the volume for 1782 [*sic*].

5. J.-P. Rabaut (known as Rabaut Saint-Étienne), *Réflexions politiques sur les circonstances présentes*, in *Pensée*, Vol. 4, Chap. X.

6. In his *Commentaire sur Polybe,* which accompanies Dom Thuillier's translation (6 vols.; 1727–30).

7. The use of "extrapolation" as a name for this mode of proference is now general, and I shall conform to this practice. Strictly speaking, an extrapolation involves treating a relationship between variables as valid outside the limits between which it has been observed. Different types of extrapolation are used in forecasting: it is an extrapolation to say: "When the average income attains so much, the expenditure on cars will attain that much" (this is based on previously observed relations between the growth of income and the expenditure on cars); it is a different type of extrapolation (with time as the independent variable) to say: "The average income will attain so much on such a date" (this is based on a previously observed rate of growth). In a loose and broad sense, people speak of "extrapolation" when they assume that a future movement will be a continuation of a past movement. But we must remain aware of the nature of our assumptions, and of their frequent complexity.

8. For references to such predictions see Sidney Schoeffler, *Failures of Economics: A Diagnostic Study* (Cambridge, Mass.: Harvard University Press, 1955.

9. A. de Staël-Holstein, *Lettres sur l'Angleterre* (Paris, 1825), pp. 23–5.

9

|||||||| ||||||||| ||| || ||||| ||||||| |||||||| ||||||||

Predictions: II

I continue my examination of the modes of proference employed in predictions.

Causality

Find a cause which will continue to act, then specify its necessary effect. This is a method of prediction based on a very sound principle. But its practical application can be badly defective, as is borne out by a passage which Rousseau wrote in 1760:

> It is, for example, very easy to foresee that England, for all its glory, will be ruined twenty years hence, and will, in addition, have lost what remains of its liberty. Everybody asserts that agriculture is flourishing on that island; for my part, I wager that it is in a state of decline. London grows bigger every day, and thus the kingdom is being depopulated. The English wish to be conquerors, and therefore they will be slaves.[1]

Consider the sentence "London grows bigger every day, and thus the kingdom is being depopulated." The first proposition is true, the second false. The period designated by Rousseau was characterized by an accelerating growth of population[2]—an acceleration which was to become more pronounced in the following century. Reliable statistics[3] for the nineteenth century invalidate his claim that the growth of London is related to a decline in the population of the kingdom: during the first forty years, the population of London doubled, and so did the total population of the land; over the entire century, the population of London increased 5.9 times, and the total population about 4.7 times. Coming at a time when the population of England was beginning to soar, Rousseau's prediction was particularly unfortunate.

Let us learn from the errors of great men. How did Rousseau derive from his well-founded forecast about the expansion of London his erroneous conclusion that the total population of England would decline? The fact that birth rates were lower and death rates higher in large cities than in the countryside was then being widely discussed. From this fact it could readily be inferred that, as the proportion of the total population concentrated in the capital increased, the unfavorable population rates of the capital would weigh increasingly upon the national-average rates. Now if Rousseau had sought to "quantify" his assumptions, deciding on some rate of increase for the rural population and some rate of inflow into town, he would have found that however high he chose to postulate the rate of population wastage in town the growth of total population would not be brutally reversed, but instead would be progressively braked over quite a number of years. Such a model would not have been a trustworthy predictor, since population rates are not stable over long periods. But at least it would have brought home to the author (this is a major function of mathematical models) what really followed from his own assumptions.

How foolish it would be to reproach Rousseau for not having used procedures foreign to his time! It was quite natural that he should use causal relationships without quantification. But perhaps we can blame him for confusing moral evaluations with positive estimates. This reasoning seems to have been as follows: He felt a strong moral disapproval of life in towns;[4] he also strongly felt that a good social state necessarily had a growing population, and a bad social state a declining one;[5] hence, postulating a perfect correlation between quality and quantity, he held that the badness inherent in urbanization would be translated into a declining population.

A discussion of Rousseau is not to the point here or else we could show how his use of the quantitative criterion often works against his qualitative judgments. What we must note is the intervention of a personal qualitative judgment in what purports to be a necessary causal relation. And Rousseau's case is by no means unique.

Causal relations in the social order lack simplicity and clarity. Which historian will attribute the course taken by such and such a phenomenon in the past to a clearly identified cause? And for each historian who does so, how many other historians will contradict him? We cannot deny the presence of a subjective element in our choice of explanations of the past. Likewise, in making a prediction, we use some "preferred" causal relation.

War provides a convenient example. It is a phenomenon with relatively clear demarcations, which has long exercised the minds of men. When we consider, however, the explanatory theses which have been eagerly embraced in the course of the past two centuries, we see that they all attribute the detested phenomenon to a cause that men wish to rid themselves of for independent reasons. When monarchy grows unpopular, war is explained by dynastic ambitions. When the nobility from whom the officer corps is largely recruited falls into disrepute, war is explained by the pride of the military caste. When the capitalist system is denounced, conflicts are explained by the struggles of entrepreneurs to further their own interests. Man finds such explanations pleasing, for they enable him to predict that an evil odious to all will be eradicated when his fight against some hated institution or social category is brought to a successful close. However childish these views, we are less prone to recognize their nature to the extent that we are more affected by the passion animating them.

But surely we can find some calm, dispassionate thinkers. What about Émile Faguet? No preference seems to have prejudiced his judgment when he extrapolated into the twentieth century the progress made in the speed and ease of transport and communications during the nineteenth century (doing so with good reason) and then concluded that as a result a tendency toward large political agglomerations would appear. He was too conscientious an observer not to notice the awakening of strong feelings of nationality, seeing very clearly that they were opposed to the agglomerative tendency even though they might sometimes appear to coincide with it:

During the whole of the nineteenth century, talk about the principle of nationalism has never ceased. The history of the principle is an interesting one: it is the history of a misconception. Different peoples felt a need to be strong, and thought they felt a need to group themselves by racial affinity. They spoke of Pan-Germanism, Pan-Slavism, Pan-Italism, and Pan-

Hellenism, giving to these confused aspirations the name of Nationalities. At heart they wanted to form large peoples, and that is something quite different.

In fact, the two aspirations are contrary. Nationality and agglomeration are not two different aspects of the same idea, but two mutually irreducible and conflicting ideas. Nationality is alive and intense only in a small people. Instead of championing large agglomerations, true nationalism is particularistic. The Belgian Revolution of 1830, which led to secession, and the formation of two small states in the place of one large one, was a true nationalist movement. That is to say, the Belgians were patriots rather than agglomerators, and preferred autonomy to power. Likewise the Irish would prefer to be weak in their own land, rather than boast of a powerful foreign landlord.

After pointing to the opposition between the nationalist and the agglomerative tendencies, Faguet went on to express his confidence that the latter would prevail in the twentieth century. But during the sixty-three intervening years, nationalism has manifested itself more frequently and with greater strength than the tendency to agglomerate and has led to the dismemberment of the Ottoman Empire, the destruction of the Austro-Hungarian Empire, and the abolition of the colonial empires. The chief fact in the history of the nineteenth century possibly is German unity. To date, the chief portent for the history of the twentieth century appears to have been the triumph of Irish nationalism: a prototype early in the century followed by many other examples. Although it is conceivable that the agglomerative tendency may yet prevail, the fact remains that Faguet's prediction would have provided us with poor guidance during the times through which we have lived. And in the confidence of his pronouncement, we may read the choice of a man more sensitive to the general than to the particular, and more responsive to order than to emotion.

A-Priorism

Here now is a prediction made by Joseph de Maistre, from his *Considérations sur la France,* which was published in 1797:

Not only have I no belief in the stability of the American government, I also lack any confidence in its specific establishments. For instance, the different towns, animated by a jealousy scarce deserving respect, were unable to decide where Congress should sit, none of them wishing to cede the honor of the position to another. In consequence, it was decided to build a new town to serve as the seat of the government. The most favorable position on the bank of a large river was chosen, an agreement to call the town Washington made, the site of all the public buildings plotted, and work begun. The map of the queen of cities is already circulating throughout Europe. And basically, nothing in all this lies beyond human capacity; to build a town is perfectly feasible. Nonetheless, there is too much deliberation in this enterprise, too much human willfulness; and the odds are a thousand to one that the town will not be built, or that it will not be called Washington, or that the Congress will not reside there.

Maistre lost his wager, and we may wonder why he ever risked making it. He knew ancient history very well, with its many instances of sudden foundations of towns. Granted, the story of the origin of Rome may be a legend, but there exists contemporary evidence for the foundation of Alexandria and we know the name of the architect appointed by Alexander. Better still, the *ex nihilo* creation of a new capital for the Russian Empire produced a great stir in the eighteenth century, and at the time when Maistre was writing, St. Petersburg already numbered three hundred thousand inhabitants.

Interestingly enough, Maistre did not change his negative pronouncement on the future of Washington when he revised his text in 1817, after he had himself spent fifteen years in St. Petersburg. His failure to make a correction presents an enigma. Perhaps the taking and burning of Washington by the English in 1814 confirmed his initial prejudice. Or perhaps we are to suppose (a gratuitous assumption on my part) that he saw in this event an analogy with the destruction of Megalopolis by the Spartans of Cleomenes. Megalopolis, too, had been built, by joint resolution, in an empty plain to serve as a seat for the nascent Arcadian federation, and it could not boast of a very long or very glorious history.[6] But if Maistre saw a parallel in that, it could only be as a result of an initial bias. How could he have formed such a bias? Certainly, he was not prejudiced against the political ability of the Americans, as is shown by his argument:

1. The British colonies in America had a king, whom they never saw: monarchical splendor was foreign to them and the sovereign seemed some kind of supernatural power, who eluded the senses.

2. The elements of democracy contained in the constitution of the parent country were in their possession.

3. Other elements of democracy had been brought over by the numerous early settlers, almost all republican, born amidst religious and political strife.

4. The Americans used the three separate powers inherited from their ancestors as a base on which to build with the other available elements, instead of sweeping everything away like the French in their Revolution.

Maistre recognized that these republicans had made a "good start," but thought they would fail where Peter the Great had succeeded. Why? The following sentence provides the transition to Maistre's negative conclusion:

That which is really new in their constitution, as resting on joint resolution, is the most fragile of all things; it would be impossible to bring together more symptoms of weakness and fragility.

Maistre did not believe the capital would be a success any more than the federal Constitution. We find them both in existence. His condemnation of the work of the drafters of the American Constitution is a priori, yet he condemns their work as an attempt at a priori creation.[7] According to Maistre, their inventions could not be realized. His "meta-politics"[8] also taught him that the French Revolution could not stop[9] and could not be crushed by the European allies.[10] It is not my intent to discuss this author, but I shall note in passing that he is at heart a Spinozist, beneath a Catholic garb.

Systems

A system can be defined as "a group of material or non-material elements which mutually depend on one another so as to form an organized whole."[11] Every social group constitutes a system; it is a tautology that the future states of a system can be known if its dynamics are completely known. In science we often have *macroscopic* knowledge of the dynamics of a system, and hence of its future states. The idea that a system-based mode of prediction is the right one was broached by

Saint-Simon, developed by Auguste Comte, and triumphed with Marx. The hold of Marxism on our minds is comparable to the hold Aristotelianism once had, and its effects on our actions are even greater—this whether we have read Marx or not and whether we acknowledge him or dispute him. I have often been struck by the unconscious Marxism of American students.

Let us see how this powerful thinker predicted. He fastens on one central concept—the transformation of the mode of production—and uses it to give the history of the human race a new coherence. The efficiency with which labor is utilized when its energies are directed on the materials of nature differs considerably in different periods of history: for the efficiency to increase, great social changes had to occur. Quite so. Marx emphasizes that progress cannot occur unless capital is accumulated and that capitalists animated by selfish interests are the necessary historical instruments of this socially beneficial process. As the accumulation of capital continues, says Marx, the number of salaried workers and the production per worker will increase. True again. The increasing production has to be consumed—as the population is transformed into salaried workers, the latter constitute an ever-increasing proportion of the total number of possible consumers, and it is therefore necessary for the workers to raise their consumption if the increased production is to be absorbed. All of which is a matter of course.

At first sight, nothing in Marx's general account points to the inevitable downfall of capitalism and to a violent social revolution. Why, then, did he make these predictions? He took it as certain that the capitalists would oppose salary increases and that a subservient state would help them to resist. By keeping salaries down, the capitalists would inevitably produce stagnation and an economic crisis. The resulting misery and the scandalous failure to utilize the means of production would provoke a social revolution in which capitalism and the coercive machinery of the state would be overthrown. But why should the capitalists act against their own interests? A subjective judgment based on contemporary evidence encouraged Marx to think they would. However, in his system of thought, the attitude of the capitalists had to be a matter of objective necessity, rather than of mere probability. The way in which he made it so is described below.

It is not the least of Marx's achievements that he was the first to stress the concept, now basic to national accounting, of "value added in manufacture." To put it very roughly, the *value added* by a firm's operations is the difference between the financial receipts from its sales and its current expenditures (not including the acquisition of new capital items) on goods and services outside the firm (thus payments to its own employees are excluded). This added value is "gross" or "net" depending on whether it is taken before or after deduction of an allowance for capital "consumed." Marx considered the "net value added." This then is a net financial product of the firm's operations, out of which both employed labor and employed capital are rewarded. By dividing it by the number of employees in the firm, one obtains the "value added per man." The increase over time of value added per man is the simplest expression of productivity gains with which we are familiar and which Marx expected. Now assuming that the value added per man is shared in unchanging proportions between worker and capitalist, both benefit: the worker's wage rises with productivity and so does the profit per man employed. Why then did Marx prophesy that the capitalist would eat more and more deeply into the worker's share, bringing about an ever sharper class conflict, impoverishment of the workers, and economic crises? His prophecy was entirely based on the supposition that increases in the value added per man would be brought about by increases in the capital investment per man, but that the increases in the value added would be less than proportional to the increases in the investment. Thus, if it was shared in unchanging proportions the reward of capital per man employed would go up as fast as productivity, but not so fast as the amount of capital invested per man, which would mean that the return per unit of capital, or rate of profit, would successively decline. In order to counteract this fall in the profit rate, the capitalists would seek an increase in their share of the value added,[12] thereby bringing about conflict, impoverishment, crisis, and finally revolution. The whole intellectual construct is admirably built, but on a quite erroneous foundation: in fact, value added has increased faster, not slower, than capital invested,[13] and this has been enough to do away with the "historical inevitabilities" pointed out by Marx.

According to the dynamic model built by Marx, social revolution arises out of the actual development of capitalism and should therefore have proved very different—the first momentous revolution took place in Russia, and, even more surprising in terms of the theory, the next in importance has taken place in China. It is worth trying to imagine how fundamentally different world history would be if Marx's prediction had come true.

We may then suppose that the revolution took place in the United States and in Great Britain, and since we are writing another Uchronia, we are free to choose our dates: say 1900 for the United States, the time of great agitation over "trustification," and 1906 for Great Britain, the time of a great defeat for the Conservatives. Here then we have two Communist states at the beginning of the century. I can hardly help thinking that communism as translated into English would be something very different from Russian communism, and would come much closer to Marx's conception of it.

The "centralized power of the state," of which Marx spoke so critically,[14] had long been the object of hostility in these countries—a favorable circumstance for action on his appeal to "smash the bureaucratic and military machine." The habits of local self-government and the practice of the "Anglo-Saxon" in running orderly meetings would have helped the "soviets," or councils, to function. Without claiming that the state would have withered away, I can see no reason why communism would have strengthened the state in English-speaking countries (and therefore, through rivalry, would have produced the same effect in other countries).

Since, by hypothesis, communism would have established itself in the most advanced countries, it follows by definition that these countries could not have set out to "overtake" the level of economic development of another state. Nothing would have paralleled the Soviet obsession with overtaking the American standard of living; the need to "force" national economic growth would not have arisen in the Communist states, and the harsh discipline introduced to this end in the Soviet Union would not have existed.

Moreover, according to the hypothesis, the new regime would have been installed in states that happened to have good natural defenses (at a time when aircraft did not count). A harsh discipline could not have been needed, therefore, for reasons of security. In short, the Communist social regime would have assumed a completely different political complexion.

It is tempting to pursue this hypothesis and to depict a Western "Communist world" instead of an Eastern one. But I have said enough to indicate how different history would have been if Marx's views had been verified in their role as predictions through the communization of advanced countries, instead of being adopted as normative doctrines first in Russia and later in China. In relation to Marxian dynamics, the victory of October 1917 is an "accident"—but of what moment! And that an accident should be able to thus change a systematic anticipation of a course of events is something that must put into question all system-based prediction in general, even more than just this particular system-based prediction.

Forms

Montesquieu writes: "If it be the natural property of small states to be governed as a republic, of middling ones to be subject to a monarch, and of large empires to be ruled by a despot, the consequence is that, to preserve the principles of the established government, the existing dimensions of the state must be maintained, and that the nature of the state will alter as its limits are shrunk or expanded."[15] Here we are given, implicitly, a conditional prediction—if a republic should progressively extend its dimensions, then it must pass by degrees into despotism. Such a prediction becomes unconditional as soon as one thinks it is certain an expansion will occur.

It is unnecessary to recall how Montesquieu established his natural relationship between the size of a regime and its political structure.[16] Rousseau treated the same subject, with greater depth I feel, in his *Du Contrat social*, where he set forth this "natural law": The larger a state becomes, the more its government will be concentrated; so that the number of rulers decreases in proportion as the population increases.[17] In that book, it seems to me Rousseau sought to contrast what must happen (in the sense of historical necessity) with what ought to be (in the sense of the demands of morality). He wished to show that a regime changes its form as the population grows and the interaction of interests becomes more complicated. The idea that an excessive size is incompatible with a given form occurs in Aristotle: beyond a certain level of the population, the organization of the state is adapted to a nation (*ethnos*) that is governed, rather than to a city (*polis*) that governs itself.[18] Galileo asserted the connection between form and dimension in a quite different field: an animal or a tree of a given size cannot naturally grow to an appreciably greater size while remaining of the same proportions and same materials; and, similarly, structures built by man cannot be made larger at will unless the design or the materials, or both, are changed.[19] In a work with fundamental implications for social science, D'Arcy W. Thompson worked out in a fascinating way the applications of Galileo's principle to the structure of living beings, and showed how internal propulsions and external pressures lead to changes in a form.[20] But let us confine ourselves to an illustration from our own field of concern. During the twentieth century we have seen the President of the United States acquire vastly increased powers. This change is consistent with Rousseau's theory, for the population has grown and the interaction of interests has become more complicated. But the change can also be explained by the growth of external pressures, in accordance with a prediction Tocqueville implicitly made in a passage comparing the powers of the President of the American republic with those of the constitutional monarch of France (under the Orléans regime founded in 1830), and in which he found that the Presidential powers were more limited in right, but above all more feeble in fact:

> If the executive power is feebler in America than in France, the cause is more attributable to the circumstances than to the laws of the country.
>
> It is chiefly in its foreign relations that the executive power of a nation is called upon to exert its skill and vigor.
>
> If the existence of the Union were perpetually threatened, and its chief interest were in daily connection with those of other powerful nations, the executive government would assume an increased importance in proportion to the measures expected of it, and those which it would carry into effect. The President of the United States is the commander-in-chief of the army, but of an army composed of only six thousand men; he commands the fleet, but the fleet reckons but few sail; he conducts the foreign relations of the Union, but the United States are a nation without neighbors. Separated from the rest of the world by the ocean, and too weak as yet to aim at the dominion of the seas, they have no enemies, and their interests rarely come into contact with those of any other nation of the globe.
>
> Clearly then, the practical part of a government must not be judged by the theory of its constitution.
>
> The President of the United States is in the possession of almost royal prerogatives, which he has no opportunity of exercising; and those privileges which he can at present use are very circumscribed: the laws allow him to possess a degree of influence which circumstances do not permit him to employ.[21]

Tocqueville does not actually make a prediction, but the purport of his words is predictive. He asserts that the strength of the executive power is connected with the importance of foreign affairs. He thereby leads us to expect that the Presidency will be strengthened if and when foreign affairs assume greater importance. Indeed, it is true as a general proposition that any "discovery" about the relationships affecting form is no more than a latent or potential prediction, and one that does not moreover pretend to infallibility, for it contains a double conditional: "*If* these circumstances arise, the form will change in that manner, *if* a good adaptation takes place." But a good adaptation is by no means assured. Accordingly, if I have discussed assertions about form in the present context, I have done so in spite of the great difference between these assertions and the other modes of prediction, and only because they are too interesting to be ignored. If, however, the methods of predicting what "must happen" are used with greater modesty, they, too, can become ways of forecasting the different possibilities of futurity.

NOTES

1. This text appears as a footnote in the *Extrait du projet de paix perpétuelle.* "But really," the reader will object, "isn't it rather unfair to an author to pick on one of his footnotes?" I am the last person to wish to be unfair to the writer I admire and love above all others. The fact is that Rousseau attached great importance to this note. He mentions it in a letter of June 16, 1760, to M. de Bastide, who was publishing the work. Rousseau writes: "There is a footnote in which I say that in twenty years' time the English will have lost their freedom; I think it is necessary to say *the remainder of their freedom,* for some are sufficient fools to think the English are still free." Even more significantly, Rousseau returned to this footnote in his *Dialogues,* in 1776, when the twenty years were almost over; and far from revising his opinion, he added: "It is worth noting that this was written and published in 1760, the time of England's greatest prosperity, during the ministry of Mr. Pitt, now Lord Chatham."

2. According to Quételet, the "doubling time" was well above a century up to 1750, but afterwards fell to less than a century (*Sur l'homme et le développement de ses facultés ou Essai de physique sociale* [Paris, 1835], 287). According to Mulhall, the population of England and Wales went from 7,020,000 in 1754 to 8,020,000 in 1780.

3. Mulhall, *Dictionary of Statistics.*

4. Thus Rousseau writes in *Émile:* "Men are not made to be packed together in ant-heaps, but scattered over the earth to till it. The more they are massed

together, the more corrupt they become. The infirmities of the body and vices of the soul are the necessary result of this too numerous concourse. Of all animals man is least fitted to live in herds. Men packed like sheep would perish in very little time. The breath of man is fatal to his kind: and this is true literally, no less than figuratively." And again: "Towns are the sinks of mankind."

5. In the chapter of *Du Contrat social* called "The Signs of a Good Government" (Book III, Chap. IX) Rousseau says: "For my part, I am always surprised that a straightforward sign should be misconstrued, or that men should be of such bad faith as not to recognize it. What is the purpose of the body politic? Surely the preservation and prosperity of its members. And what is the most certain sign that they are being preserved and are prospering? The number and increase of the population. No need then to look any further for the disputed sign. Other things being equal, the government under which the citizens most increase and multiply—without artificial schemes, colonies, or naturalization of foreigners—is infallibly the best: that under which a people declines and decays is the worst."

6. Yet contrary to Maistre's wager about Washington, Megalopolis was actually built, bore the name designated in the joint resolution, and served as the seat of the federal diet. It is perhaps not superfluous to add that Philopomen and Polybius were born there.

7. *Essai sur le principe générateur des constitutions politiques.*

8. "This new expression seems a most appropriate invention to denote *the metaphysics of politics,* which do exist, and are a science deserving the entire attention of observers" (from the preface to the *Essai sur le principe . . .*).

9. Thus: "The more one examines those who appear to be the most active figures of the revolution, the more one finds something passive and mechanical in them. It cannot be said too often: it is not men that conduct the revolution, but the revolution that uses men. People speak rightly when they say the revolution is self-moving."

10. Rousseau provides another notable example of prediction by "a-priorism" in his famous declaration about Russia (*Du Contrat social,* Book II, Chap. VIII): "The Russian Empire will want to subjugate Europe and will itself be subjugated. Its Tartar subjects and neighbors will become its masters and ours. To me this revolution seems inevitable." See Voltaire's objections in the relevant footnote in my edition of the *Contrat* (Geneva, 1947). *Gouvernement de Pologne* contains Rousseau's a priori motives for his prediction.

11. See, for instance, *Vocabulaire technique et critique de la philosophie.*

12. *Das Kapital,* Book III, Part III.

13. See my article "Le coefficient de capital," *Bulletin SEDEIS,* No. 1821, Suppl. 1 (May 20, 1962).

14. See Karl Marx, *La Guerre civile en France* (Paris: Editions Sociales Internationales, 1953), p. 39.

15. Montesquieu, *L'Esprit des lois,* Book VIII, Chap. 20.

16. *Ibid.*, Chap. 1–19.

17. *Du Contrat social,* Book III, Chap. II.

18. Aristotle, *The Politics,* VII, 4, 1326b.

19. Galileo Galilei: *Discorsi e Dimostrazioni Matematiche intorno à due nuove scienze . . .* (Bologna, 1655).

20. D'Arcy W. Thompson, *On Growth and Form* (Cambridge, Eng., 1916). (Subsequent editions were published in 1942 and 1961.)

21. Alexis de Tocqueville, *On Democracy in America,* Part I, Chap. 8.

10

Historical Prediction
and Scientific Prediction

It is unquestionably true that we are able to make safe predictions, and everything we call "progress" rests on successive extensions of the field they embrace. I shall start by emphasizing this point, as a preliminary to defining the conditions of safe prediction and to distinguishing the areas where such conditions are in a greater or smaller measure wanting.

The Predictive Content of Knowing

The patent for an invention contains a guaranteed prediction; in effect, the inventor says: "With those materials and that procedure, you will obtain this result. And you will obtain this same result each and every time you follow my recipe." Large plants are built to utilize new processes, but only because industrialists are confident the relevant predictions will be continually verified.

Nowadays, a society possessing and utilizing a large and growing number of recipes is said to be "advanced." All the productive processes going on all over the world as I am writing are founded on confidence in the efficacy of the predictions associated with them. At the same time, scientists are conducting repeated experiments in laboratories to determine whether certain elements, placed in mutual contiguity under certain conditions, will in fact give a particular final result. If his experiments are conclusive, a scientist will assert that the same result will be obtained whenever the same initial situation is reproduced; and thus a new prediction will be added to our "stock in trade."

It cannot be denied that every practical recipe involves a confident prediction. The fruitfulness of a scientific theory is generally measured in terms of the predictions that follow from it and are found to be verified. The punctilious will add that a theory can never be established for all time by means of these same criteria, since a new theory may be able to account for the very same phenomena and for something more besides: what is actually established is the prediction suggested by the theory and later verified.

The progress of science and technology thus amounts to a building up of our corpus of predictions. And if this corpus constantly grows, there is, a priori, a likelihood that it will gradually absorb those areas where uncertainty now reigns.

I would not be so bold as to set limits on scientific prediction; but surely I can emphasize its special characteristics without being accused of imprudence. A scientific prediction is an assertion about an outcome: situation A will be followed by situation (or event) B. The prediction is timeless in that B is not announced for a given day or hour, but as the consequence of A whenever A occurs. A prediction is based on the law-determined behavior (legality) of the objects to which it applies; in consequence, it was long thought that scientific prediction held only for things, and not for man. If people now think otherwise, with reference to predictions based on statistical laws, the validity of such predictions seems to be restricted to cases where individual aberrations do not affect the result. But above all: scientific prediction guarantees the coming of B only if the initial situation is really A. If the initial situations have no more than a similarity between them, although it so strikes us as to make us regard them as identical, we shall find that B follows on some occasions and not on others, and we shall be unable to improve our prediction of B until we have improved our understanding of the meaningful traits of A.

The Alchemist's Mishap

The alchemist's mishap provides an illustration of this important point. I would be reluctant to call liars those men who claimed in the course of the centuries to have succeeded in making gold or silver. They were studious men and for many generations the only ones to conduct experiments. Their dedication to their quest seems incompatible with deliberate fraudulence. It is far more plausible, in my view, that certain alchemists really did obtain precious metals in individual experiments or series of experiments,[1] but after knowing the rapture of success found themselves sadly unable to reproduce their result. The minerals they used were always impure, and certain batches were bound to contain some gold and silver. On finding gold or silver in his crucible, the alchemist would think that he had discovered the secret of transmutation, when he had merely succeeded in refining the metals. And if the impurities were lacking in the next batch of minerals, the experiments would fail.

The alchemist's mishap[2] strikingly illustrates the necessity of minutely analyzing the initial conditions in experiments designed to establish a predictive and scientific proposition. Once a proposition is shown to be well grounded, it entitles us to predict B with complete assurance only if the initial situation A is exactly reproduced; and, hence, the great pains taken in industrial chemistry to use identical substances and identical procedures, so as to obtain an identical final product.

The Principle of Sufficient Similarity

Identical initial conditions lead to identical results. This is a fundamental postulate of our thought, and no doubt corresponds to what used to be called an innate idea. Our ways of proceeding depend on it: we reproduce the same initial conditions when we wish to obtain the same result. All our confident predictions also depend on it: the result will be the same as before, because the initial conditions are the same as before. But even in nature, and a fortiori in human affairs, the "same as before" is but an approximation, an impression of similarity, a subjective judgment. The livelier the impression of similarity, the more confident we are that the situations identified by our judgment will come in the same sequence as before. Yet the points of similarity that strike and convince us are not necessarily the ones that are relevant to the production of the expected result; the alchemist's experience is a case in point. Or the similarities may be relevant, but a difference which in our eyes is insignificant may inhibit the result we have assumed.

Event B has come out of situation A. This much we know. But which traits of the complex situation *A* are meaningful for the production of *B*? Learning to distinguish such traits is the essential apprenticeship of the scientist. We tend to think there is no difficulty—at least in principle —about finding them by means of well-conducted experiments; yet the matter is not as simple as that, since non-conclusive experiments were conducted for so long. But the difficulties are even greater when we cannot manipulate the initial conditions as we please, and have to confine ourselves to observations relating to very complex situations.

The Difficulties of the Meteorologist

Science, for all its remarkable achievements, does not enable us to predict the weather, in spite of observations conducted for three centuries—since Torricelli's invention of the barometer—and the continual development of the means of measurement we employ. We do not have to look far to find the reason for this failure: the initial situation is still too little known for us to predict its sequel, and the past initial situations, whose sequels have been observed, are likewise too little known. Significantly enough, the use of radiosondes led not long ago to the discovery of air streams at high altitudes; this indicates that ground observations may leave out data of crucial importance. The gathering of facts has made enormous progress, but our picture of them is still far from adequate. I think it is safe for me to say that a theory of meteorological phenomena could not be constructed out of meteorological data alone, and that the theories constructed in meteorology are based on physics, a science in which complete observations can be conducted in limited and controlled experiments. But simulation techniques are useful only in determining the effects springing from identified factors; the intervention of other, insufficiently understood factors can nullify the effects we anticipate.

The predictive capabilities of this science are very limited. Because of the importance of weather forecasts for the national economy, the Council of the American Meteorological Society issued the following statement for the express purpose of damping false hopes:

Weather forecasts prepared in some detail are possible for two or three days in advance. The reliability of the prediction, however, decreases progressively after the first day. Forecasts of the weather expected three to seven days in advance must be issued in less specific terms than the shorter-range predictions and are ordinarily restricted to a statement that the temperature will be higher or lower than the normal for that time of year and that predominantly wet or dry weather will prevail. It is also possible to say with some degree of reliability whether or not the latter part of the period will be significantly warmer or cooler, wetter or drier, than the first part.

For periods of one week to one month in advance, the average temperature and total precipitation for the same period can be compared with the normal temperature and precipitation with some skill. However, the present status of meteorology does not permit a forecaster to specify day-by-day variations in the weather any more than a week in advance.

Forecasts for periods of more than a month in advance are sometimes attempted. These may say, for example, that the next season will have an abnormally high (or low) temperature or precipitation. The success of this type of forecast has not yet been demonstrated and at the moment such forecasts must be considered as experimental.

The position of the American Meteorological Society is that individuals or organizations that publish forecasts for conditions more than one month in advance mislead the public if they do not clearly describe the forecasts as experimental and of unproven value. Furthermore, the society holds that the issuance of detailed day-by-day weather forecasts for more than two or three days in advance is misleading and is not justified by present meteorological knowledge.[3]

It is admirable that scientists should concur in an attempt to specify the limits to which their confidence extends. In the given case, their capacity for prediction does not reach very far. Maupertuis once said:

> The first means that presents itself [for forseeing the future] is to derive from the present state the most probable consequences for the future state: but this does not go far. . . . We can scarcely arrive at an assured science in this way.[4]

And meteorologists can indeed tell us why "this does not go far." Weather forecasts are mainly based on the observation of large "pressure systems," which last only a few days. It is impossible to say where the next pressure system will appear, for the large pressure systems of the future are recruited from among a host of small ones now in existence, and we do not know which of these will grow and which will not. Thus, in relation to a date sufficiently far in the future, the present is charged with non-specifiable possibilities.

Presages

Considering that even now we are unable to foretell the weather by means of its determining factors, it is not surprising that mankind should remain attached to presages and omens. The scientists confess that a study of air movements does not enable them to predict a period of abnormal cold more than a month in advance. But in the autumn of 1962 everybody in my countryside foretold a hard winter, pointing to such signs as the abundance and brightness of red berries on rockspray and firethorn. They were using the oldest of all methods of prediction: the reading of presages or omens.

The interpretation of signs comes naturally to a rural population whose life is shaped by the cycle of the seasons. Anomalies such as drought or unseasonal rain and late or excessive frost affect the means of livelihood. Adverse variations greatly affect the standard of life; they are discussed throughout the ensuing year, and the unusual events which preceded them recalled and seen as premonitory signs. And thus adages like this old French one come into existence:

> Si corneille a nid bas et merle haut
> Les beaux mois fondront en eau;
> Si merle niche bas et corneille haut
> L'été sera sec et chaud.[5]

Or this old English one:

> If the cock moult before the hen,
> We shall have weather thick and thin:
> But if the hen moult before the cock,
> We shall have weather hard as a block.[6]

These sayings are prognostications based on the "observation of birds," and thus conform to the etymological and historical meaning of "auspices" (from *avis,* bird + *specio,* to see): like all peasants, those of Latium studied the behavior of birds for precursory signs of the weather. The use of auspices is not, in principle, an illegitimate form of prediction, for the procedure is open to verification; if a good correlation is found between certain unusual types of avian behavior and the characteristics of the following season, the disconformities are valid indicators, even though we are quite unable to explain how the weather is connected with them. Cicero went too far[7] when he rejected the thesis of his brother Quintus that a properly *ascertained* correlation has some efficacy as a prediction even if the underlying reason cannot be found.[8] Cicero would not set any store upon a series which could not be rationally justified. Two different conceptions confront one another in his treatise—science as ascertaining, and science as what is understood. Most scientists today would take sides with Quintus. However, we generally would not spend time trying to check a correlation between phenomena if it seems a priori contrary to reason that they should be linked.

The Romans used observations of nature in predicting the outcome of battles, as well as in forecasting the character of the seasons. It is not repugnant to reason to suppose that, within a complex ecological system affected in all its parts by the seasons, the subgroup "birds" may perceive the character of the coming season before the subgroup "man." A supposition of this type deserves to be checked, and after corroboration it can be utilized. But it is repugnant to reason that the behavior of birds should indicate the outcome of military and political events, which are of a quite different order.

For predictions of political and military events, the Romans also relied on haruspices—soothsayers who inspected the entrails (*exta*) of sacrificial bulls.[9] To us it seems quite ridiculous that the assassination of Caesar should have been announced by the fact (?) that no heart could be found in a bull that had been sacrificed. The "omen"—quite apart from its utter improbability—has nothing in common with the slaying of Caesar except that both events are "out of the ordinary."

Abuses such as those are not a reason for rejecting all prediction by means of omens. No other way is open to us while we lack a knowledge of causes. And this method is more rational than we suspect if effects which matter to us happen to reach us after effects which are of no importance in themselves but are "leading indicators" thanks to their greater celerity. Think, for example, of warriors who have absolutely no knowledge of gunfire until suddenly shells begin bursting in their midst, an event they can hardly ignore. In a lucky moment they might notice that a distant flash precedes each explosion, and they would be quite right to trust this presage. A presage is unerring if one and the same cause is the source of two "waves," one slow and mighty, the other quick and little:

our reception of the small disturbance warns us of the shock to follow. Close relationships of this kind are readily grasped. More remote and complex ones can be found by looking for correlations of time-series— an easy task since the invention of electronic computers. But until we know what is responsible for a given correlation, we do not know whether we may expect it to meet the next test.

Everyone will agree that a prediction by signs is radically inferior in nature to a prediction by causes. The fact remains that we regard a good correlation as an important step toward an explanation.

On Divination

My reference to Cicero's treatise gives me an opportunity to turn to good account the frequent gibe that forecasters are mere "diviners." There is some justification for the term, particularly if it is taken in its widest but least common sense. Adopting this usage in the work which provides the epigraph for my book, Gaspard Peucer (Philipp Melanchthon's son-in-law) treated divination as a generic term applying to all forms of exposition of the future and undertook to distinguish the legitimate ones from the illegitimate.[10] He defined as *physical divination* all arguments from causes to effects, that is to say, all arguments in which a prediction of future effects is extracted from causes known and corroborated by universal experience.[11] In other words, what we would call scientific prediction came under the general heading "divination," with the adjective "physical" as classifier. However, his way of speaking was very unusual, and the more general practice was to separate rational prediction from divination. Thus in St. Thomas:

> The name of divination is not used if a man foretells things that happen of necessity, or in the majority of instances, and which can be foreknown by human reason. . . . There are certain arts for the foreknowledge of future events that occur of necessity or frequently, and these do not pertain to divination. But there are no true arts or sciences for the knowledge of other future events, but only vain and false devices inspired by the devil.[12]

Where did Aquinas draw the line between a rational and legitimate *praenuntiatio* and divination? His examples are very telling: we can predict an eclipse with certainty, and with less certainty rain or drought and the recovery or death of the ill.[13] These effects result from causes producing them of necessity or with great regularity. But matters are quite different if the causes do not in themselves have a definite propensity to produce a given effect: and those "rational powers"—human beings—are causes such as these. We can see Socrates run or walk, but we could not predict that he would do so, for it was in his power to act otherwise.

Here Aquinas distinguishes free agents from factors that are subject to a strict *legality* (a natural necessity to behave in a certain way). In practice, the distinction remains valid even for a philosopher who most denies free will—he will tell us an agent performed of necessity an action we regard as the paradigm of a free one; but he will not go so far as to claim that identically the same action is equally necessary for every other person placed in the same circumstances. Such a philosopher will concede that men cannot be substituted for one another in such a way that the behavior of one would on all occasions be exactly congruent with that of another. He will further admit his incapacity to predict the behavior of a given man in many different circumstances. And he will thereby concede more than is required to establish the *illegality* of human behavior. But if human behavior is *illegal* (whether or not it be called "free"—as it is simpler to do, and as I think right) then surely St. Thomas was justified in saying that it is the subject of divination rather than of rational prediction. Here it becomes important to discuss the notion of "statistical legality."

Statistical Legality

Economic and social forecasting rests on the postulate of the *statistical legality* of human behavior. Although this postulate is fundamental, it has not, to my knowledge, been precisely formulated—no doubt because "statistical legality" is too rich an idea to be readily set forth.

In each definite group of human beings, the number of ways in which people will behave in a particular set of circumstances is not infinite: some ways of behaving are rare; others are more common; and one way of behaving is more frequent than any other. The one that is more frequent than any other (though not necessarily more frequent than all the others taken together) is called the *modal* behavior. In all ages and societies, men have had the notion of "modal behavior." The mere fact that one way of behaving was unquestionably and regularly more frequent than any other was enough for men to be aware of it, long before they thought of counting the different ways. They regarded it as typical.

With the coming of statistics, the calculation of averages became possible. An average is not the same thing as a mode: in a given population, the average number of children per household is most likely not a whole number and is therefore a number of children which is found in no household; whereas the mode is the number of children most frequently occurring in a household. Thus the mode expresses a tangible reality, but one which is not the whole reality of the group. The average is a summary of all the realities, but expresses them in a form which corresponds to no tangible reality. The two concepts are different, but we tend to identify them. It is characteristic that the distribution we call "normal" is the distribution in which the mode and the average coincide, yet it is only one out of an infinite number of possible distributions.

Modern statistics does not stop at modes and averages. An effort is made to prepare tables showing in the fullest possible detail the specific frequency of each different case. Whatever form the distribution may take, one feels in a strong position for prediction if it can be assumed the distribution will not change or will be subject to a regular deformation. Let me give some simple examples.

Suppose we feel entitled—for reasons that need not concern us here—to assume that in, say, ten years' time, the total personal income in some country will have increased in some fixed proportion. It is often postulated that the growth of incomes does not affect their structure. What does this mean? Not, to be sure, that any two persons in the population will see their real incomes (before tax) increase in the same proportion. Nonetheless, something very precise is meant. To illustrate what this is, let us suppose that during the initial year the wealthiest 5 per cent of the population receives 24 per cent of total personal incomes, while the poorest 20 per cent receives 6 per cent; thus the total income of the top 5 per cent is four times as great as that of the lowest 20 per cent. In addition, let us suppose that the second wealthiest 5 per cent of the population receives 10 per cent of total personal incomes, while the second poorest 20 per cent also receives 10 per cent. To postulate a stable distribution is to assume that the initial proportions characterizing it will not be changed by the general growth of incomes, whatever changes may or may not take place in the membership of the different income groups: in the terminal year, the top 5 per cent will still have a total income four times as great as the lowest 20 per cent, and the second wealthiest 5 per cent will still have the same total income as the second poorest 20 per cent. I shall not discuss whether the postulate of a stable incomes structure is founded,[14] for I have considered it only by way of example.

However, I must stress how important the postulate is in practice. For instance, in a fundamental report on the future of social progress in India, the authors assume that the pre-assigned target of raising the average income of the second poorest 20 per cent to a certain level in fifteen years cannot be reached without an over-all rise of incomes in roughly the same proportion.[15] It is not that the authors wish to maintain the existing distribution, simply that they think it has the same sort of "inertia" as one finds in physical phenomena.

On the contrary, the change of certain structures is sometimes assumed—for instance, the structure of consumption expenditure by all the households of a country. Thus, in a conjectural inquiry into the evolution of consumers' expenditure in France between 1960 and 1985, it is assumed that food expenditure will drop from its 1960 value of 36.8 per cent of total expenditure to 21.7 per cent in 1986, whereas expenditure on transport and telecommunications will rise from 7.8 to 12.9 per cent.[16] Here it is assumed that the structure undergoes a regular deformation so that for each 1 per cent rise in the average income per capita the real expenditure on food will go up by only 0.42 per cent of its previous value, whereas the expenditure on transport and telecommunications will go up by 1.6 per cent (i.e., the two types of expenditure have a different elasticity).

Economic and social forecasts would not be possible without the notion of "statistical legality." Its applications are innumerable and not always equally felicitous.

Quételet and the Average Man

If "legality" in the statistical sense was introduced into social science, Quételet's observation that "illegality" in the juridical sense exhibited certain regularities had a great deal to do with it. Quételet's discovery furnished him with one of his principal themes:

In everything which relates to crimes, the same numbers are reproduced with a constancy that is unmistakable. This is true even of crimes which seem most beyond human foresight, such as murders, which are generally committed at the close of motiveless quarrels or under other seemingly accidental circumstances. Experience nevertheless proves both that murders are committed annually in pretty nearly the same number, and that the instruments used to commit them are used in the same proportions.[17]

This famous statistician held that men's actions, taken in the aggregate, were invariant. The uniformity of crime rates appeared to him to strikingly corroborate his view.

Quételet was, to my knowledge, the first to invent the "average man" (i.e., the Average Frenchman or Average Whatever-Kind-of-Other-Man), who was to enjoy so successful a career in our own century and embodies the popular notion of statistical legality:

The man that I consider here is the analogue, in society, of the center-of-gravity in bodies; he is the mean about which the social elements oscillate; he is, if you like, a fictitious being for whom everything takes place in conformity with the average results obtained for society. If we try to establish, so to speak, the basis of a *social physics,* we must consider this man, without dwelling on special cases or anomalies, and without inquiring whether such or such an individual can attain a greater or less development in one of his faculties.[18]

The words "a social physics" clearly indicate Quételet's hopes for a science properly so called, based on the new invention of the "average man." In chemistry a pure body is obtained by the elimination of impurities through analysis. In sociology a stable behavior is to be produced by the elimination, through aggregation, of individual accidents:

Above all, we must lose sight of man considered on his own, and regard him only as a fraction of the species. In stripping him of his individuality, we get rid of all that is merely accidental; the individual peculiarities that exercise little or no influence over the mass will become effaced of their own accord, allowing the observer to seize the general results.

But there is one very important difference. Once a pure body has been isolated, we can conduct controlled experiments to see how it will behave in conditions varied by us at will, whereas the behavior of the average man is a function of a state of things that we do not control. To say how phenomena will be changed by an anticipated cause, we are reduced to using historical or analogical precedents. Thus, in considering how some type of consumption will change in relation to income, we may hold that this consumption will have the same elasticity as in some previous period in the same country, or that its elasticity will decline with increasing income in the same way as observed in some other country. More refined methods will later take the place of these crude hypotheses. For instance, we may distinguish the consumption pattern of new members of a given income group from that of established members and assign the new-member pattern to everyone we expect to come into the group each year. And thus we move from hypothesis to hypothesis, basing ourselves on detailed observations. And in consequence our predictions acquire a better basis in reason, but to attribute to them the same certainty as scientific predictions would be going too far.

The Intervention of New Causes

New and unforeseen causes will intervene, whose effects we could not calculate even if we were forewarned. Let us consider, by way of example, the forecasting of cigarette consumption in the United States. Before the correlation between cigarette smoking and lung cancer had been asserted by researchers, the forecaster obviously could not take into account the future impact of a still-unknown assertion. Nor could he be expected to take notice of it when the first findings were published, but only after further confirmation appeared. Now that there is no doubt left about the consensus of medical opinion and its vigorous assertion, the forecaster must make an estimate of the impact. But how is he to proceed? It is not a matter of assessing what can be expected from the reinforcement or weakening of factors whose effects on cigarette consumption are roughly known from previous observations. A new cause has intervened.

What potency can be attributed to fear as against habit? How much fear? How many cigarettes fewer?[20] But there is more than just the direct impact of fear upon inveterate smokers. The government may feel responsible for lessening the appeal of cigarettes, and thus the authorities may request less brandishing of cigarettes by television and film heroes—

how will this affect teen-age behavior? And if it lessens the acquisition of the habit by teen-agers, does that guarantee that many of them will retain non-smoking habits when adults? However rough the approach indicated here, surely it indicates that in such a case a useful forecast could not rest upon the established "legality" of the behavior of the average man.

NOTES

1. It is by no means conclusive, but still significant, that on several occasions medals or coins were struck with "alchemic gold." See E. J. Halmyard, *Alchemy* (London, 1957).

2. The mishap sometimes turned into a tragedy. Krohneman, after being made a baron, was hanged. The most recent instance is that of James Price, who, after making gold and silver in the presence of reliable witnesses in Oxford in 1782, was ordered by the Royal Society to reproduce his experiment under the supervision of three specially appointed men of science. Price poisoned himself on the day they were to appear. One may suppose that he had simply made a mistake, having used impure substances, and that, his supplies exhausted, he was driven to despair by his inability to obtain the same results with a new batch of minerals.

3. A declaration of the American Meteorological Society in September 1957, quoted in *Long Range Weather Prediction,* a publication of the PEP, Vol. XXVIII, No. 458 (January 29, 1962).

4. Maupertuis, *Lettres,* Letter XVIII.

5. G. Bidault de l'Isle, *Dictons de nos Campagnes* (2 vols.; Paris, 1952).

6. *Oxford Dictionary of English Proverbs.*

7. See *De Divinatione.*

8. There lies the "hitch": so many premonitory sayings are poorly checked.

9. Both modes of prediction are mentioned in a sentence which also records the decline in their credit: "*Nam ut nunc extis (quanquam id ipsum minus aliquanto quam olim) sic tum avibus magnae res impetriri solebant.*" (*De Divinatione,* I, xvi.)

10. "Commentarius de praecipuis generibus divinationum, in quo a Prophetiis autoritate divina traditis, et a Physicis conjecturis, discernuntuartes et imposturae Diabolicae, atque observationes natae ex superstitione et cum haec conjunctae; et monstrantur fontes ac causae Physicarum praedictionum: Diabolicae vero ac superstitiosae confutatae damnantur ea serie, quam tabella praefixa ostendit . . . Autore Casparo Peucero D Wittenberg 1574." His work is a fascinating encyclopedia of superstitious practices contrasted with those he believes rational.

11. Peucer, p. 16 *bis* (in his work the rectos alone are numbered).

12. *Summa Theologica,* IIa, IIae, questio xcv, art. I.

13. St. Thomas' distinction between these degrees of certitude is marked by his use of the phrase *per certitudinem* in the former case, and *non quidem per certitudinem, sed per quamdam conjecturam* in the latter.

14. The available data indicate a constant relation between the second 5 per cent (from the top) and the second 20 per cent (from the bottom), but not between the top 5 per cent (whose share is diminishing) and the poorest 5 per cent (whose share before transfers does not appear to be increasing). See Simon Kuznets, "Quantitative Aspects of the Growth of Nations: VIII. Distribution of Income by Size," *Economic Development and Cultural Change,* XI, No. 2, Part II (January 1963).

15. The report I refer to here is a document prepared by the Perspective Planning Division of the Planning Commission of India. It is called *Perspective of Development 1961–1976, Implications of Planning for a Minimum Level of Living* and was issued in August 1962. Mr. Pitambar Pant was in charge of the work.

16. The document in question is a study of the possible evaluation of consumer expenditure submitted by M. Delors (from the Commissariat au Plan) to the Groupe 1985. The reader should understand that both this document and the Indian report just referred to are regarded by their authors as hypotheses rather than "predictions."

17. A. Quételet, *Sur l'Homme et le développement de ses Facultés, ou Essai de physique sociale* (2 vols., Paris, 1835), I, 7. (An English translation was published in Edinburgh in 1842.)

18. *Ibid.,* I, 21.

19. *Ibid.,* I, 4.

20. *Wall Street Journal,* August 8, 1963 (New York)

Part **III**

WAYS OF
CONCEIVING
THE FUTURE

11

Process

and Action

The sciences of nature have predictive import, but treat man as an insignificant or an exogenous agent. Man is an insignificant agent in relation to stellar and meteorological phenomena, and an exogenous one in relation to, say, chemical experiments. The second case is of interest to us and deserves a simple illustration.

Conditional Prediction

Consider a predictive and scientific proposition of the form "Bodies B_1, $B_2, \ldots B_n$ placed in mutual contiguity under conditions $C_1, C_2, \ldots C_m$ give result R after H hours." This general proposition is transformed into the particular prediction that R will result at some specified time T, only if we assume that the bodies are "placed in mutual contiguity" H hours before T. A chemist leaves an assistant to carry out an experiment, returns home, and looking at his watch, says: "Jack will start the experiment in 5 minutes, so we will have the result in 4 hours 5 minutes." His prediction may be very wrong—not because the experiment takes more than 4 hours, but because his assistant does not begin it at the specified time.

The scientific and predictive proposition becomes a *historical* prediction: that is to say, it acquires a datable term of expiration as soon as we assume a datable intervention by an exogenous human agent. In speaking about what will happen in 4 hours 5 minutes, our chemist is really making two predictions at once—one bearing on the behavior of things, the other on the behavior of a man.

We can clearly distinguish in this simple example between the definite process of things and the triggering of the process, which depends on the aleatory behavior of man. Is there anything resembling this model in human affairs? Yes, if we can form general propositions about the political order. Let us suppose that the "positive law of bodies politic" put forward by Montesquieu and Rousseau[1] is in fact well established. According to this law, we recall, authority becomes more concentrated in proportion as a people grows; thus changes in population lead to mutations of the regime. Implicit in the law is a prediction of Caesarism, but on one condition: "If the people grows (beyond a certain size)." Therefore the prediction will not necessarily be accomplished. Associated with it is the advice: "Limit the size of your state to avoid the transition to Caesarism."

We have here, on the one hand, a process that is held to be certain if the requisite conditions are satisfied, and on the other, a human behavior that can lead to the process or can interrupt it. But it is different from the previous example in that human behavior now has a *twofold* role: it is both internal (endogenous) and external (exogenous) to the process supposed to be certain. Men are *submitted* to the process (as objects), but are also *masters* of it (as acting subjects); and this twofold role of men is characteristic of the social and political order as a whole.

Three different positions can be taken with regard to the Montesquieu-Rousseau law—always assuming it is valid.

1. Primus says: "That is the process, and that the result. Take heed, and stop the determining factor, for you are masters." His warning is presented in the form of a conditional prediction associated with a suggestion of the course of action to take.

2. Secundus says: "That is the process, and that the result. But it is possible to intervene in various ways and thereby affect the result. Different interventions would be effective to various degrees and some are more likely than others."

3. Tertius says: "That is the process, and included in it is the impossibility that Primus' appeals will have any effect on its inevitable result." In short, Tertius refuses to dichotomize people into "objects" and "acting

subjects." Human actions are already taken into account in the process; they cannot be expected to stop it.

Attitudes

If we are determined to predict human affairs, we will be inclined to adopt the position of Tertius, who traces one and only one *line of the future*. If we want to make men act, we shall also insist on a *line of the future*, asserting that it can be deflected only through the adoption of Primus' suggestion. And the more Primus is taken with his idea, the more he will be concerned to present it as the only way of deviating from an otherwise ineluctable course. Thus the wish to predict and the wish to persuade conspire to impress on the minds of men the idea of a line of the future, and to dissuade the forecaster, Secundus, from opening the fan of possible futures.

It is true to say that our understanding naturally prefers a unique prediction to a multiple forecast. Each representation of a possible future costs the mind an effort (if the representation is a reasoned one, and not a mere daydream), and it is not our habit to start by repeating the effort several times in order to then choose from the possibles before us the one we think is most probable. To spread out the fan, then shut it again, and pass from a multiple forecast to our most probable prognosis—this is not a procedure that comes naturally to us. On the contrary, we start by imagining *one* future sequel to the present state. And having done so, we feel attached to this first-conceived future because of the investment we have made (the mental effort) and even more because of the possession we have obtained (a subjective certainty about the future). Further efforts to imagine other futures would be to make a new investment only to devaluate our acquisition: we would be working to dispossess ourselves of a certainty.

And to do so is very sound, yet we hesitate. After making a headpiece, Don Quixote tested it by striking it with his sword. The headpiece shattered. He reassembled it, but this time did not strike it, for fear of again losing a possibly worthless helmet. Our own minds are similarly inclined.

By the mere fact of our predisposition toward a unique prediction, we tend to reject the view that choices capable of affecting a process, made by men as thinking agents, are somehow outside the process. We lend a willing ear to Tertius when he tells us that the choices are taken into account in the process: "Everything is weighed, measured, and counted."

Let us return to our example of atmospheric pollution in an urban center.[2] Tertius says to me: "Certainly, every owner of a car contributing to the pollution is free to buy or not buy, use or not use his car. Yet you will agree that whatever the freedom of car owners, we can count on the number of cars increasing conformably with a process we can approximately calculate."

I readily admit his point, and agree that there is, in consequence, a "natural course" of pollution.[3] But if human behavior has so far been conceived as endogenous to the process, I also conceive it as exogenous (thinking now of measures taken by the authorities) and capable of correcting the natural course with greater or less rapidity.

Here Tertius attacks me sharply: "You say the authorities will intervene sooner or later, and more or less energetically, and regard their intervention as autonomous. According to you, the promptness and degree of alteration in the natural course will depend on decisions made by the authorities. But you will grant me that the intervention will take place because of the pollution, that one is unlikely as long as the pollution is low, and that it is beyond all probability that there should be none once the pollution is high. Why then do you refuse to recognize the authorities' action as a mere retroaction, a natural phenomenon whose model we know very well: a phenomenon which builds up, exponentially sets off— by the mere fact of its growth—inhibiting forces which retard and eventually halt its progress, resulting in an equilibrium or in periodic fluctuations. You have agreed to call the pattern of development the 'natural course'; but you claim the restraints it will undergo are artifices willed by man; for my part[1] I say that the corrective actions generated by the phenomenon form an integral part of it, and that in the true 'natural course' the growth is restrained by obstacles it has itself generated. Therefore, all human actions, the authorities' no less than the car owners', enter into the process."

Mere Retroaction?

The thesis just propounded by Tertius flatters our intellect; a global conquest of reality is a pleasing notion, and so too is the fancy of usurping divine prescience. But the thesis is shocking to common sense, and clashes with the "mores" of our understanding, which are represented in our ways of speaking.

All of us recognize processes in human affairs, and without this awareness no social science would be possible. A "process" is a succession of events we can describe and discuss as though they fell within the province of the physical sciences. The process of inflation provides a trite example. If the volume of incomes grows without a corresponding rise in productivity, the swelling flux of purchasing power exerts a pressure on conumers' markets, and price-rises depending on the elasticity of demand and propagated by diffusion will result. If the imbalance between supply and demand causes an increase of imports from abroad and keeps usual exports at home, there is an absorption effect complementary to the price-rise. The words "volume," "flux," "pressure," "elasticity," "diffusion," "absorption" are all taken from the physical sciences. And we discuss measures for slowing down and stopping the process in similar terms.

If we now consider whether it is likely that the minister of finance of a certain government will take some particular anti-inflationary measure, we begin to speak a different language. We have to discuss an action rather than a process, and appraise the will of a man rather than understand the interplay of forces.

Does this change of language correspond to an objective difference, or to an illusion of our thought? Should Tertius argue for illusion, saying that an anti-inflationary action is no more than a retroaction sparked by the inflation itself? I can answer him. In the aftermath of the two world wars, we have seen sufficient examples of the inflationary process. If its development automatically leads to an anti-inflationary retroaction forming an integral part of the whole process, the curves showing the course of inflation in different countries ought to have a family resemblance. No such kinship exists. A difference of government is associated with differences of policy and line of development.

The Contrast between Process and Intervention

The principle underlying the present essay is this: the mind conforms to observable "mores" when it foresees the future, and the prerequisite for improving them is to examine them. It is, I think, pertinent to stress that the mind habitually contrasts *process* and *intervention*. When we recommend a public action, we do so to modify what seems bound to come about in its absence. Our advice is designed to undo our prediction. The probable future that needs preventing is sometimes the result of an action taken by an agent from the same category as the one whom we advise (the now-classical case of the two-person game), but more often than not it is the result of a process.

Without attempting to "define" a process, I wish to recall the general acceptation of the word. We generally would not speak of a process in referring to the intended result of an agent's conscious action, but would do so in referring to a phenomenon which arises from a complex concurrence of actions taken by agents who in no way intend to produce the phenomenon. For instance, it is evident that the successive rise of prices, characteristic of the inflationary process, is an effect, and not a consciously sought goal. On the contrary, to slow down or stop the rise is the goal of an anti-inflationary policy. The intervention has a *final cause;* the process has only *efficient causes.*

To be sure, all the actors inside the frame of the inflationary process have their purposes or goals. The workers who demand raises wish to regain a lost purchasing power; the merchants who mark up their goods wish to regain profits wiped out by rising costs; and so on. But even though the process results from the pursuit of all these particular goals in combination, they are not of the same dimension as the process, whereas the goal of anti-inflationary intervention is.

For an intervention to have a chance of working, it must be of the same dimension as the process: the action of the intervening agent must balance the pull of the process.[4] Clearly, then, the one decision of this agent is not of the same order as the decisions taken by each of the agents whose actions daily feed the process. And just as it would be unreasonable to consider individually the behavior of the agents who are carried along in the process, so is it reasonable to consider the behavior of the agent able to perform a balancing action. The intervention is on the scale of the human will; the process running its course is not. And thus it is appropriate to use different languages to explain the process and conjecture an intervention.

Specificity of the Event

Essential to the development of the sciences as sciences is the study of processes. We identify processes very crudely by such generic terms as inflation, revolution, purge (*hot,* rapid processes), urbanization, and industrialization (*cold,* extended processes). The examples available to us in each "family" are too few in number and too rich in peculiarities for us to discover easily a typical structure of an identified process; yet in naming the process we prove that we have some "idea" of it, which, however small its validity, we can improve. I do not propose to describe how, and shall confine myself to emphasizing that in order to speak about processes we borrow concepts from the physical sciences. And we may legitimately do so, notwithstanding the freedom of the individuals participating in the process, for the most likely behavior—given the very large number of individuals—occurs with such an overwhelming frequency that on the macroscopic scale everything takes place as though the agents were objects with fixed propensities.[5]

It would be useful to undertake a careful critique of the circumstances entitling us to treat human behavior as *legal* (a task I have no ambition of performing here). To say that a knowledge of the average movement is sufficient for a knowledge of the movement of the whole is to evade the problem: it is a platitude, for an average is a relation containing our unknown quantity, the global movement, in the numerator. What needs to be considered is this: we substitute for the multitude of agents an ideal agent deprived of all individual peculiarities (for instance the *homo oeconomicus* of classical economics), or alternatively—adopting a more modern method based on statistical distributions—a "representative sample" in which individual characters are weighted.

Two remarks are called for here. First, if we neglect an unusual behavior or weight it insufficiently, a freak effect can make us go wrong. In a society with an annual quota of murders, it is not a matter of indifference that one of the victims should be Henry IV of France. But the overlooking of a substantial effect produced by an action of small weight seems to be unavoidable.

Things are different for the agents of exceptional weight who figure in the system. It is a matter of indifference to the railways if I decide to take my sons on a journey I normally make alone, but not so if the minister of war requires railway facilities for an important movement of troops. A man speculating on the rising price of gold will not worry about determining whether another speculator has taken a different position, but it is of cardinal importance for him to know that the monetary authorities are planning a massive intervention to lower the price.

If it is unimportant for us to know each particular decision taken by the very numerous agents of small individual weight who feed the process, the same does not hold for the weighty decisions which may intervene. Such decisions can inject the specificity of an event into the course of a process. They are usually taken by a very small number of men to whom important ways and means are made available by the existing political or social order. And consequently there is nothing illogical in the commonplace curiosity about any seat of great power (and hence of great possibilities)—that driving curiosity which would have us ask Lesage's Lame Demon, could we procure him, to lay open the roofs beneath which such decisions are taken. The number of decision-makers is too small for us to postulate the statistical legality of their behavior: the great importance of their specific characters and individual motives must be recognized. Popular opinion is well able to divide men in positions of authority into two contrasting categories, dependent upon the originality of their behavior. The Regulars do not obtrude their personality upon their decision-making, so that their decisions are much what you would expect from a nameless "someone" in that position under these circumstances. In contrast, the Originals make decisions bearing the seal of their individual character.

Obviously decisions made in seats of power are least unexpected, better foreknown if made by Regulars. Further we must note that whenever a decision is made by a numerous body each member of which opines individually (is not bound by party discipline), personal characteristics are damped down by numbers. It is perhaps not out of place to recall that "democratic philosophy" called for such damping down, and to contrast the recent trend in even the oldest democracies toward the personalization of authority, which affords the maximum opportunity for the display of individual character.

"Who sits up there" thus makes a major difference (as it did in the similar circumstances of the Roman Empire), and it seems foolish not to recognize that individual decisions are historical causes in their own right. I find it hard to understand how eminent authors, such as Engels[6] —and a great many others—can have held or propounded the opposite thesis, which carries with it inadmissible implications. If taken seriously, it would drive us to acknowledge in every past conqueror or tyrant the necessary instrument of a preordained "becoming," staged by that secular Providence, evolution! Now it may well be true that the situation of France in 1799 and that of Germany in the winter of 1932–33 called for a "strong man." But surely it is plain that with someone other than

Napoleon the fifteen-year recrudescence of the European war would not have occurred, and with someone other than Hitler genocide would not have been conceivable. Therefore individuals in high places are true causes, and we miss this if we rely exclusively upon a "macroscopic" approach.

It is legitimate and serviceable to use the language of social physics in predicting that a given process will lead to a great concentration of power; but as to the use made of this power, that is the object of speculations of another kind.

Let us consider a case at first sight very favorable to the foregoing thesis of endogenous retroaction. Two great industrial countries simultaneously reach the same extreme of economic depression and unemployment. In the same month, a new leader comes to power in each country and begins a vigorous struggle against unemployment. Both leaders expand the economic activity of the state, and make constitutional changes (such as strengthening central power at the expense of local powers) designed to place the state in a lasting position of authority over the economy. Thus the role of these two men seems to conform to the retroaction model not only with regard to the hot process of the immediate crisis, but with regard to a cold process of long-term economic development, which calls, we may suppose, for a more active role of the public powers.

The example is well suited to justify the idea that an intervention is a mere retroaction and that men who play an important role on the political scene are simply playing a historically necessary role. The date? January 1933. The leaders? Roosevelt and Hitler.

However striking the parallel, it will be granted that the differences are more outstanding. While it is true that Hitler solved unemployment, built the *Autobahnen,* and launched the Volkswagen, these are hardly the things for which we remember him. It will not be claimed there is a necessary connection between his economic role and his war[7] and genocide. If similar circumstances led two men to adopt certain analogous policies, common sense compels us to acknowledge that these circumstances also *permitted* them to follow other, very different policies, each according to his own inclination.

Thus the process provides the occasion for the event but does not determine its nature. What Hitler was going to do could be foreseen far better by listening to his speeches than by studying the process. The fact, so great in its consequences, that a Hitler instead of a Roosevelt took power in Germany was likewise unforeseeable by a macroscopic method. For if we ask, speaking in generalities, which of the two countries set the greater store by culture (at the time), then surely the answer is Germany. Yet it gave itself a self-taught leader, while Roosevelt had received an excellent education. If we further ask where is indifference to family origins a matter of principle, the answer is the United States, which gave itself a patrician President, while the Germans subjected themselves to a *déraciné*.

The calamities of the forties were quite foreseeable, in rough outline, from 1930 on, but not through the understanding of processes alone.

The Knowledge of Processes

Nothing is more difficult than to foresee the actions of a man, particularly a power-drunk politician. Cicero did not foresee that Octavian, his favorite, would deliver him to the daggers of assassins. The accession of Caligula was the occasion for general rejoicing.[8]

Thus any systematic effort at forecasting must rest on the understanding of processes, and we would be fools not to devote ourselves to this task on the lame pretext that such understanding does not enable us to make complete predictions. The understanding of processes is essential to an advisory forecast. The forecast in 1930 of a deteriorating economic and social situation, breeding discontent and opening the door to an adventurer, would not have sufficed for an exact prediction of the sequel, but it would have served as an urgent warning to oppose the process that facilitated the career of the adventurer.

Although our knowledge of social and political processes is inferior— in both actual and potential development—to our knowledge of natural processes, it is sufficient for us to make timely interventions that have some chances of success, and to put "forces" to work as Comte expresses it so well.[9] This is of enormous worth, and in my opinion, all that we can hope for.

Auguste Comte's Dream

There are, however, some intellects, and not among the least, that demand more. They want to understand the whole of history as a single process for the mind to grasp. Comte regarded political science as a "special physics"—a "social physics"[10] that could "unveil the future" through observation of the past.

> The aim of every science is foresight (*prévoyance*). For the laws established by observation of phenomena are generally employed to foresee their succession. All men, however little advanced, make true predictions, which are always based on the same principle, the knowledge of the future from the past. For example, all men predict the general effects of terrestrial gravity and a multitude of other phenomena sufficiently simple and usual for the least capable and attentive spectator to be aware of their order of succession. The faculty of foresight in each person is measured by his science. The foresight of the astronomer who predicts with complete precision the state of the solar system many years in advance is absolutely the same in kind as that of the savage who predicts the next sunrise. The only difference lies in the extent of their knowledge.
>
> Manifestly, then, it is quite in accordance with the nature of the human mind that observation of the past should unveil the future in politics, as it does in astronomy, physics, chemistry, and physiology.
>
> The determination of the future must even be regarded as the direct aim of political science, as in the case of the other positive sciences. Indeed, it is clear that knowledge of what social system the elite of mankind is called to by the progress of civilization—knowledge forming the true practical object of positive science—involves a general determination of the next social future such as it results from the past.[11]

It seems to me that our philosopher was confusing scientific prediction and historical prediction—two very different things, as the following illustration will show. A contemporary of Comte, Nicolas Sadi Carnot, formulated an important scientific law about the motive power of engines.[12] Carnot's principle was designed to be valid for all time: an "intemporality" quite different from "historicity." Carnot did not propose a formula expressing the future growth of the total power harnessed in engines, nor one describing how the distribution of the total power between locomotives, steamers, and other engines would change.[13] Historical predictions such as these lie outside the field of physical science. And likewise in an even simpler case: a physiologist is acquainted with the effects of alcohol on the body, but his science does not tell him whether the percentage of alcoholics in some town or some country will increase or decrease; a prediction of the use men will make of alcohol is outside the province of physiology.

Whatever place scientific prediction holds in a historical prediction, the latter comes into existence only through the making of a prediction about human actions. Contrary to what Comte says, science does not unveil the future: its role is both less ambitious and more useful. The scientist of today who speculates about the state of the atmosphere after a series of atomic tests conducted at some particular intensity, or about the state of some country after bombing by another power in a military attack, does not *predict* certain future states but warns us that they would result from certain assumed human actions.[14]

The sciences of nature generally do not yield unconditional historical predictions, except in the case of future states *recurring* in virtue of the *structure* of a system proofed against our intervention. The prediction of the next solstice is an example. Historical prediction in astronomy can of course reach much further into time than this, the reason being that the astronomical order is indifferent to human action.

If, then, we argue by analogy with the sciences of nature, we cannot, I think, infer that we should be able to know the future of man, as Comte imagined. As our sciences develop, and with them our power, it seems to me there will be a greater variety of possible futures, depending on the use we make of this power.

The System of Mankind

Even in the most materialistic account of mankind, we do not arrive at a certain prediction of our future states. For if mankind forms an open system determined by its ecological relationships, the nature of these relationships will change according to the state of our knowledge, and we cannot predict the future state of our knowledge.

However, there is in our day a great intellectual propensity toward regarding the whole of history as a single process, in relation to which all actions and choices cease to be determining, all of them being endogenous to the process. And one facet of history most lending itself to this view is the question of population. The proliferation of man since the middle of the seventeenth century is a process bound to strike the imagination. We may legitimately treat the phenomenon in terms of social physics, but then it is paradoxical for us to treat the framework of political geography as a rigid one in our extrapolation of population trends. If the phenomenon is comparable with physical phenomena, it cannot be compartmentalized by the *ideal* lines of frontiers. There must be a tendency toward an equalization of the density, a leveling of the distribution over inhabitable regions;[15] immigrants or invaders must exert pressure on the less filled "national parks." There will be "housing wars," more rational, popular, and terrible than any conflict in the past. Who would be blind enough to deny this possibility? But also, who would be so much a fatalist as to make it into a certainty?

Processes and Forecasting

If we understand that processes exist in human affairs and grasp their dynamics as well as possible, we stand to gain everything in the spheres of both intellect and utility. We gain nothing in the intellectual order, and lose a great deal in the field of action, if we insist on integrating all history into a process that embraces all human actions. What is important is to find points of fulcrum on which we can exert pressure, thereby deflecting the course of events in one direction rather than another. The commonsense distinction between process and action is therefore salutary.

We want to forecast in order to act; hence there naturally follows a classification of processes according to their relationship to action. But first, let me recall the sense in which I am using "process": the evolution of a phenomenon which is not a *goal* chosen by a human will but the effect of a complex concurrence of actions not consciously aimed at the effect. Thus the evolution of the phenomenon can be seen as a "natural course." And let me recall the distinction made in Chapter 6 between the "dominating future" and the "masterable future": a future dominating an agent at one level may be masterable by an agent at a higher level. Thus we could say that inflation is a dominating process from the standpoint of the municipal authorities but is masterable by the national authorities. In other words, the national authorities are, it seems to us, provided with ways of counteracting the phenomenon, while the municipal authorities are not. But thinking now of another process—the growth of the national population—would we say that the national authorities have means of stopping the increase? I rather think not. And about the growth of the total population of the earth, we would say readily that governments who agreed to stop the process would find their power unavailing.

Some processes are absolutely dominating. For this it is not necessary that means of counteracting the process be inconceivable; it is sufficient if they are inapplicable.[16] The existence of social processes whose run is thus dominating needs no emphasizing: our contemporaries are hardly more convinced of anything else, and this commonplace notion[17] is in continual use in perfectly "naïve" forecasts. Quite rightly so, too, for in recognizing a process as dominating, we are able to say that the future scene will differ from the present in such a way and such a direction. Confidently foreseen changes provide *future data* that can be important even if they remain "fuzzy,"[18] and whose value increases if we can roughly quantify the course of the phenomenon and associate specified magnitudes with successive future dates.[19]

This is how we place foreknown elements on the future scene. These *foreknowns* act as props and also as constraints, forming a frame within which our thought represents the future.

The forecaster's first task is to consider what changes are likely to be produced by dominating processes, seen as *strong and powerful tendencies,* during the period under consideration: he ascertains the foreknowns. His search for the foreknowns is something quite different from the derived prediction of aspects held to be immediately inferable from some given foreknown. Very often such a derived prediction turns out to be incompatible with the influence of some other foreknown (we shall see some examples). He must therefore start by exhibiting all the foreknowns, then test their coherence, and afterwards see whether something seeming to follow from one of them is compatible with the rest.

Just as the foreknowns must be checked against one another, so must they be checked against the structural certainties.[20] The latter, we recall, are structural features of the present, which our thought automatically carries forward into the future; I compared them to dikes extended from the present into the future. There may be a conflict between the *transferred presents* and the *foreknown futures.* All this pertains to the problems of coherence of the future scene, which are easily neglected, quite understandably, for a question about the future usually bears on some particular aspect that we hope to grasp without referring to the whole. We sometimes succeed, but more often this is a source of error. We shall see what our reliance on a tendency can lead to.

NOTES

1. See my paper "La Théorie des formes de gouvernement chez Rousseau," in the periodical *Le Contrat social* (November–December 1962).

2. See Chapter 4.

3. I am still assuming, for simplicity, that cars are the only source of pollution.

4. This manner of speaking should not suggest that the intervening agent necessarily has a force he can directly apply to restrain the pull of the process. It is sufficient for him to know of, and do away with, a determining factor of the process, or to trigger another counteracting process.

5. My formulation differs appreciably from the classical one of Quételet, which is worth quoting:

"All observations tend to confirm the truth of this proposition, which I proposed long ago, that *everything pertaining to the human species considered in aggregate is of the order of physical facts;* the greater the number of individuals, the more does the influence of the individual will disappear, leaving predominance to a series of general facts, dependent on the causes by which society exists and is preserved. These are the causes which must be ascertained, and as soon as we know them we shall be able to determine their influence on society in the same way as we determine effects from their causes in the physical sciences."

(Adolphe Quételet, *Sur l'homme et le développement de ses facultés, ou Essai de physique sociale* [2 vols.; Paris 1835].) The double title is characteristic, indicating a shift from the traditional approach to another. The italics in the quotation are Quételet's.

6. "That such and such a man and precisely that man arises at that particular time in that given country is of course a pure accident. But cut him out and there will be a demand for a substitute, and this substitute will be found, good or bad, but in the long run he will be found. That Napoleon, just that particular Corsican, should have been the military dictator whom the French Republic, exhausted by its own war, had rendered necessary was an accident; but that, if a Napoleon had been lacking, another would have filled the place is proved by the fact that the man has always been found as soon as he became necessary: Caesar, Augustus, Cromwell, etc." (Friedrich Engels, Letter to Heinz Starkenburg, January 25, 1894, in Karl Marx and Friedrich Engels, *Correspondence* [London: Martin Lawrence Ltd., 1934].)

7. Those who still think that men make war to get out of an economic mess should note that the economic situation and unemployment were completely remedied in the Third Reich well before Hitler unleashed his war.

8. *Princeps exoptatissimus,* says Suetonius, who depicts the throng pressing along his way and lavishing tender names on him, calling him their luminary and their child: *"sidus"* et *"pullum"* et *"puppum"* et *"alumnum"* appelantium. (*The Twelve Caesars,* III, xiii.)

9. "In general, when man appears to exert a great influence, it is not due to his own forces, which are extremely small. It is always forces external to him which act for him, according to laws over which he has no control. All his power resides in his intelligence, which puts him in a position to know these laws by observation, to foresee their effects, and subsequently to make them work in combination to produce the goal he sets before him, always provided he utilizes these forces in accordance with their nature. Once the action has been produced, ignorance of the natural laws makes a spectator, and sometimes the actor himself, attribute to the power of man what is only due to his foresight." (*Plan des travaux scientifiques nécessaires pour réorganiser la société* [May 1822], published as the third part of the General Appendix to the *Système de politique positive* [Paris, 1929] IV, 94–5.)

10. *Ibid.,* p. 130.

11. *Ibid.,* p. 118.

12. Nicolas Sadi Carnot, *Réflexions sur la puissance motrice du feu et sur les machines propres à développer cette puissance* (Paris, 1824).

13. Mulhall's statistical estimates are of some incidental interest: the total power in the world, in thousands of h.p., was 1,650 in 1840, 9,380 in 1860, and 34,150 in 1880. At the last of these dates, the distribution was: 21,240 in locomotives, 7,670 in fixed engines, and 5,240 in steamers.

14. A scientist would be the first to say that such resulting states are not the object of rigorous forecasts.

15. This talk of equalization of the density should obviously be taken as referring to the useful surface rather than to the geometrical surface.

16. We must understand that an intervention is exogeneous, but also that an intervention is subject to conditions and limits.

17. The idea is commonplace chiefly in regard to the changes that people are aware of—those grouped under the name of progress.

18. Thus when Faguet pictures the twentieth century, he foresees that the speed of communications will increase a great deal, and much more between large agglomerations than between these and smaller centers. In this case, it is unimportant that he fails to quantify the march of the phenomenon over time (my reason for using the adjective "fuzzy"). But in other cases, the value of a prediction depends on its being quantified as a function of time.

19. For instance, the Paley Report (*Report of the President's Commission on Raw Materials* [5 vols.; Washington, D.C., 1952]) contains numerical estimates of the world consumption of energy in 1975.

20. Chapter 6.

12

The Changing Scene

The present is like a scene before us, offering itself to our eyes. A part that is unknown ceases to be so the moment our sight fastens on it. I could drive a car through a village, keeping a lookout only for oncoming cars or children crossing the road. But stopping at the main square, I immediately obtain an over-all impression, and if I linger I can pick out an increasing number of details.

If I stay I can build a model of the village and, provided I am indiscreet, I can push my way into the houses, note their interior arrangement, and eventually elaborate my mock-up down to the smallest details, situating each house and even each armchair in relation to some central landmark (as for instance the church).

Now I think of the future. A few days of observation are enough to give me a sense of different movements. A dealer in antiques passes through, taking with him some old furniture. A van arrives and new household goods are delivered. New buildings are started, and over there alterations are being made at a dangerous crossroad. I would like to model the village as it will be in twenty-five years' time. I know many things will be unchanged, for instance the church, but many others will suffer a displacement, or disappear, or will be quite new. Can I anticipate these modifications so as to construct from my present mock-up another representing the village twenty-five years hence? Clearly, I cannot.

The Present Can Be Charted but Not the Future

The word "chartable" designates—fairly precisely, I think—a way of treating the present that does not hold for the future.

When we want to imagine the future changing of our village, the most simple and common way is to visualize a strong current running through it and deforming it.

Let us change scales: now consider the African continent, whose cities we want to imagine as they will be in half a century. Our thought is guided by the idea of an urbanizing stream. If we hypothesize the growth in the total African population and in the percentage of town-dwellers, we can hazard a guess as to the total urban population. But how will this population be distributed among the different cities? We should answer this more readily if we hypothesized the growth country by country, instead of for the continent as a whole. But would we be entitled to base hypotheses on a political map liable to change in ways we cannot foresee? Suppose that in 1913 a thousand experts were asked to draw the political boundaries of Europe in 1963. Not one would have come close to the truth.

Thus we cannot *foresee* the future scene in the way we see the present scene. We can fasten our attention on powerful currents transforming the present scene, but even if we have understood them well, any inferences we draw about the future may be upset through the influence of unforeseen, volatile elements.

On the Speed of Currents

It is remarkable that currents strongly affecting the future are in general fairly well perceived. None has been of greater importance over the last two centuries than the increasing production per worker through technological progress. It seems that forecasting of this trend was fairly common in England as early as the first quarter of the eighteenth century, since in 1724 Swift made it the butt of his ridicule. His unjust satire fortunately preserves for us the very clear ideas then prevailing on the subject.

Swift represents the world of science by the Flying Island of Laputa, inhabited by mathematicians and hovering over the terra firma of Balni-barbi. He relates that some inhabitants of Balnibarbi once paid a visit to Laputa, and returned "with a very little Smattering in Mathematics" and "full of Volatile Spirits acquired in that Airy Region":

> These Persons upon their Return, began to dislike the Management of every Thing below; and fell into Schemes of putting all Arts, Sciences, Languages, and Mechanics upon a new Foot. To this End they procured a Royal Patent for erecting an Academy of PROJECTORS in *Lagado:* And the Humor prevailed so strongly among the People, that there is not a Town of any Consequence in the Kingdom without such an Academy. In these Colleges, the Professors contrive new Rules and Methods of Agriculture and Building, and new Instruments and Tools for all Trades and Manufactures, whereby, as they undertake, one Man shall do the Work of Ten. . . .[1]

"One Man shall do the Work of Ten"—Swift's words are a precocious statement of what we call the "increase in productivity." And he successfully related the increase to the causes which, acting in combination, did in fact produce it.[2]

But the striking statement "one Man shall do the Work of Ten" calls for a comment on the speed of the trend. A vast erudition would be required to say at what dates, and in what fields, it became possible for one man to do the work given to ten in 1724. But as to the tenfold increase of the production per worker *for the working population as a whole,* we can estimate (with a large margin of error) that it was attained in about 1950.[3] Consequently, if Swift's contemporaries had thought of the trend as a rapid one (a matter of one generation), they would have committed a practical error far greater than the conservative who would have quite denied its existence.

The importance of assigning a speed to a "course" of things is thus clear. Outcomes are quite different according to the speed, as a political example will serve to illustrate. A number of people, from the time of Louis Philippe on, were struck by the growth of the two colossi—the expression was in current use—Russia and the United States, foreseeing that they would eventually relegate the old powers of Europe to minor roles.[4]

It follows, by the simplest of analogical arguments, that the opposition between Russia and America should dominate the twentieth century. And we would consider a prophecy to this effect made in about 1840 to be of great moment. Yet its predictive value would have been nil, or worse than that, negative. Such a prophecy, accepted by diplomats, would have generated the expectation that in any worldwide conflict the United States would "naturally" or "logically" intervene in the opposite camp from Russia. In actual fact, the United States has intervened on the same side as Russia in both world wars. But the situation would no doubt have differed had Russia and America achieved as early as 1895 the prepotency that has been theirs since 1945. Their rivalry would have weighed decisively on the international scene, and presided over international alignments far different from the ones we have known. Thus the rate at which the phenomenon of Russo-American superiority develops is of great importance in practical prognostications.

However, it must not be thought that the speeds alone are sufficient for good predictions. Consider the historical scene at the beginning of the century and imagine just one different *event:* the crushing defeat of Japan in the Russo-Japanese War.

Russia, thenceforth Suzerain of Japan and China, would have represented a threat to the United States, giving immediate effect to their potential opposition. They would have confronted one another in the Pacific, and hence the United States would have regarded Germany, the power on the opposite flank of its enemy, as its natural ally. The alignment of powers would have changed: it is difficult to think of England acting in consort with Russia in 1914 in the absence of the defeat of Tsushima. And thus we see how much influence an aleatory event can exert on the general course of things.

But this effect of a particular event on the general course of things (an effect to which I attach great importance) is not our subject just now. We are speaking about the course itself, of a known character and direction, and are indicating the importance of estimating its speed. A trivial example will suffice to show that a forecast of a change in some particular direction, if unaccompanied by a specification of the speed, can give rise to very different behavior depending on the speed the hearer assumes (even when unconscious of so doing). Suppose that two of us are told: "The cost of living will double"; one of us may imagine the process taking two years (a 41 per cent increase annually), while the other thinks of thirty-six years (a 2 per cent increase annually). The appropriate behavior is clearly not the same in the two cases. Thus an assertion about a course is ambiguous unless a speed is specified.[5]

A Course of Things and Its Reflections

What I mean by "reflection" here is the illumination of phenomenon *B* by our forecast of phenomenon *A*. If I regard the dated course of phenomenon *A* as an assured thing, I naturally try to make the fullest use of my mental "asset." I therefore look for phenomena which seem to me in some way linked with *A*, and making use of the known interrelationships, I derive dated propositions about those other phenomena. In fact, I have no hesitation in arguing transitively:

I foresee such a dated course of *A*
Moreover, I count on such a relation between *A* and *B*
Therefore, I foresee such a dated course of *B*
Moreover, I count on such a relationship between *B* and *C*
Therefore, I foresee such a dated course of *C*
And so on.

It is evident that the forecasts of *B* and *C* rest on the forecast of *A* and will reflect any mistake about *A*. But they also depend on "articulations"—the relations postulated between *A* and *B*, and between *B* and *C*. We can go wrong about *B* not only because of a mistake about *B*, but also because of a mistake about the connection between *A* and *B*. And in the case of *C*, added to these two sources of error is the possibility of a mistake about the articulation between *B* and *C*.

Thus if we wish to draw inferences from a forecast, we should carefully examine the relationships between phenomena, in order to reduce errors due to wrongly formulated articulations.

Suppose, for example, an economist wants to derive a forecast of the growth of per capita private consumption from a forecast of the rise of the output per man-hour. His articulations must take into account these facts: production per worker may move up more slowly than production per man-hour because of a decline in the number of man-hours per worker; production per inhabitant may move up more slowly than production per worker because of a decline in the ratio of workers to total population, a change which may be due to demographic or sociological factors; again, disposable income per inhabitant may move up more slowly than production per inhabitant, owing to an increase in the share of the national product taken by investment or public consumption. About each of these articulations the expert forecaster must make certain assumptions, and with their help he reaches a tentative conclusion about the increase in disposable income per inhabitant, linked with his initial assumption concerning the rise of production per man-hour. From his estimate of the increase in disposable income per head he will now derive forecasts concerning specific consumptions: as the income per head rises, different forms of consumer expenditures rise at different rates; the relation of each such rate to the rate of increase of income, giving a ratio higher or lower than one, is known as a "specific elasticity." And thanks to such derivations, he can, speaking now in terms of the population as a whole, translate his sketch into a demand for so many more cars, so many more tires, and so forth.

How many causes of error! No doubt. But the economist has a guarantee in the "circularity" of his procedure. Associated with the change in total consumer expenditures is a change in the structure of consumer requirements; this change has to be matched by a change in structure of the goods and services made available. When he comes to scrutinize what will be called for, he may well find—to take a frequent case—that the requirements include more imports than we can expect to balance by exports of goods and services, and this will force us to damp down our expectations.

Or again he will find that the demand for services will move up far more sharply than the demand for industrial consumer goods. This is annoying if both the present level of production per man and its expected increase are lower in the services sector than in manufacturing. This means that we must anticipate a heavy shifting of people from manufacturing to services, and that we have to take into account the dampening influence of this transfer upon the average productivity increase. Such considerations are foreign to daydreamers, who pattern their picture of over-all or average productivity gains upon what is occurring in this or that sector which is now undergoing a process of automation: such people generalize from a localized phenomenon, without realizing that its natural result is to shift people away from the locus of its occurrence to activities where it is not occurring, so that its speed is not pattern-setting for the whole.

The economist has to see the whole picture and he must see it in detail.

Coherence is one of his intellectual constraints—the different sectors must supply one another with adequate inputs for the desired outputs. Specificity is the other—the plant is localized and specialized; men dislike changes in location and jobs; the distribution of skills does not necessarily match the job structure. The system contains strong viscosities, which mere calculations would let us forget. The economist has to elaborate his picture down to concrete and specific details before he can establish that an abstract "possible" is a genuinely real one.

Coherence

Forecasts in society and politics are a different matter. We can hardly be surprised at this, since forecasting is an established discipline in economics and not in the fields we are concerned with here. In society and politics, a man jumps from a forecast he regards as certain to another he believes follows from it, without explicitly formulating his minor premise about their interrelation, so that this premise escapes criticism by the reader and even by its author.[6]

It is important to distinguish two types of coherence. It is one thing to say: "You cannot extract water from this receptacle in excess of its capacity." It is another to say: "You cannot pour water into this receptacle in excess of its capacity; if you do so, it will overflow." Call these propositions A and B. Proposition A stands for a type of coherency-condition that no forecast should ever contradict. On the other hand, proposition B stands for a type of possibility that must be allowed for.

The economist might say: "Consumption will certainly not rise by 15 per cent next year because the resources are inadequate, but it does seem likely that incomes will rise by 15 per cent." And he will indicate what effects the imbalance between nominal demand and actual supply should have on prices and the balance of trade.

A forecast of a type-B incoherency may be called a "critical forecast." Suppose that at the beginning of 1929 a commission of American experts makes a forecast of economic and social changes during the coming decade. If it contains no warning of an economic crisis, its authors can expect little credit for it after 1931. However, it is sometimes possible to consider "general trends" without forecasting "accidents."

It is reasonable to formulate a "war-excluded" economic forecast, for war is exogenous relative to the economic process; but it is not reasonable to formulate a "slump-excluded" economic forecast, for the forecast is never so useful as when it warns us an economic crisis is possible, since on this preventive action can be taken. Similarly, in politics a forecast confined to activities allowed in the constitution is worthless if there is a possibility of violence, revolution, a putsch, or a *coup d'état*. And this is one of the major difficulties of political forecasting—how does one foresee that things are going to take a "critical turn"?

There is little difficulty if the critical event has long been ineluctable, long been inscribed in tendencies where certain men teach us to decipher it. And if they are able to interpret the past, why should they not illuminate the future? For my part, I am inclined to think that the crisis is avoidable almost until the last moment. The elements have slowly built up, but we retain a certain freedom of action in relation to them, a freedom which assumes great importance in the eye of the onlooker. But on these occasions, there occurs a singular phenomenon which a simple analogy will explain. Suppose that a chess player does not know that a bomb has suddenly been staked on the game. If he loses, the bomb will be exploded. A spectator knowing about this "payoff" follows the game with unusual interest, and is appalled to see the man play worse than usual and make stupid blunders. Then suddenly the crisis is apprehended: a moment of numbness followed by catastrophe.

But what is the nature of the crisis? I regard it as a "change of state"—just as in chemistry. Yesterday the scene presented a familiar aspect. Those volatile elements, men, formed, in aggregate, a scene with some perfectly static or *solid* parts, and with other, slowly changing or *viscous* parts. And in the scene there was also a little *volatility,* but on an insignificant scale in relation to the whole: a partner changing his mind, a thief breaking into a shop. But today the aspect changes: heat increases the volatility of the elements; effervescence threatens all stability. That which was solid or quasi-solid becomes soft and takes unforeseen forms depending on how the effervescence gathers up in brutal thrusts.

Retz gives a memorable description of the Fronde's first day:

> I cannot convey to you the consternation that appeared throughout Paris in the first quarter of an hour after Broussel's arrest, nor the agitation that arose after the second. Sadness, or rather dejection, took hold even of children: people looked at one another, unspeaking. Suddenly there was an outburst, excitement, running, shouting, and a shutting of shops.[7]

This great writer was obviously simplifying, but that is what we need. He is careful to point up the insignificance of Broussel, who provided the occasion for the tumult. He emphasizes that the Parliament of Paris, whose opposition to Mazarin slowly grew and sharpened, did not wish for nor even imagine the violent course the conflict was to take:

> Not one of all the men who held forth that year in the Parliament and in the other sovereign courts had the least vision, I do not say of what was to follow, but of what might follow. Everything was said and done in the spirit of a law-suit.[8]

Retz gives us a sense of "derailing" from procedure to riot. I have often fancied that the whole art of politics consists of maintaining, on the inside, sufficient confidence between the parties to the discussion, and on the outside, sufficient confidence in the progress of the discussion, so that the spirits of disaffection shall remain prisoners of the "green-cloth," lest by escaping it they rise up as ogres of discord.

But what is important for us just now is simply to represent the crisis as a change of state in the scene and to stress that in forecasting we cannot assume that nothing of the kind will take place: indeed we must take into account its possibility and evaluate its probability.[9]

A Work of Imagination

It is extremely difficult to estimate the probability of a political crisis. Consequently, many thinkers claim that in forecasting we should discount the possibility of one occurring. But how can this opinion be upheld when the political events in question can determine our lives? To bolster it, one would have to maintain that the over-all course of things is not changed by momentous events. I believe this is false, but even if it were true, how could we neglect events capable of affecting us cruelly? For my part, I believe that events can generate new waves which affect the course of history. For example, if Turgot had established himself as firmly as Richelieu in the ministry, then, considering the enlightened opinion in his support and the admirable administration ready to serve him,[10] all the positive achievements of the French Revolution might well have resulted from reforms he had in fact started. Suppose this had happened; the history of the world would have been altered, for mankind would have known neither the Jacobinic myth of sanctified terror nor the Napoleonic myth of messianic despotism, both of which have played so large a part in the misfortunes of our own century. A wise man who might have foreseen the positive changes that would be effected (with or without a revolution) could certainly not have foreseen the myths spawned by the Revolution and their consequences.

Thus, to exclude a crisis is, I think, absurd. A forecast is never so useful as when it warns men of a crisis, because it spurs them to prevent the event if it is masterable, or to take shelter if it is dominating (the symbolic example is Noah, and the all too historical example, the European Jews in 1939).

If our doctors of social science tend to give crisis-excluded forecasts, the reason lies, I think, in their psychological inclination. A crisis is abhorrent to the reasonable man, a time of distasteful frenzy, ruled by absurdity. The scenes of a crisis are visions for which the rational mind can find no place. Neither Condorcet nor Faguet could conceive of the dramatic crises lying ahead.

But there is something more: a forecast of a crisis requires the use of rational faculties, but also something more, which I shall try to convey. Consider this image again: the social scene consists of solid structures, heavy viscous tendencies, and volatile elements. A crisis is a raising of the temperature, which increases the volatile parts, liquefies viscous parts, and disintegrates solid structures. A disequilibrium is a symptom of change and can be grasped by the rational mind. However, a man can see changes yet have no vision of the coming conflagration. Here we may usefully speak of *tactile agnosia*—a concept introduced by Jean Delay[11] in connection with an experiment in which a subject, a woman called Modeste, was blindfolded and given a pencil to identify. While able to describe all its characteristics—cylindrical, long, smooth, flat at one end, sharp at the other—Modeste had great difficulty in recognizing the object as a pencil.

> She recognized stereometric bodies best of all, because their nature can be mathematically deduced from a correct analysis of their parts. The process of recognition is an intellectual reconstruction, an analysis followed by synthesis; but in our opinion this *mediate* process is abnormal, at any rate in the adult mind.

Normal recognition is immediate: it comes before any analysis or synthesis, and is an immediate apprehension of a significance.

Delay mentions Ernst Cassirer's distinction between "pregnant perception" and discursive knowledge based on the interpretation of signs. This distinction provides some valuable hints about the problem of forecasting. As "serious" thinkers, we do not want to put forward anything about the future unless it is deducible from observable signs. But as a result there may well be a self-censoring of "pregnant forecasts" which would make us say "revolution ahead" the instant certain signs appeared. I will not dwell on this, for I am interested in forecasting insofar as it can be made into a systematic activity and am therefore well aware of the danger of assigning a role to a psychological process that cannot be discussed. It was by conjuring up a process of this kind that Maupertuis drew Voltaire's most stinging gibes. However, the secret nature of the process does explain why men who want to use ostensible procedures are reluctant to take into account a crisis, which can be sensed much more easily than it can be argued.

My aim in this book is to describe the "mores" that our minds conform to in fore-thinking. And therefore I had to mention "pregnant forecasting" since this process unquestionably occurs and gives rise to very strong feelings of subjective certitude. Because of its hidden nature, this psychological process can have no place in a field of activity that is to be systematic, disciplined, justifiable, and discussible. In any case, there is no reason for thinking that the conclusion the mind immediately jumps to in "pregnant forecasting" is reached by different procedures from the ones the mind uses in discursive forecasting, nor for thinking that such a conclusion is objectively more certain. What happens is no doubt just an acceleration of the working of the mind. But as long as these intellectual operations are not formulated, they cannot be criticized and so do not belong to a discipline of forecasting.

Decision and Horizon

In what follows, forecasting will be brought into closer relationship with decision-making.[12] Forecasts can help us to make decisions whose necessity we are already aware of, and can suggest that decisions we have not previously thought of will need to be faced. Our need to take decisions and our ability to make them are the chief practical justification of forecasting. Not all efforts of the imagination are forecasts, but only those which should sooner or later become operative. And hence forecasts have a limited horizon: they are concerned with only a limited portion of the future.[13]

We treat forecasting as an art tied to practical needs.

NOTES

1. Johnathan Swift, "Voyage to Laputa," *Gulliver's Travels*, first published in 1724.

2. One essential cause is missing: the use of non-biological sources of energy.

3. Deborah Paige estimates that the annual output per man grew at an average annual rate of 1.2 per cent from 1857 to 1959. It was surely lower in the preceding period: a generous estimate is 0.875 per cent. For the period 1857–1959, see the study by Deborah Paige, P. J. Blackaby, and S. Freud in the *National Institute Economic Review* (July 1961).

4. We would do an injustice to Tocqueville if we singled him out for seeing what others had also seen. A passage written by Napoleon III in *Des idées napoléoniennes* (published in 1839) is of incidental interest: "*Je le dis à regret, je ne vois aujourd'hui que deux gouvernements qui remplissent bien leur mission providentielle; ce sont les deux colosses qui sont au bout du monde, l'un à l'extrémité du nouveau, l'autre à l'extrémité de l'ancien. Tandis que notre vieux centre européen est comme un volcan qui se consume dans son cratère, les deux nations orientale et occidentale marchent, sans hésiter, vers le perfectionnement, l'une par la volonté d'un seul, l'autre par la liberté.*"

5. In a later chapter, I shall indicate that when the change per unit time is expressed as a percentage of the initial value, the word "speed" gives an inadequate psychological idea.

6. It is sometimes asserted that scientific progress encourages an analytic approach, reduces the tendency to accept arguments from authority, and is therefore conducive to democracy. The idea behind this assertion is that scientists are in the habit of testing theories, but it should not be forgotten that none of us is competent to test propositions outside his own field. It is just as plausible to assert that scientific progress accustoms us to accept propositions that we cannot check. It is clear that neither of these relationships is stated in a rigorous manner, and that it would be difficult to confirm or refute the assertions.

7. Retz, *Mémoires,* entry for August 26, 1648.

8. Retz, *Mémoires* (Paris: Édition Petitot, 1825), I, 238.

9. In politics, the critical change of state is a sudden heating of the parts. In economics, a depression is a slowing down; a heating up appears only in the world of finance (for instance, panic at the stock exchange). The word "crisis" is better suited for sudden and violent changes, whereas the word "depression" is particularly suited to a slackening in production and employment. This cooling down is gradual, and therefore an intervention has far more chances of being effective than in explosive, political crises.

10. The part played by the administration in the positive achievements of the Revolution has never been sufficiently recognized. We need a history of the government officials; it would show that they were responsible for most of the boons that we attribute to politicians.

11. Jean Delay, *Les Dissolutions de la mémoire* (Paris, 1942), pp. 42 *ff.*

12. See the present author's "Les Recherches sur la décision," *Futuribles* No. 23 *Bulletin SEDEIS* (January 20, 1962).

13. One might wish to disparage the methods of economic forecasting by pointing out how impossible it was for an economist in 1910 to forecast the demand for men's hats in 1960 on the basis of the growth in incomes. But this comment can be turned against its author by asking why the hat-making industry in 1910 could possibly want to know its 1960 sales. On the problem of "horizon," see Franco Modigliani and Franz E. Hohn, "Production Planning over Time and the Nature of the Expectation and Planning Horizon," *Econometrica* (January 1955).

13

Conjectures and Decisions

This chapter ranges from Thucydides to Morgenstern. It indicates that conjectures have always been needed in decision-making, and outlines the position assigned to them in the modern theory of games and decisions. In this way the point is made that a better process of decision-making calls for a better framing of conjectures. Also an attempt is made to consider whether modern methods of calculating probabilities can help us to form conjectures.

"For Fear That . . ."

Let us consider Thucydides' famous work. It almost seems as if this marvelous writer set out to indicate the role conjectures play in men's decisions. The history opens with the Corcyraean affair. Corcyra, a Corinthian colony in the Greek sense of "an independent state founded by families of Corinthian origin," was torn by political strife. Corinth had a chance to intervene, and might have forced Corcyra to join its alliance, which was then regarded as an instrument of subordination. Athens, without being directly involved, was frightened by one conjecture. The chief naval powers were Athens, Corinth, and Corcyra. Individually the last two cities were much weaker than Athens; together they would have been stronger. To make matters worse, Corinth was in league with Lacedaemon (Sparta). Against the military supremacy of Lacedaemon and its Peloponnesian allies, Athens could set its naval supremacy. But if Corinth were to subjugate Corcyra, Corinth would become the greatest naval power, enlisting this might in behalf of the Lacedaemonians, who already had the military advantage. On the other hand, Athens could intervene so as to make Corcyra its ally, thereby strengthening, instead of losing, its position as mistress of the seas. And therefore Athens intervened.

The Potidaean affair provides another illustration. This city, too, was a Corinthian colony, and a tributary ally of Athens. It built fortifications and went so far as to extend a wall along the side of the city facing the sea. The intention could only be to keep Athens, the ruling naval power, out. Therefore Athens ordered the Potidaeans to raze the wall and deliver hostages, and upon their refusal, Athens laid siege to the city, thus helping to start a war. By the end of two years Athens was deep in difficulties: to escape the continual and unopposed ravaging of their land by the Spartans, the rural population of Attica had taken refuge within the city walls, crowding into the temples and living in such conditions that there was an outbreak of the plague. Popular opinion rose against Pericles and longed to sue for the peace the moderate Lacedaemonians would grant if Potidaea were set free. To quell the discontent, Pericles delivered a speech in which he presented the following conjecture: if you allow Potidaea to separate from us, all our other tributary allies will think that they too are authorized to separate; we shall be deprived of the forces they now are bound to supply, and what is worse, we all have to fear these former auxiliaries, for their behavior will be inspired by resentment of our present domination. Deriding those who hoped gratitude would repay an act of renunciation, Pericles conjectured the consequences so vividly that he carried the Athenians with him, persuading them to continue fighting.

I have taken but two examples. There is not a single speech, reported or imagined by Thucydides, that could not serve to illustrate the role of conjecture, particularly in the form of pessimistic surmises: "This will happen unless you do what I advocate."

Conjecture is so important that one surmise is often set against another in joint deliberations. Sometimes a part of a conjecture is accepted, but not the whole. When Archidamos, king of Sparta, spoke against war, he acknowledged that the Lacedaemonians had sufficient military might to ravage Attica with impunity, but urged that such easy victories would not decide the outcome of a long war. When the Athenians decided on the disastrous expedition to Sicily, they argued this course was necessary to prevent the Syracusans from uniting the island under their rule. Nicias opposed the venture while granting that Sicily might well fall under the sway of Syracuse (this was no doubt a tactical error on his part). His plea was that Sicily divided was more dangerous than Sicily united: it was easy for the Lacedaemonians to conclude an alliance with a few individual cities, but unlikely that the island, once united, would want to wage war on Athens. His conjecture seems a feeble one, and this might account for its defeat in the assembly.

The feeble conjecture was overruled when the time came for decision; the mistaken conjecture led to disaster when the time came for action. It is almost as if Thucydides wanted to make us aware of these relationships. In the descriptions of Alcibiades' political maneuvers in the Argos affair, and of his playing off of Tissaphernes and the Athenian army in Samos, Thucydides depicts how this schemer instilled different conjectures in different men, so as to make them move according to his will.

The Mistaken Conjecture

A mistaken conjecture can be disastrous. When Napoleon undertook the invasion of Russia, he decided to occupy Moscow as a means of attaining his ultimate goal—the Tsar's acceptance of Napoleon's conditions for peace. All the contemporary evidence suggests that Napoleon identified the two objectives, the occupation of Moscow and the capitulation of the Tsar, thinking the one would certainly lead to the other. Yet that unquestioned conjecture was unfounded. And this was sufficient to bring about his ruin. The burning of Moscow, an event human foresight could not provide for, was merely an accident highlighting the real state of things: often when men put themselves in an untenable position, accidents smite them.

Through a mistaken conjecture Hitler was made chancellor of the Reich. The president, Hindenburg, had no wish for him, but wanted a government with a parliamentary majority such as his own favorite, Papen, had been unable to find. Papen had no wish to serve Hitler, but wanted to make use of the Nazi parliamentary group. Several times, he tried to buy Hitler's support cheaply by offering him the vice-chancellorship, which is as much as to say, nothing at all. His offers were declined.

Goebbels wrote in his diary: "It is clear the system is at bay. To help it now would be criminal." But in the elections of November 1932 the Nazis lost two million votes, not long after the shock of Gregor Strasser's resignation. This was the moment when Léon Blum thought Hitler had been definitely debarred from power, and the moment when Papen thought he could catch his fish: Hitler could be offered the chancellorship. It was of course understood that only two out of the ten ministers in the cabinet would be Nazis. Unlike first Papen and later Schleicher, Hitler would have no special powers and would lack the president's support if the majority should go against him in parliament. Used by others and worn out, Hitler would eventually yield his forces to some more serious associate.

We all know the price Europe paid for this incorrect surmise.

While it would be pointless to draw up an unending list of mistaken conjectures, it is most useful to distinguish between those in which the error was accidental and those in which the error was systematic. Prominent examples of the latter type include conjectures assigning to a certain actor a behavior that is regarded as natural because of its frequency, when in fact this behavior should be recognized as unlikely in view of the actor's visible character. Thus the inclusion of the Communist party in a postwar government coalition did not have the same futurible weight as the inclusion of some other party. The signing of the Munich Agreement with Hitler did not have the same futurible meaning as it would have had with a Stresemann or a Brüning.

Some conjectures are unfounded because of the overlooking of a specific factor; others are fundamentally unsound. Thus it would be very difficult to adduce a single instance in which economic sanctions had the conjectured political results. And I am using the term "economic sanctions" in a very broad sense, covering both the "continental blockade" directed against England by the revolution and the empire,[1] and the so-called "blockade of Germany," from which the British government expected such great results in 1939.

If one forces oneself to make explicit the conjectures entering into a decision or a policy, then many mistaken conjectures will be rejected. And it is sufficient to clearly state the conjectures for the absurdity of certain ways of behaving to be perceived.

The military organization of France between the wars was absurd in its very principle. It was exclusively defensive, at a time when our alliances with Poland, Czechoslovakia, Rumania, and Yugoslavia bound our allies to attack Germany's eastern flank in the event of Germany attacking us, but likewise clearly bound us to take the offensive against Germany in the event of its attacking one of our Eastern allies. To openly choose a purely defensive strategy when our treaties called for an offensive in one of two possible situations (and the more probable one at that) was a fantastic inconsistency, which I once called the "fatal error of the national defense."[2] As a result, the possibility against which we refused to provide became inevitable; thanks to our policy, Hitler could surmise with negligible chances of error that the French army would not budge if he attacked in the East. True enough, we did not declare war over Czechoslovakia, and though we declared war over Poland, we did not fight it. So that when the German army attacked France, there were no Czech or Polish armies left to tackle the aggressor from behind.

Such folly is impossible if a problem is openly stated in terms of considered possibilities and appropriate actions. One of the great merits of the modern theory of "games and decisions" is that it requires actors to state decision-problems clearly. I wish to discuss this discipline briefly.[3]

Formulation of a Decision-Problem

Consider a man who is choosing between two or more possible actions; call them $a_1, a_2, \ldots a_n$. These actions are mutually exclusive, and the choice, once made, is irreversible. It will be assumed that the man has no grounds on which to base his choice except the better or worse results of each action.

If the universe were stationary and the actor the only cause of change, then each action would correspond to one and only one result. Because of his preference for one of the results, the actor would simply choose the action that is certain to bring it about. But the real universe is not stationary: it "moves," and during the time needed for an action to unfold, things change, and among them things related to the outcome of the action. We call a combination of future circumstances affecting the result of the action a "state of the world."[4] The combination of circumstances is, we understand, *independent* of the will of the actor, but *relevant* to the outcome of his action.

Our actor starts by considering a future state of the world: call it s_1. Letting his thoughts dwell on s_1, he decides that the best action for him to take is a_3, as the outcome of this action in the state of the world s_1 is, he finds, preferable to the outcome of any other action. Suddenly he realizes that s_1 is by no means the only possibility: the future combination of circumstances may in fact be s_2. And the outcome of a_3 in the state of the world s_2 is, he finds, particularly undesirable. He thus realizes that to choose an action he must consider every possible outcome, that is to say, the outcome of each action against each state of the world.

The Array of Outcome-Values

All the possible outcomes of all the possible actions can be found if the possible states of the world are listed *exhaustively*. The set of outcomes can be written in the form of an array. For a simple explanation of how this is done, assume that the number of contemplated actions is three and the number of states is four.

Write each state at the head of a column and each action at the head of a row. Thus a table is formed in which the total number of compartments is equal to the number of actions multiplied by the number of states. In each compartment, write down the outcome corresponding to the action at the head of the row and the state at the head of the column. The outcome obtained when the action a_2 meets with the state s_3 can be represented by the intuitively obvious notation: r_2 and r_3, or $r_{2,3}$. By convention, this is generally simplified to r_{23}, but I shall not conform to this usage here, leaving the comma to indicate clearly the meaning of the indices.[5]

		STATES			
A		s_1	s_2	s_3	s_4
C					
T	a_1	$r_{1,1}$	$r_{1,2}$	$r_{1,3}$	$r_{1,4}$
I					
O	a_2	$r_{2,1}$	$r_{2,2}$	$r_{2,3}$	$r_{2,4}$
N					
S	a_3	$r_{3,1}$	$r_{3,2}$	$r_{3,3}$	$r_{3,4}$

Now replace each outcome by the value[6] the decision-maker attaches to it: call these values $V_{1,1}$, $V_{1,2}$, etc.[7]

This new table shows the different possible values which result from each different action against each different state. If possible, the table should be completed by assigning a probability to each of the states. Since, by assumption, they have been exhaustively listed, the sum of their probabilities should be equal to unity.

The table, with the probabilities designated by $\alpha_1, \alpha_2, \ldots \alpha_n$, is written out below.

		STATES (with the probabilities in parentheses)			
		(α_1)	(α_2)	(α_3)	(α_4)
		s_1	s_2	s_3	s_4
A C T I O N S	a_1	$V_{1,1}$	$V_{1,2}$	$V_{1,3}$	$V_{1,4}$
	a_2	$V_{2,1}$	$V_{2,2}$	$V_{2,3}$	$V_{2,4}$
	a_3	$V_{3,1}$	$V_{3,2}$	$V_{3,3}$	$V_{3,4}$

Expectation and Assigning the Probabilities

All that remains is the choice of an action. If the probabilities of the states of the world are known, the criterion adopted is the "expectation." To find the expectation of an action, multiply the values resulting from that action in different states by the corresponding probabilities of obtaining the values, then add the products together, and divide by the number of states. It was assumed that the decision-maker assigned values to the different possible outcomes of a given action; that different outcomes were possible only because different states of the world were possible; and that the decision-maker knew the probability of each different state. Each value results from the combination of a given action with a given state. Therefore, the probability of a given value is evidently the same as the probability of the corresponding state of the world. Thus the expectation of the action a_1 is:

$$\frac{V_{1,1}\alpha_1 + V_{1,2}\alpha_2 + V_{2,3}\alpha_3 + V_{1,4}\alpha_4}{4}$$

The action with the highest expectation will be chosen.

But what if the probabilities are not known? To answer this, a delicate discussion of the notion of probability would be required.

When we say that the probability of throwing a one with a die is ⅙, we rely on an immediate perception of a symmetry so constituted that in a long series of throws a one turns up with a frequency of ⅙.[8] This frequency is an *objective probability*.

Suppose now that a businessman estimates that the chances of a particular bank making a loan to a given company are ⅙. Clearly, this numerical estimate is simply the expression of an opinion. Another businessman might make a very different estimate. What we have here is a *subjective probability*. Most writers on the subject think it is legitimate to use subjective probabilities when objective probabilities are unknown (as they are in human affairs). A man behaves rationally if he weights a state according to the degree of likelihood he attaches to it.

But if we are to accept this principle, the decision-maker must be able to estimate the probabilities. Some writers claim fictitious bets should be used for this purpose, but in my opinion this is a method of questionable value.

Criteria of Choice

What are the criteria of choice if subjective probabilities cannot be estimated? Daniel Bernoulli once likened ignorance of probabilities to equiprobability. If we accept this, the expectation of the action a_1 will be:

$$\frac{V_{1,1} + V_{1,2} + V_{1,3} + V_{1,4}}{4}$$

This is the principle of Laplace. There are many other principles, particularly those of Wald, Hurwicz, and Savage: they can be found in the special literature on the subject.[9] The *minimax* criterion must, however, be stated because of its importance and fame: find the largest loss for each action—the loss in the worst state for that action—and choose the action associated with the smallest loss (the minimum of the maximum losses).[10] This criterion is an extremely cautious one: it is particularly recommended in a game against an opponent who is determined to make you lose, but less so when the situations confronting you are not the work of a hostile mind.

Conception of the States of the World

Although game theory is a very important subject and interests me greatly, I shall not discuss it further, for I have said enough to indicate the relationship postulated in it between conjectures and decision-making. As indicated above, a problem of decision is supposed to arise because the individual does not know which of several states of nature will actually prevail. In other words, the individual does not know which one of several *possible futures,* each independent of his own will, is to be verified. It is important to note that these possible futures are treated as *data* of the problem. The standard textbook on the subject says:

> With respect to any decision problem, the set of "states of nature" is assumed to form a mutually exclusive and exhaustive listing of those aspects of nature which are relevant to this particular choice problem and about which the decision-maker is uncertain.[11]

Consider this statement carefully. It is assumed that the decision-maker knows the possible states of nature. That is to say, he can face the decision-problem only if he is equipped with views of the future, which are, we maintain, the result of conjecture. I shall not dwell on this here, for my next chapter is concerned with the work of conjecture that is linked with the making of decisions.

Consider the statement again. The decision-maker is supposed to have an *exhaustive* listing of the states of nature. Paradoxically enough, we cannot take this assumption lightly without taking it seriously, but taking it seriously we are in danger of despairing. If we start by treating it simply as a recommendation, we find we are urged to consider whether we have rightly conceived the possible states and to make sure we can think up no further possibilities. But we cannot stop with this.

It is not enough for us to list *some* states of nature: we must list them *exhaustively.* In order to avoid any ambiguity, it is worth recalling that we are considering the future state of the decision-maker's environment; this state is independent of his will and of his action, and is of interest inasmuch as his knowledge of it affects his choice of an action. At the present time, the future state is seen as a set of *states of the world,* each one of which is a possible state at the contemplated instant or period of future time. If you like, picture this set of states as a fan bearing one of the possible states at the future date on each of its leaves. When the time comes, the state that has actually prevailed is ascertained. I shall speak of this known state as the "event." Thus, at this point of our discussion, the states of the world, the plurality of which corresponds to the variety of states possible *ex ante,* has to be distinguished from the event, whose singularity corresponds to the uniqueness of the state observed *ex post.* This matter is so delicate that we cannot be too careful about the language we use.

To say that the listing of states of the world must be complete is simply to say that the fan must include the event. The question is whether, or when, or under what conditions, we can know that such an exhaustive listing is possible. In everyday life we often hear the exclamation of regret: "If only I had thought that . . ." or "If only I had imagined that. . . ." Coming from a reasonable man, who knows what he says, such an exclamation indicates that his actions led to an unwanted result because of an unforeseen event—an event not included in the set of contemplated states of the world.

"The event was possible since it has occurred, and therefore the decision-maker should have included it in the states of the world." Would we speak like this? No; there is no one who would adopt so stern an attitude in all circumstances.

Let us pause to consider further the case where the agent is frustrated by an unforeseen event. I wish to call such an event a "disconvenience," my reasons for this being as follows. The decision-maker, who considered certain states but not the one which became the event, had in a sense imposed a convention of his own devising on the world: "Nature, you may produce these states of the world, and none other." But nature broke his "convention" by producing an unforeseen event. This event is disconcerting: nature and mind are in harmony or in concert only as long as the former produces no event the latter has not acknowledged as a possibility.

Some worlds—the closed and well-regulated worlds constituted by games—completely conform to an imposed convention. When a gamester throws a die, it will land with one of six known faces uppermost. When the roulette wheel is turned, the ball will land in one of the thirty-six known compartments. It is part of the very nature of a game that the actual outcome is uncertain, although it will come from a set of known outcomes.

In the world of man, the situation is quite different. The actor does not come provided with an exhaustive list of the possibilities. It is quite natural that the actual event should sometimes lie outside the set of imagined states. I would even go so far as to say that an actor in the real world could not be identified with a gamester without a paradox resulting. The game player's universe is specially designed so that chance may reign within a fixed framework, and so that perfect knowledge of the states of the world may be combined with perfect ignorance of the actual event. Whereas in the real world causality is far more important than chance. And so, if our knowledge extended, like the gamester's, to the complete set of possible states, we could not at the same time be completely ignorant about the event that will actually occur.

Arbitrary Classification of the Future

There is always one way of exhaustively listing the states of the world; but this way is *logical* rather than concrete. The simplest and most certain way of exhausting the possibilities is provided by the law of contradiction. We may always say: "The future state will be like this . . . or will not be like this." We thereby impose our "convention" on the real world, which has no alternative but to produce this event or not to produce it. Once again we are masters of the game; but with what real benefit?

The binary distribution of the future is of no use for decision-making unless probabilities are assigned to the two branches of the alternative. To know that the sum of these probabilities is, by the law of contradiction, equal to unity is of no help. The proposition "A nuclear war will take place before 1970 or will not take place before 1970" is useless. Furthermore, if the event we are concerned with is measurable, nothing prevents us from dividing the future into as many states as we like. For instance, we can say that in 1970 the price of an ounce of gold will be: 1. less than $35; 2. exactly $35; 3. more than $35 but less than $50; 4. more than $50 but less than $70; 5. more than $70. But have we done anything more than fit a grid formed in our mind onto reality? If we wanted to we could have cut out the grid differently. It would be absurd for us to regard these five possibilities as equiprobable simply because we have five "pigeonholes," assigning a probability of ⅕ to each possibility. This becomes obvious as soon as we create a sixth "pigeonhole" by subdividing, say, "pigeonhole number 4" into a $50 to $60 group and a $60 to $70 group. If each of these six possibilities were equiprobable, they would each have a probability of ⅙. Yet we have no reason to think that the likelihood of, say, "pigeonhole number 3" (less than $35 but more than $50) has suddenly decreased. (This specific example illustrates an argument made famous by Shackle.)

Logical tools can always be used in order to set up an arbitrary classification of states. But such a classification is of no use in decision-making unless a weight is assigned to each state thus defined. The theoreticians tell us that the decision-maker weights the states according to the subjective probabilities he gives them, or, as Shackle would say, according to his degrees of belief in them. But before he can assign these subjective probabilities or degrees of belief, the decision-maker must draw on some idea of the natural processes in the real world that should bring about this or that state. That is to say, the decision-maker must, in order to weight states that are arbitrarily defined and therefore exhaustive of the universe of calculation, speculate about the probable events of the real world, and since the "possibles" of the real world cannot be exhaustively listed, he must inevitably *choose.*

Thus, according to the theory, conjecture is a necessary part of the process of decision-making, either in imagining the states or in assigning probabilities to arbitrarily defined states. One important point, however, must be noted: the effort of conjecture, which presupposes a mental choice, is more likely to lead to the consideration of just one state rather than to the distribution of probabilities over different states. The conjecture often takes the form "I have strong reasons for believing in such and such a state of the world."

NOTES

1. See the present author's *Napoléon et l'economie dirigée, Le Blocus continental* (Paris, 1942).

2. See my article, "L'Erreur mortelle de la Défense nationale," *Revue hebdomadaire* (April 15, 1939).

3. I have discussed it at greater length in "Les Recherches sur la décision," *Futuribles,* No. 23. The reader should also look up the comments of experts in *Futuribles,* No. 26, and the elegant and concise exposition of the subject by M. Barbut in *Mathématiques et sciences humaines,* No. 2 (January 1963).

4. Or a "state of nature."

5. I have observed that persons unfamiliar with this notation are bothered, if only for an instant, by the unexpected number ($_{23}$), whereas the mind immediately grasps that here $_{2,3}$ denotes $_2$ and $_3$.

6. This value is often called the "utility," now that the word has been revived by John von Neumann and Oskar Morgenstern in their famous *Theory of Games and Economic Behavior* (Princeton, N.J.: Princeton University Press, 1944).

7. This substitution must be carried out even if the outcomes take the form of sums of money. For a subject who has $100 the outcome "— $120" is not symmetrical with the outcome "+ $100" because "— $120" represents total ruin, the negative value of which is much greater than the positive value associated with winning $120. I shall not insist on this point, for the outcomes in the fields we are concerned with do not spontaneously assume a numerical form.

8. There is much discussion about whether frequency is the definition of probability or is simply the verification of probability. A man who defends the former of these positions will object to the use of the word "probability" in the sense it is given below. See Rudolf Carnap, *Logical Foundations of Probability* (Chicago: University of Chicago Press, 1950).

9. For a short bibliography see the present author's "Les Recherches sur la décision," *Futuribles,* No. 23 (January 20, 1962).

10. The *maximin* criterion is as follows: find the minimum payoff of each and choose the act associated with the maximum of these payoffs.

11. R. Duncan Luce and Howard Raiffa, *Games and Decisions* (New York, 1958), pp. 276–8.

14

The Pragmatism of Conjecture
and a Few Consequences

Here I wish to examine conjecture in relation to its effect on action. The connection between conjecture and action is at its clearest when an agent pins a decision on an estimate of the probability of some facet of the future. Let us take a simple example: before making a large loan to a firm in some foreign country, a merchant bank consults a political expert about the risk of nationalization in that country. The decision-maker asks for an opinion on a specific question about the future, and this opinion will be of determining importance for his action. Many other factors enter into the decision, but these have already been taken into account, and the specially requested forecast is marginally determining. Here the effect of the conjecture is direct: the conjecture is of maximum efficacy. Real cases cover a very wide range, with this situation as a limit.

Let us consider this same example, but assuming now that the bank's directors overlooked the possibility of nationalization. Just when they are about to grant the loan, a forecaster warns them the firm may well be nationalized before the bank has recovered its investment. The logical connection between conjecture and decision is the same as in the former case; the psychological relationship alone is different. In the former situation, the bankers chose an expert whose authority they trusted, thereby showing how much importance they attached to the question. Their decision was pinned on the forecast from the very start. In the latter situation, they often, and indeed almost always, regard the forecaster's warning as bothersome, if not positively meddlesome, so that they take no account of it. Thus even though the forecast may have the same truth value in both cases, it will have a different efficacy.

But the two situations are substantially the same: they differ only with regard to the decision-maker's reception of the forecast. There is a well-defined decision-maker, a well-defined decision "in the making," and a well-defined question about the future. There is also the answer to this question, which, if it is believed by the agent, will affect his decision. A conjecture which is addressed to an agent with regard to a decision he is making and which, if believed, will affect his decision can be called an *ad hoc* conjecture.

Ad Hoc *Forecasting*

In the world of business almost all conjectures are *ad hoc* and are produced only on request. One might submit a forecast to a friend or a public authority on one's own initiative, but not to a business concern. In business a forecast is generally requested by a specific agent for the purpose of a specific decision and is requested only because there is doubt in the agent's mind. Consequently, the forecast bears only on the area of doubt, which is seldom as wide as in the example considered above. The type of thing a company wants to know is the likely market for the goods it buys or sells, that is to say, the most probable future values of well-specified variables. It is a fundamental characteristic of such an *ad hoc* forecast that the area of doubt is clearly demarcated. Because this type of forecasting is extensively used, particularly in the United States, it has helped to shape the popular notion of forecasting. It is not certain a priori that the methods valid for problems of this kind are best suited to provide inspiration for forecasts of other kinds.

In the public sector it is also becoming increasingly common for a decision-making authority to order a forecast. For example, a government might ask its experts if the economy is going to take a downtrend, or if an existing recession will continue, and if their answer is Yes it will prepare a deficit budget. Or consider a much more ancient practice—for centuries the diplomatic envoy has been used by his government as a "predictor" of the behavior of the power that he is accredited to.

I have just used the word "predictor," for it seems to me that in all these cases of forecasts required *ad hoc* by the decision-maker a definite prediction is what he is after: he does not want to know all the possible states and their respective probabilities; instead he wants the predictor to commit himself to one of the states and to suggest that it is so probable as to allow a decision to be based on it. We may picture the situation as follows: the decision-maker is possessed of several of the factors entering into his decision; these are his *data.* But he is short of one *datum* because he is in doubt about a *futurum,* yet he wants to make his decision as though he were possessed of a *datum* on this point too. And so he decides to use the anticipation supplied to him by the forecaster as a *pseudo-datum,* and asks for it to be formulated as precisely as an accomplished fact.

In other words, the agent wants to make a decision relating to the future in the same way as he would pass a judgment relating to the past,[1] and to this end he avails himself of the predictor as of a witness testifying on some particular point of the future.

I think this attitude of the decision-maker (with its concomitant relationship to the predictor) is more common than any other. But many others are observed. Thus the rash agent refuses to see anything but the splendid result such and such an action will give, assuming the most favorable conditions, and hence feels no need for a forecaster to speak to him about risks of which he is aware but deliberately sets aside.

Forecasting of Consequences

A forecast is "ancillary" if it is produced in response to a precise question asked by the decision-maker. A very bad decision is often based on a very good ancillary forecast. For instance: a typewriter company asks for a forecast of the market for electronic computers, and on the basis of the prognostication branches out into this type of manufacture, then goes bankrupt. But the forecast is, as it turns out, perfectly correct; other factors in the decision were the ones at fault. Or: the Japanese government of 1941 consults a naval expert about the chances of success on a surprise attack on the American fleet in Pearl Harbor. The expert predicts success, and on the basis of this prediction the government decides on war. The operation succeeds as predicted, but the war ends in disaster. In these two very different examples, the ancillary prediction was admirable, the decision abominable.

The decision-maker is inclined to limit his request for a forecast to some particular question about which he is in doubt, reserving for himself the general handling of the decision-problem, into which he inserts the particular, limited prediction he has obtained. It is up to him to make the decision, therefore up to him to foresee its consequences. Few men in positions of authority are disposed to welcome an account of the consequences of their decisions.

Yet the ablest of men can be blind to consequences evident to another —such was the case of Talleyrand at the Congress of Vienna, where he prepared the French disaster of 1870. As a prize for its decisive part in Napoleon's defeat, Russia absorbed the portion of Poland taken by Prussia at the end of the preceding century. By way of compensation, Prussia wanted to absorb Saxony, and the allied powers were prepared to assent to this. Talleyrand alone stood in the way of the scheme. This opposition constituted one of his main policies at the Congress of Vienna, and he excited great admiration because he succeeded in denying to Prussia what it hoped for and securing the survival of the kingdom of Saxony, by compensating Prussia with the left bank of the Rhine, on which it had no designs. The abbé de Pradt wrote not long afterward:[2]

> There are two invariable principles underlying France's relations with Prussia: alliance and distance. The one is the means to the other.
>
> Yet all of France's work throughout the Congress went into alienating Prussia and forcing it to draw nearer to her own frontiers. And this resulted, at a stroke, in destroying an alliance and creating an enmity. This fatal mistake arose from the persistence with which France defended Saxony; for it is to be observed that, in contrast to everything she did for Saxony, France seemed quite undisturbed by the thought that opposition to Prussia meant Prussia would have to draw its frontiers closer to those of France. Many notes were passed about the incorporation of Saxony, but not a single note dealing with the disadvantages attendant on establishing Prussia on France's doorstep, between the Meuse and the Rhine as well as between the Rhine and the Moselle.

Talleyrand's conduct is a memorable example of inept forecasting. The strange part of it is that to this day "Talleyrand at the Congress of Vienna" is singled out as the paradigm of negotiators. And it is hardly surprising that minds trained to have so little regard for consequences should have invented the Polish Corridor in 1919 or the four-power control of Berlin inside the Russian zone of occupation in 1945.

In fact, men involved in a grand settlement are rarely clear-sighted as to its consequences. Completely taken up with the past which they wish to conclude, they fail to recognize the promises of disorder they have inscribed in the order they have instituted. It is easier for the uninvolved observer to perceive the consequences, and this constitutes a strong argument for criticism from the point of view of "What will come of it all?" Unfortunately, the critic is often powerless to raise his voice above the hue and cry set off by his not conforming to the immediate requirements of the situation.

Often, too, a criticism in terms of consequences is mistaken for a defense of a present interest. In France between the wars some tried to argue that rent controls were leading to a critical shortage of housing. In vain. They could only be speaking as landlords' advocates. And those who attacked France's policy of sticking to the gold standard as strangulation of the economy were accused of connivance with speculators.

Nobody would be so mad as to claim to predict all the repercussions of a given decision. But consequences of major importance can often be predicted with great assurance. Unhappily such a forecast is almost always ineffective, whatever its potential utility. The agent with the power of decision, having opted in favor of the measure whose dire consequences the forecaster traces, sees the forecast as an argument supplied to his opponents, and needing therefore to be suppressed or discredited.

Argumentative Forecasting

A forecast that a contemplated action will have this or that consequence is an argument for or against its adoption. In all cases of conflict between the proponents and opponents of a given action, the forecaster who presents the series of outcomes plays into the hands of one or the other, even if he sees himself as a neutral party and describes the consequences without evaluating them. Members of the public who become acquainted with the forecast form a good or bad opinion of the action according to the values they attach to the consequences. Therefore, if the consequences announced by our forecaster are apt to result in a bad opinion of the measure, its advocates try to keep the forecast quiet, while its attackers try to exploit the forecast to the fullest. In proportion as the latter succeed in this, the former acquire an interest in discrediting the forecast and its author. And to do so is not very difficult, for the detractors from the measure mix the forecast helter-skelter with a jumble of other arguments of a very different quality; thanks to these compromising associations, rejection of the forecast as the work of an interested person or "partisan" may well be secured. Indeed, according to the dialectic of the forum, the proof of partisanship lies in the adoption of the forecast by a party. The forecaster cannot even have the consolation of serving the "right party," for at times he will point to the bad consequences of a measure desired by men with whom he is generally in sympathy, and thus will supply weapons to men whose outlook is alien to his own.

The forecaster dreams of a state of things in which his conjectures about the outcomes of an action would be received with equal interest by all participants in the decision, who would then divide up according to their preferences for different results. Nowadays the expert tends to take a clearly adopted stand in relation to the politician, which can be summed up by this little speech: "You responsible politicians," says the expert, "are about to make a decision. Yet you have not calculated the consequences of the action you are contemplating. I will work them out for you. And hence you will have a proper understanding of the matter when you decide—as it pertains to you and you alone to do—whether the advantages outweigh the disadvantages."

The decision-maker does not willingly assent to this division of labor. Surely this would amount to allotting the expert too much space in the surmising forum. And what about the decision-maker's loss of prestige should he concede that the expert can see further than he can himself? To make matters worse, it seems that the expert proposes to take for himself everything to do with intelligence, leaving the politician with, so to speak, the emotive parameters. Suppose a minister wants to levy a tax. The expert will show that it will have low yields and bad economic effects, thus forcing the minister to become aware of the value he attaches to hitting a certain category of citizens or a certain kind of activity, and thwarting him because he will be unable to expect or promise concrete results, which were not his reason for suggesting the project but served as its ostensible justification. Or suppose the minister wishes to decree the handing in of all private gold-holdings with compensation at a rate well below the current quotation. The expert tells him such a decree will require oppressive operations by the police and would in any event result in the collection of little gold. Without, for all that, abandoning his project, the minister will be angered at standing convicted of irrational judgment about hoarders of gold.

Generally speaking, it seems difficult to separate the "objective" discussion of the consequences of a measure from the discussion of the measure proper. The champions of a measure are too liable to assume desirable consequences simply because they desire the measure—and its adversaries are too liable to assume undesirable consequences simply because they do not desire it—for the discussion of consequences to be easily made a thing apart, a preface to the making of the choice.

Forecasts Not Linked to Decision-Problems

So far I have spoken about forecasts that are linked to a decision-issue moved by the decision-maker himself. Such a forecast is ancillary if it is supplied by the forecaster at the request of the decision-maker, who wants an indication of the outlook before making up his mind. It is a forecast of consequences if the forecaster represents to the decision-maker the probable outcome of the policy he is contemplating.

But it must not be assumed that the agenda drawn up by a public authority is well adapted to the problems arising in the social body. To refute any such notion, it is sufficient to look at the position allotted to the Algerian question in the French parliamentary debates during the two years before the explosion of October 1954. Therefore, the forecaster must not be tied to the authority's agenda. Neither must he be restricted to forecasts made within the specific framework of the question the authority is considering. At the beginning of the Gaullist regime, experts were asked for forecasts bearing on the economic development of Algeria and situated within a social and political framework which did not last. The forecasts were invalidated because they were linked to a hypothesis imposed by the authority.

The forecaster renders great service by devoting his attention to problems he is given without questioning the framework in which they are set. He renders still greater service by calling attention to developments that are not part of the business in hand. Take a simple and, nowadays unlikely, example. Deforestation of a country threatens to result in large-scale erosion, yet the problem is not being dealt with. The forecaster must "disclose" the problem and bring it to the fore. Take another example, which is part of recent history. In 1963 it was observed that the road network of Paris was basically the same, with minor alterations, as in the days of the Second Empire.

> At that time the entire conglomeration numbered 2 million inhabitants, 100,000 horses, and 20,000 handcarts. It now contains close to four times as many inhabitants, whose individual purchasing power is on average four times as great. It also contains 280,000 trucks and buses, 1.3 million cars, and 1.1 million two-wheeled vehicles.
>
> Yet since that time Paris has not changed in its main outlines.[3]

The congestion now prevailing is associated with costs which are quantifiable and others which are not. It ought to be possible to "quantify" the time lost in slow-moving traffic or in finding a parking place, and to make a rough estimate of its cost. Of much greater importance, however, is the nervous exhaustion and bad temper resulting from this state of affairs. Such damage could have been averted by a clearly formulated warning, a forecast insistently and unhesitatingly stated so that the problem might be forestalled.

Such a forecast should have been perfectly easy. It is obvious that an increasing number of vehicles on a more or less unchanged road network will exert growing pressure. A simple extrapolation of the growth in car-ownership would have sufficed for the purposes of an adequate policy. An adequate forecast for action could be framed simply by thinking of the problem. Is it possible that nobody thought of the problem? Surely not. What was lacking was the proper formulation and enhancement of this natural and simple forecast, and an insistence compelling attention. There is in all this an important psychological factor.

The Status of Forecasting

The agent who makes the decisions can act without a forecast even though it is available. In fact a no-meeting between the forecast and the decision seems to be quite in the order of things. The agent's failure to understand or listen to a warning is one of the main themes of Greek tragedy, but it is no less a feature of our own world. An observer sees countless instances of governors refusing to see a clearly drawn future. It seems that the exercise of power, which is like a great stretching out of the hand, is accompanied by a shrinking of vision. Perhaps the reason is that this hand is not merely muscle for manipulation but also nerve for the sense of touch, so that the immediate pressures the hand encounters or provokes inform the governor's brain and there extinguish the eye's information, vision. Be this as it may, the man with the least foresight is, other things being equal, the man in the seat of power. We expect a man in a high position to see far, so that the lowly observer thinks that a future development which seems almost obvious to him is far better discerned by the responsible authority. He feels it would be an impertinence to offer a forecast. And if he decides to submit one, he has to besiege the appropriate man; yet how can this man receive whomsoever claims to have a useful view of the future? If at length the forecaster is given a hearing, he is likely to be met with a certain good-natured tolerance, of which diplomats are past masters, and which will always be the best way of brushing off useful advice. And so the forecaster is flummoxed.

A good forecast cheapens for want of attention. A man who might refine his forecast if he knew it would be taken into account is disposed to vulgarize it if he knows it will not. He produces it in private conversations, is led into exaggeration and then into caricature—he starts out with something valid and ends up with an absurdity. Another forecaster, of a more prudent cast, seeing how it all degenerates into a game, will prefer to say nothing. In this domain the misjudgment of a value easily leads to its debasement.

Things would be quite different if forecasting had its forum, its market, its exchange—the name does not matter provided there is an audience neither indifferent nor gullible, a body of enlightened amateurs. Such a body would be in principle receptive and in practice selective: they would sort out the fantasies and the reasoned conjectures. Let us use an analogy that should not be taken too far. Forecasting is always part of the activity of individual man, serving as an input for his own behavior. Such forecasting is then "homework," utilized by none other than its author. Beyond this, there always have been authors of forecasts who, like artists of former ages, addressed their work to some important patron or again peddled their wares to some likely "customers." A quite different stage is reached if a fair is organized, to which a variety of forecasters bring their wares for public exhibition. This allows all willing "visitors" to take cognizance of the forecasts made and to compare them, but also, and this is essential for the advancement of the art, it enables the artisan forecasters to learn from one another and to improve their rude products. It has been the chief purpose of *Futuribles* to set up such a fair, indeed more than a fair, a stable marketplace. To pursue the analogy, such exhibition offers an incentive for the "industrialization" of forecasting, that is, production involving a concourse of minds and systematic procedures.

It is obvious that a forecast of too special a nature will not arouse widespread interest, and that a forecast with too short a range will not lead to discussion. And it is clear that the surmising forum cannot serve as a floor for forecasts bearing on the results of actions heatedly debated in the political forum: for if the forecasters were to discuss such matters their passions would prevent the free questioning and argument appropriate to an examination that is to be as rigorous as the nature of the subject allows. Thus the forecasts proposed in the surmising forum should be in some measure removed from the event to which they refer, and in some measure independent from decisions in the making.

Another name suggested for the surmising forum was "exchange." The most regularly quoted "forecast-values" will be questions of general and lasting import. The "future of education" will always be quoted, for, in a society endowed with changing knowledge, education must undergo successive modifications, calling for decisions taken long in advance.

If a problem is the subject of widespread concern, speculations about its future aspects are seen to be important. Thus as the family shrinks from a three-level structure to a two-level structure (parents and children living apart from grandparents) while longevity increases, the life of the aged becomes, both in its actual forms and in its financial aspects, an object of forecasting.

Forms once regarded as "immovables by their very purpose" are also becoming objects of forecasting. Political forms are an important example. Men always thought political institutions had to be sacred—with good reason too, for it is highly dangerous to make a game out of the rules of the political game. They thought the institutions had to be maintained, allowing for no change unless corruption made their replacement necessary. The temper of our time is utterly different. We regard them as evolving. And whether this frame of mind is imprudent or not, the fact remains that it "mobilizes" these institutions as objects of forecasting.

More generally, the idea of change is so germane to our time that all forms seem destined to change and are therefore objects of conjecture.

The Forecast's Kinds of Utility

A very general forecast is not useful in the same sense as an *ad hoc* forecast. An interesting theory of relevant anticipation has been elaborated by Modigliani and Cohen.[4] For a given agent at a given moment of time, an opinion about the future is relevant if approaching decisions will differ depending on whether or not he believes in it; an opinion is irrelevant if his actions are in no way affected by it. This is tautologically true. But these authors go so far as to say: "Don't devote resources to estimate particular aspects of the future if, no matter what you might find out (with due consideration to what you might conceivably find out), you would not be led to act differently from the way you would act without finding out."[5] This is a good maxim of economy in the sense intended by its authors: that is, only factors capable of affecting the result should be brought into decision-making. The rule is an obvious one, leading to no difficulty except in its application. But the maxim is a very bad one if it is held to deny the utility of a long-range speculation able to illuminate future decision-problems and suggest new ones. If a long-range speculation is to be of seminal value, it must amount to something more than an anticipation of the future value of specified variables, with a simple extension of the horizon beyond the range relevant to a present decision-problem. For if nothing more were needed, it would be better to estimate these distant values at the intermediate moment of the future when they become relevant to the decisions then being made. A long-range speculation should be a structural forecast rather than a point forecast. And since we cannot know in advance which and whose decisions it will be relevant to, it is naturally of general interest. This is not to say that it is the business of the state. One of the aberrations of our time is the idea that anything of general interest should be done by the state.

Again I say that we need a forum in which forecasts are proposed and debated. It is vital that a large number of competing propositions be offered. A monopoly in the previsions' market would be particularly dangerous. It suffices to bring forecasting to bear on its own development for us to perceive political dangers of no small size.

An Example of a Beckoning Forecast: the "Leisure Culture"

What is taken to the surmising forum is a topic of general concern to society, a topic which forecasters try to sort out between them. For instance, the growth and use of leisure time is a fashionable object of speculation. Let us consider how the topic could be handled. This will show us how, by formulating the problems, a forecast "beckons" us to make decisions.

To start with let us try to define a much-trafficked idea. We live in a society as opposed in principle to idle luxury (*rentiers*) as to idle poverty (unemployment). The idea of leisure is bound up with the idea of work. The mind connects the development of leisure time with the development of productivity: a greater output per man-hour means that each worker can purchase more goods and work fewer hours. But at what rate will a man's working hours decrease? Here the forecaster must consult the economist about the future growth of productivity, and in his reply the economist will mention that if society uses accretions in productivity in order to reduce the hours of work, then the rate at which the productivity grows is correspondingly smaller, for the growth of productivity is linked to the growth of production.[6] The forecaster does not, however, linger long over the problem of the actual value of the growth rate because all kinds of general considerations do not depend on it.

The first question he takes up is the way in which the hours of work will be reduced. Very different forms are conceivable, and the forecaster's choice between these forms or between the relative weights to assign them presents him with a problem. The reduction is generally thought of in terms of a shortening of the work week, yet this is by no means the only possible form, and we may wonder whether it will be the most important form in future.

If we think in terms of the individual worker's year, we find the amount of hours worked on the one hand nibbled by sick leave, on the other hand deliberately cut down by annual holidays. Greater concern for people's health brings more liberal granting of sick pay, thanks to which the worker need not hasten back to the job. The facilities of travel enhance the attraction of the long vacation; in my country the paid vacation was suddenly introduced (by Léon Blum, 1936), and most warmly appreciated; its successive lengthening figures as one of the main demands of unions, the pattern of four consecutive weeks being at present generalized.

Let us now extend our vision to embrace the entire life of the worker. Not long ago, a lifetime of work began at fourteen and ended by death at about sixty. The average age of entry into the work force is being successively raised, while on the other hand retirement benefits allow the ending of earning activities long before death, which is being increasingly delayed. Thereby, in the average worker's life, the ratio of hours worked to hours lived undergoes a successive decline.

Indeed, the ratio of hours worked to hours lived should presumably be taken for the nation as a whole (including children, invalids, etc.) to give us an over-all view of the subject and to permit comparison of the various measures which affect this ratio.

In considering how the time spent by the nation at work is reduced, the forecaster will establish certain rough and ready equivalences in order to fix these forms in his mind. The total number of working hours is reduced more or less equally by: 1. cutting one hour off the effective work week;[7] 2. granting an extra week of annual leave to every worker; 3. deferring the age for starting work by one year; and 4. lowering the age of retirement by two years. This classification gives the alternatives. Which of these possibilities actually prevails[8] depends on an unconscious and complex process; thus workers sometimes demand a concession which, it later turns out, was not the one they were really after (operatives are inclined to demand a shorter work week but then spend the spare hours awarded to them doing overtime, whereas they do in fact make use of their annual leave). The choice between these alternatives becomes increasingly conscious as the problem is more clearly formulated.

The forecaster makes prognostications about the relative importance of these different forms. For example, he will argue that as work becomes less tiring and is carried on under better conditions a man assured of greater longevity will wish to postpone complete retirement. Social resistance to enforced retirement will grow, particularly as the gap between salaries and pensions spreads wider, for this gap will be difficult to narrow if the percentage of old-age pensioners is on the increase.

In connection with the length of the work week, the forecaster will note that time spent commuting must be added to time actually spent at work. He will think it no less important to reduce the length and discomfort of journeys to and from work than to reduce working hours and remedy working conditions. Thus he will be drawn into conjectures about the relationship between work locations and residence locations, and about the growing importance of good transportation facilities and adequate roads and highways.

Perhaps he will decide that the reduction of the total number of working hours in a worker's life will not consist in lopping off several years at one end with the introduction of earlier retirement, nor in nibblings thanks to successive subtractions from the work week, but of "large packages"—that is, two annual holidays instead of one, then later three, so that the working year grows to resemble the school year. Hence he will speculate about transportation problems connected with holidays. The daily ebb and flow resulting from the distance between work areas and residential areas is a feature of our industrial civilization, but no less a feature is the huge holiday migration that now comes once a year and in the future possibly will come twice or three times a year. The forecaster must estimate the likely flows and analyze them in terms of attraction of different holiday resorts and repulsion of the usual places of abode (from which it is often essential to escape).

An economist is naturally led into speculations about the effects of leisure time. Let us consider its effects on current consumption. The weekend or annual holiday does not result in any extraordinary expense for the worker who spends his leisure time digging in his garden, working on his house, walking to nearby places having trees and grass, using public sports facilities, participating in talks about municipal affairs, pursuing a course of study, reading a library book, and looking at television. But his household budget is heavily strained if holidays imply large expenditures for travel, lodging, and board. Even though he is paid for his holiday, his budget runs at a deficit, and to make it up he later demands overtime work. And thus spendthrift leisure tends to extend the work week and so counteract the effect of rising productivity.

The influence of the vast holiday migration on national improvements is far greater. I refer to expenditures by individuals, businesses, or public authorities, on anything to do with the environment of life. We have seen in France and are still seeing an enormous influx into towns and cities, which grew more and more choked until they burst, spreading like formless lava over the surrounding countryside. Nothing has been done for the amenity of life in towns. It is not surprising that men escape from them in noisy hordes as soon as they have the opportunity, using their cars—weevilers of treed and grassy cells in towns—as a means of reaching some more pleasant place. But since men's desires are thus bent on holiday resorts, it naturally follows that the priority for improvements is given to resorts occupied for a season rather than to towns occupied the whole year round. This is an economic paradox. Sooner or later, interest will be "reconverted" to the improvement of the usual environment, and the task will be immense.

These concerns of the economist join with those of the humanist, who is concerned that leisure be employed as much as possible in the healthy exercise of body and mind. But how can one ask young people to take exercise on a sports ground before or after work if there are none within reach? The discrepancy between the leisure activities preached by the humanist and the available facilities is jarring. And to set it right is difficult, owing to the pressure of population on urban space.

Of all the facilities presupposed by a leisure culture, only one has appeared in France—radio and television. A harsh judgment on the free dissemination of spectacles is a manifestation of intellectual snobbery, particularly detestable when the programs allot so large a part to education as in our own country. The forecaster should ponder whether the proliferation of channels may not raise the quality of one channel at the expense of another, more popular one, to the great impoverishment of the greater number. If so, there will be a problem in need of solution.

My intention here was simply to indicate how a vague idea in the air becomes, as soon as one stops to consider it, a source of questions, which start out by being very general, as they were above, but can be made more and more specific when discussed with the appropriate experts. It is interesting that regardless of one's starting point in a procedure of reflection about the future the same questions crop up, seen from different angles. One always ends up with calls for choice and action.

NOTES

1. On the contrast between making a decision and passing a judgment, see the present author's *The Pure Theory of Politics* (Cambridge, 1963), Part V, Chap. 2.

2. Abbé de Pradt, *Du Congrès de Vienne* (Paris, 1815), I, 212–13. The author discusses the same theme in *L'Europe après le Congrès d'Aix-la-Chapelle* (Paris, 1818), pp. 78–9.

3. Délégation Générale au District de la Région de Paris, *Avant-projet de programme duodécennal pour la région de Paris,* p. 41. Later in the same document the picture is filled out by a reference to underground means of transport. I quote: "A little more than half a century ago, a plan for an underground network of public transport was rapidly carried out on the initiative of the engineer Bienvenue. In fifteen years, between 1900 and 1915, 92 kilometers of track were put into service; the remainder of the present network, a further 77 kilometers, has been gradually built since that time." (P. 42.) In connection with subways, it is worth observing that we French flatter ourselves in claiming to take as broad a view of things as our grandparents, for we have undertaken nothing as new or as broadly conceived as the Métro.

4. Franco Modigliani and Kalman J. Cohen, *The Role of Anticipations and Plans in Economic Behavior and Their Use in Economic Analysis and Forecasting* (Urbana: University of Illinois Press, 1961).

5. *Ibid.,* p. 22.

6. See M. Vermot-Gauchy, *Futuribles* Nos. 53, 54, and 55.

7. I speak of the "effective work week" because the only practical effect of many legal or contractual reductions in the work week is simply an increase in the rate of pay for hours that are turned into "overtime."

8. I am omitting effects due to the increasing number of women seeking employment; not that these effects should be neglected, but my concern here is simplicity.

Part IV

QUANTITATIVE
PREDICTIONS

15

On Quantification

The chief meaning of the word "forecasting" is, to the modern mind, *the forecasting of figures*. This is quite understandably so, for we live in an age of rapid technological change. Each particular decision to put new apparatus, machinery, and plant into operation depends on quantitative forecasts about physical performance (technical forecasts), costs (budgetary forecasts), and generally about profitability (commercial forecasts). For instance, a multitude of quantitative forecasts is required before a decision is taken to manufacture a supersonic plane for transatlantic flights, and airlines want to make their own quantitative forecasts before placing their orders.

Generally speaking, quantitative forecasts (which will turn out to be good or bad) preside over all investment decisions both in the private and public sectors of the economy. The forecasts are of different kinds and varying rigor—but the least rigorous are not necessarily the least influential. A rough estimate of an influx of people into one region and a population decrease in another region is sufficient for the state to plan the building of schools or for a cement-maker to choose the location of a new plant.

Since quantitative forecasts help to guide important decisions, it is hardly surprising that there is a strong and growing demand for them. But besides having this directly utilitarian purpose, with which we are all familiar, they help to shape our picture of the world. Our minds are so constructed that a phenomenon somebody points out is far more likely to strike us if it is given a quantitative expression. Thus an attempt was made over ten years ago to bring home to American public opinion the poverty of the "underdeveloped nations" (as they were then called) by ranking their per capita Gross National Products along a scale graduated in dollars. This quantification was designed to make people aware of a real gap, and in terms of this purpose it did not matter that all serious economists condemned the principle on which the comparison was based.[1]

Quantification is useful for exposition but even more useful in forecasting.[2] We all know the population is growing, but we sense its growth far better if we are told that the annual rate of increase of the population was three per thousand in 1650–1700, four per thousand in 1750–1800, five per thousand in 1800–1850, and six per thousand in 1850–1900,[3] and that it jumped to seventeen per thousand in 1950–59,[4] about six times the rate prevailing in Louis XIV's time. These figures prepare us for the forecast of an annual growth of twenty per thousand in the last quarter of the century.[5] Our imagination is stirred even more if these growth rates are expressed in terms of the time the population needs to double. In the first half of the nineteenth century, the growth rate corresponded to a duplication period of 139 years, then fell to 84 years in the first quarter of this century and 62 years in the second quarter; right now, in the third quarter, the duplication period is 41 years, and in the last quarter it will presumably drop to 36 years.[6] Whatever risks are inherent in the application of this quantification procedure to the future, how telling these figures seem!

During one and the same year, 1958, a forecast is made of world population in the year 2000, and another is made of automobile sales in the United States during 1959. These quantitative forecasts have the same form, but serve different social purposes. The "short" prognostication informs professional decisions. The "long" prognostication informs the thought of the more conscious fraction of mankind. It "makes one think" as the commonplace, very apt expression goes. For instance, it makes one think that the emphasis will shift from optimal utilization of labor to optimal utilization of natural resources. The notion of "productivity," in its simple sense of the relationship between output and input of labor, comes from the United States, whose economy was characterized in its origins and growth by scarce manpower and abundant resources. The figures given in the Paley Report[7] for the per capita expenditure of natural resources in the American economy would not be reproducible on a worldwide scale for a foreseeable world population of more than six billion.

The "natural wealth," which economists have traditionally left out of their calculus because its cost in human labor is nil, will have to be included because of its growing scarcity as people make increasing use of it. The Industrial Revolution is often compared to the Agricultural Revolution, which five thousand years ago turned our hunting forebears into tillers of the soil. In my opinion this comparison is based on an error—the Agricultural Revolution was a transition from destructive exploitation to cultivation, whereas the Industrial Revolution was primarily, though not entirely, exploitation at a much higher level of technology, and it still remains for us to introduce cultivation and conservation of our resources. Demographic pressure, and above all the increasing per capita consumption of natural resources, will eventually constrain us to do so.

Although this question is probably the most important of man's temporal cares, it is not my subject here. I mentioned it simply to show in what way questions are suggested by forecasts of the relatively long term.

Quantitative forecasts of the long future are suggestive in a wide range of fields. For instance, the biologist Bentley Glass estimates that biological findings now appear in some 20,000 periodicals, and that by the year 2000 this number will rise to 120,000, publishing a total of something like 6 million articles in the course of a year.[8] Our attention is by its very nature a rare commodity: it cannot be spread out over an unlimited number of demands. Glass tells us that to read 2,000 articles a year he would have to devote half of his working hours to the task. His figures suggest that the probability of a "meeting" between a given information and a reader will decrease very rapidly. The reversal of this increasing tendency toward noncommunication of information will become increasingly important.

It would be interesting to discuss how that could be achieved, but we shall not go into this; it suffices for our purpose to give a new example of the mental stimulus that even a very rough quantitative forecast can provide.

Thus quantitative forecasting has two functions: it can contribute to the solution of specified problems, and it can make us catch sight of new problems.

In this chapter I shall be concerned with the "prehistory" of quantitative forecasting, and in the next with the form it has taken in short-term economic forecasting. Then I will indicate what role quantitative forecasting plays when longer periods, say, fifteen to twenty-five years, are considered: that is what interests me most of all, the horizon discussed in terms of possible futures in the surmising forum.

Quantitative Forecasting: Demographic Origins

The first long-term forecasts were about population. I wish to consider at some length a forecast concerned with the populations of Russia and the United States, published by the abbé de Pradt in 1819. This forecast is particularly interesting, for Pradt's object was to examine the relative strength, present and future, of the different powers, and it was in the context of this political forecast that he had recourse to a demographic forecast. He believed that "the dominion of power was transferred from France to Russia" when Napoleon marched France from arrogance to disaster. But that was not all—Russia, already the first power of Europe, would see its strength grow even more in relation to the rest of Europe. One of the causes of Russia's growing strength was, Pradt thought, that country's growing population, and in discussing this point, he incidentally mentioned the United States:[9]

> The increase of population in Russia is of the same degree as in America, and for the same reasons: the open spaces, the abundance of livelihoods, and the progress of civilization. The United States started in 1778 with 2.5 million inhabitants, to reach 1818 with 9 million inhabitants. It has been calculated[10] that in 1920, and perhaps before, their population will exceed 100 million. Nothing can stop this: the same causes which gave them their first million will also give them their hundredth. In population it is the same as in trade: the difficult million is the first, not the last. Russia possesses more than 45 million inhabitants—a fine starting point and a solid basis for further progress. This population is the result of fifty centuries of barbarism and one century of attempted civilization. What size will the population not attain when civilization spread throughout the empire can produce the same favorable changes over the whole body of the monarchy as in the parts civilization has already reached? Make no mistake, in a hundred years' time the population of Russia will exceed 100 million men: the spaces to contain them await them; the earth offers

a virgin bosom to nourish them; trade bids them come; industry will train pupils to provide for them; a varied climate will favor every kind of cultivation; a thousand rivers will carry the products of art and nature. There is not one cause that can halt this progress: and there are a thousand to hasten it.

This writer's thought was clearly guided by the idea of space: he foresaw analogous populations filling analogous spaces in one hundred years' time. But if he had argued on the basis of analogous growth rates in Russia and America, he would have forecast very different populations for the two countries since there was such a difference in their initial populations. His forecast for the United States was amazingly accurate, and his forecast for Russia, as that country was then understood, fell only a little short.

Pradt did not aspire to more than a rough guess within the context of a political question. In contrast, many other nineteenth-century writers undertook systematic calculations of increases in population. Their arguments, rather than their numerical estimates, are what concerns us here.

All these writers started with Malthus' principles[11] that 1. the population grows by geometrical progression if there are no obstacles, and 2. there are obstacles checking this growth. Once these principles were adopted, it was natural to express the actual growth as a sum of two terms, one an exponentially increasing function corresponding to virtual growth at the "natural" rate of increase, the other a retardation function representing the influence of obstacles. In order to write a "law of population," it was necessary to express the retardation function in some form. But there was a difficulty: "The nature of the function measuring the obstacles opposed to indefinite multiplication of the species is unknown."[12] Accordingly, it was necessary to make a hypothesis about its form.

The virtual growth rate given by the exponential term is constant, that is to say, a constant proportion is maintained between the population added in each period and the population present at the beginning of the period. Thus the number of men added per unit time becomes greater and greater, increasing without limit. That seemed impossible. It therefore seemed reasonable to assume that the growth rate would slow down increasingly. Verhulst chose the simplest possible mathematical expression combining the underlying exponential tendency with increasing retardation of the growth as population increases: to obtain his expression it suffices to write the instantaneous growth as the sum of two terms, a positive term proportional to the present population, and a negative term proportional to the square of the population in excess of some given level. If one wants to do so, one can write the second term in such a way that it reinforces the first term up to a certain level of the population, and only then begins to work against the first term.[13] Verhulst's law of population gives an S-shaped curve for the total population as a function of time.

The S-shaped curve applies to a great variety of natural and social phenomena[14] and is deservedly famous. But we may ask whether the natural process of saturation[15] described by this curve is suitable for human populations, since they do not use their environment "monotonously." If mathematicians had existed in the days when man lived off wild animals, they might well have described the growth of population by an S-shaped curve, but in time its upper asymptote would have been "punctured" in consequence of the change to agriculture. It is surprising that Pearl found an almost perfect correlation between Verhulst's law and American population statistics;[16] an excellent agreement was obtained when Pearl published his findings in 1920,[17] and what is more, the agreement continued to hold for all the population censuses up to 1950, when the population took an upward sweep not predicted by the curve.

We should note that according to Verhulst's law the population approaches an upper limit, which it does not exceed.[18] Pearl was much less happy in his attempts to use the law to forecast the upper limit of world population: in 1930 he gave the upper limit as 2 billion, and in 1939 he revised this figure to 2.65 billion.[19]

Demographers have introduced various refinements in the twentieth century, but in general they have not had much luck with their forecasts. In the United States the 1960 population census showed that forecasts prepared twenty-three years earlier by President Roosevelt's National Resources Committee, and even forecasts prepared a mere thirteen years earlier by the Bureau of the Census,[20] were very wide of the mark. Yet the forecasters[21] had tried to encompass reality by presenting their forecasts in the form of wide-open "forks." This notwithstanding, their highest figure for the 1960 population was 25 million short in the 1937 forecast, and 22 million short in the 1947 forecast!

In Europe we are more familiar with the errors made by the Princeton demographers,[22] who conducted a study of the future population of Europe for the League of Nations in 1943. They forecast the French population would be 39 million in 1960, 38.1 million in 1965, and only 36.9 million in 1970!

As I said at the outset, all this is "prehistory." It would be absurd to adduce past errors in order to pass judgment on the predictive capacity of present-day demography, a science which has developed a great deal, in France particularly under the stimulus of Alfred Sauvy. But the errors are evidence that a curve fitted to past data offers no guarantee that future values on this curve will be valid. Difficult calculations must not be allowed to mask the simplicity of the underlying assumptions.

Growth Rates

I wish to offer a few critical reflections on Verhulst's two main ideas—natural growth and its obstacles. My reflections will be naïve, but for me to consult my own forces rather than the general utility and refrain from asking questions which must be asked, for fear I shall be harshly judged for asking them badly, would in the given case be tantamount to vanity. Besides, any forecaster must first have a just measure of his own inadequacies and must then strive to master the timidity this sentiment inspires in him.

Growth, a phenomenon of much interest in forecasting, can be formulated in very different ways, and each of these ways has a different effect on the mind of the hearer. Let me take a specific example: car production in France from 1953 to 1963. The total output was 368,300 in 1953, 924,400 in 1958, and 1,481,700 in 1963. Let us consider three different ways of expressing this growth:

1. Comparing the annual output at five-year intervals, we find that the 1958 output increased by 151 per cent relative to the 1953 output, whereas the 1963 output increased by only 60 per cent relative to the 1958 output.

2. Comparing the annual output at five-year intervals, but this time in terms of units of production, we find that the 1958 output was 556,000 cars in excess of the 1953 output, whereas the 1963 output was 557,000

cars in excess of the 1958 output. Thus the increase in physical quantity was the same in both cases.

3. Adding up the total number of cars produced in successive five-year periods (1954–58 and 1959–63), we find 3.1 million cars were produced in the first period, and nearly twice as many (more than 6 million cars) in the second.

These formulations are all "true," but the second and third are more concrete than the first. Yet the first formulation is commonly employed in the form of an *average* rate of annual growth, which in the second of the periods considered above would work out at about 10 per cent. It is precisely because this formulation is abstract, universally applicable to all objects, and highly tractable to mathematical calculation that it is generally preferred by specialists. But its use is attended by serious drawbacks. To start with, there is a danger of misleading the uninitiated. For instance, suppose we say that the growth slowed down from the first period to the second. Though correct, this is misleading. For this talk brings to mind the notion of "speed" and in common usage "speed" denotes the derivative of a physical quantity with respect to time, so that one might think that a decreasing number of units is added to the annual output, when in fact the number is increasing.

But the language of growth rates conceals a far bigger danger, to which even specialists are vulnerable. It induces an unconscious prejudice—the idea that a constant growth rate is "normal." What is crucial for us here is not to discuss the "obstacles" that may prevent the growth rate from remaining constant, but to examine why it should be assumed that the growth rate ought to remain constant in the absence of obstacles. In some cases there are strong reasons for assuming stability, but in others there are none, and it seems to me that we tend not to distinguish between these cases. For biological growth (obstacles aside), it is indeed natural to make such an assumption. Just as the parent cells have divided, so will the offspring cells divide: it seems evident that this dynamic process is invariant by its very nature. But our actual reason for postulating a constant growth rate is that the engendered effect is itself a generating cause, perfectly homogeneous in kind with its own generating cause.[23]

So strong a "sufficient reason" as this is not always available. Not by a long shot, and in particular not in economics. It is certainly not true that last year's products are all factors of next year's output, nor that they are factors of an invariable kind, nor again that they are the only factors.

A concrete phenomenon cannot grow in extent at a uniform rate (*ratio*) without a sufficient reason (*causa*) in concrete reality. In finance the law of compound interest has always seemed somewhat scandalous because men feel that the law is not grounded on sufficient reason. Suppose somebody speaks to us in this vein: "If your family or company lends a sum of money to some other family or company at 3 per cent interest compounded annually, then you can recoup that sum five times over at the end of fifty-five years, ten times over at the end of seventy-eight years, and more than nineteen times over at the end of a century." Unless we are completely lacking in any sense of reality, we must object: "That will be possible, assuming the currency does not depreciate in value, only if the borrower displays enough 'industry' to augment the value of his material resources by no less an amount than the growth of the paper-value of the loan."[24]

Much use is made of growth rates in forecasting. They are a great convenience, for they enable us to translate a hypothesis into figures and to elaborate it in detail. But at the same time quantification clothes a hypothesis with respectability, with the result that the hypothesis may well meet with too favorable a reception in the mind. The forecaster must beware of letting his audience think that a growth is a "natural datum" when it is in no way guaranteed. The best way for him to put his hearers on their guard is by describing his reasons for assuming growth—reasons which become weaker and weaker as he moves away from the realm of biology.

Let us consider a quantity which has become the object of much attention: the Gross National Product per worker per year (the "productivity"). Who would actually claim that future growth of this quantity at such and such an average rate is a matter of historical necessity. Deriving inspiration from the high growth rate observed in France since the war, some forecasters assume that growth will be maintained almost unabated during the next twenty years.[25] Others criticize this assumption, saying it is based on a temporary growth rate, which is boosted abnormally high because the economy is "making up" for time lost in the Great Depression and in the war. These critics suggest that a "secular rate" based on a much longer past provides a better ground for a forecast.[26] While forecasters have very different opinions about future growth rates, they do at least agree that the future they forecast is not inevitable. The optimists do not believe the growth rate they are hoping for is "natural" (it would lead, we should note, to a fifty-seven-fold increase in the output per man over a period of one century), any more than the pessimists believe the secular rate they propose is "natural": it may seem quite modest, but projected backwards it would give a successively smaller individual output in each preceding generation, until so minute an output is obtained as to be utterly implausible.[27]

The causes of the rise of production have varied in the past and will vary in the future. It is only in the absence of concrete hypotheses about changes in the causal factors that one assumes, as a first approximation, on the basis of the principle of *in*sufficient reason, that the growth rate will remain the same as in the base period. But this can only be a stopgap confession of ignorance, and after making it, one should set out to break down the complex cause into as many particular factors as possible, assigning to each of them its respective share in the final result. This is a work of extreme difficulty,[28] filled with pitfalls, for the factors separated by the mind are not autonomous,[29] and yet are not linked to one another by constant relations. Some very good authorities doubt that this "unscrambling" is possible given the present state of the statistical data.[30] If so, this is a reason for trusting to the past. But we must realize that reliance on the past is merely a Bayesian conjecture: we have no guarantee the growth rate will hold in the future except that it held in the past. And in such a case, our credence must have a short horizon, as was once noted by Condorcet.[31]

In the above example, there is another reason for limiting the horizon. The Gross National Product is not invariant with respect to institutional changes,[32] and in my opinion it is likely that the concepts we now use in calculating it will be modified in the future.

Obstacles to Growth

The supposition that obstacles to growth increase in proportion to growth actually achieved is intuitive.[33] It often proves false. The history of shipbuilding affords a striking example. Ships were gradually made larger and larger in the course of the centuries, but there seemed to be an upper limit to the size they could reach since a vessel lacked strength unless certain portions of its frame were made all of one piece. Some of the most important of these parts were the transom "knees," for which crooked timbers of the required shape were produced by forcing oak trees to divide as they grew. But the trees had to be cut down in their prime, for otherwise the timbers would not have the necessary solidity. This condition limited the size of the timbers, and hence the size of the ships. For this reason, the most famous naval architects in the days of wooden ships thought it would be impossible to build ships in excess of a certain fixed tonnage.[34]

A change of shipbuilding materials was sufficient to dispel this limitation.

A more up-to-date example was recently suggested to me.[35] Think of an electronic apparatus with a very large number of cells. Suppose the probability of a breakdown in one of the elements is 1/500,000. The number of cells must be kept far smaller than 500,000 since if it is not then, logically, the apparatus would always be out of order. The number of cells cannot be increased unless the probability of a breakdown is reduced, but it obviously cannot be reduced indefinitely. Better yet, a way must be found for the apparatus to automatically repair a breakdown in its elements. The probability of a breakdown in one of our nerve cells is, I understand, much greater than the probability of a breakdown in a present-day electrical element, but the human organism has an advantage in that the breakdown of an element automatically triggers a replacement circuit. And this, I am told, is the property scientists are now trying to imitate.

Exhaustion and Breakthrough

Our feeling that a progress gradually exhausts the conditions for its pursuit is justified, but it must be corrected by the observation that breakthroughs occur thanks to human ingenuity. Suppose our communications system depends on message-bearing runners, as with the Incas. The speed of transmission will rise considerably during an initial period, after which further improvement of the roads, better selection of the runners, and increases in the number of relays will lead to smaller and smaller accelerations. A breakthrough will occur when the runners are replaced by couriers on horseback. But if, at this stage, anyone attempted to specify the "necessary limit" beyond which the speed of transmission could not be increased, he would, as we know, go wrong.

The Roman Empire was marked both by the atrocities presented to the populace as spectacles and by the efforts of its architects to make these horrible entertainments available to as many spectators as possible. Progress in accommodating a mass audience reached a halt with the construction of the Coliseum: and until television came, this limit was not broken.

These simple examples serve to remind us of the general validity of the S-shaped curve, and at the same time, of the possibility it will be invalidated. According to D'Arcy W. Thompson, the two ideas of a quantitative limit on growth and of a breakthrough thanks to a qualitative change were coupled by Galileo:

> He said that if we tried building ships, palaces, or temples of enormous size, yards, beams and bolts would cease to hold together; nor can Nature grow a tree nor construct an animal beyond a certain size, while retaining the proportions and employing the materials which suffice in the case of a smaller structure. The thing will fall to pieces of its own weight unless we either change its relative proportions, which will at length cause it to become clumsy, monstrous and inefficient, or else we must find a new material, harder and stronger than was used before. Both processes are familiar to us in Nature and in art, and practical applications, undreamed of by Galileo, meet us at every turn in this modern age of cement and steel.[36]

I wish that paragraph could be always present in the mind of the forecaster, drawing his attention both to the natural and continuous process of growth exhausting itself and to the event that leads to a leap beyond the asymptotic limit once perceived.[37] We see straight away the difficulty this coupling of notions entails in quantitative forecasting. For the forecaster will first assign a "law of exhaustion" (Verhulst's *loi d'affaiblissement*) to a phenomenon he is considering, and then he will want to take the "breakthrough" into account: but how can he foresee this event before the means of producing it is known? And even if the means is apparent, he will not necessarily recognize it. By about 1900, cars could be numbered in the thousands and many car races had already taken place—yet did anybody see that this expensive plaything would serve as a springboard for progress in transportation? And who would have dared to predict that in one generation's time this means of transportation would account for ten times as many passenger-miles as the railways?[38]

Besides, in an age of technological progress, ought one to think, in the singular, in terms of a breakthrough, or, in the plural, in terms of a series of cumulatively acting breakthroughs? Our picture is, in the former case, of a jump from one S-shaped curve to another,[39] and, in the latter, of a successive "translation" of an S-shaped curve.[40] The latter of those viewpoints is familiar to the economist: the efficiency of capital inputs "ought," assuming invariant technological knowledge, to decrease along the same S-shaped curve, but, in actual fact, the efficiency of capital inputs increases—a situation visualized in terms of a translation which more than compensates for the bending of the curve.

On Mathematicization

The value of the above remarks is at best suggestive. When those powerful thinkers Quételet and Verhulst described growth by a mathematical expression, they were giving form to initial suppositions they had chosen as well as they could by philosophical meditation over concrete knowledge derived from observation. Mathematical minds applying themselves to social phenomena should come up with important results.

But the social scientist who lacks a mathematical mind and regards a mathematical formula as a magic recipe, rather than as the formulation of a supposition, does not hold forth much promise. A mathematical formula is never more than a precise statement. It must not be made into a Procrustean bed—and that is what one is driven to by the desire to quantify at any cost. It is utterly implausible that a mathematical formula should make the future known to us, and those who think it can would once have believed in witchcraft. The chief merit of mathematicization is that it compels us to become conscious of what we are assuming.

To conclude, let us note how the light shed on facts changes according to which one of the equally legitimate ways of describing them is adopted. Take these very simple facts: an Atlantic crossing took 15 days in 1838 (with the *Britannia*), 100 hours in 1935 (with the *Normandie*), and 8 hours in 1960 (with a Boeing 707 jet). We may say that the *Normandie* was 3.6 times as fast as the *Britannia,* and that the Boeing 707 was 12.6 times as fast as the *Normandie.* The second increase seems much larger than the first. But not if we describe the facts in this way: the *Normandie* represented a time-saving of 9 days 20 hours compared with the *Britannia,* whereas the additional time saved by the Boeing 707 airliner was much smaller, a mere 3 days 20 hours. And compared with the previous saving, the 4.5 hours to be saved by the supersonic jet seem insignificant.

Thus the same material change can be quantified in terms of progressively greater gains in speed, or in terms of progressively smaller economies of time. I will not here press my feeling that the latter expression is the more relevant for social cost-benefit analysis. I am content to illustrate by this very simple instance the general proposition that we should not limit our description of a material change to a single mode of mathematical expression. Such a limitation implicitly biases conclusions.

The danger increases as we move away from physical magnitudes to aggregates which are a matter of conventions, and to ratios of such aggregates. It should not be lost sight of that all such sophisticated quantification has implied a choice of concepts, that is, a philosophical exercise. Designers of statistics are indeed philosophers, however unwilling to claim the name, and are fully aware that different aspects of reality can be lit up if alternative sets of concepts are used. This is of great importance for attempted quantification of the long-range future. Not so for short-term forecasting to which we now come.

NOTES

1. Estimates of the Gross National Products (GNP's) in terms of the respective national currencies were simply converted into dollars at the current rates of exchange. Colin Clark, who compared various GNP's in *The Condition of Economic Progress* (1940 and 1951 edns.), was well aware of the unsoundness of such a procedure. The magnitude of the errors thus committed was pointed out by Milton Gilbert and Irving B. Kravis in 1954. It is worth noting that the comparison was between countries with similar institutional structures. The errors become even greater as the difference in the institutional structures increases (see *Problems in the International Comparison of Economic Accounts* [Princeton, N.J.: National Bureau of Economic Research, 1957]), but the United Nations continues to publish such comparisons.

2. Cf. the United Nations, *The Future Growth of World Population* (New York, 1958).

3. A. M. Carr-Saunders, *World Population* (1956).

4. *Statistical Yearbook of the United Nations* (New York, 1960).

5. This figure is implied by the 64 per cent growth over 25 years (1975–2000) given in *The Future Growth of World Population.*

6. To obtain the "duplication periods" I converted the figures for the percentage growth per quarter given in the United Nations document referred to in the previous note.

7. *President's Report on Raw Materials* (5 vols.; Washington, D.C., 1952).

8. Bentley Glass, "Information Crisis in Biology," *Bulletin of the Atomic Scientists* (October 1962).

9. Abbé de Pradt, *L'Europe après le Congrès d'Aix-la-Chapelle* (Paris, 1819), pp. 36–8.

10. I have been unable to trace the calculation to which Pradt refers.

11. According to D'Arcy W. Thompson, Malthus was indebted to Richard Wallace's *Dissertation on the Numbers of Mankind in Ancient and Modern Times* (Edinburgh, 1753). Wallace suggested that the difference between the natural growth (a sixfold increase every hundred years) and the growth actually observed should be regarded as a measure of the obstacles.

12. Verhulst, *Notice sur la loi que la population suit dans son ses accroissements, Corr. Math.,* ed. A. Quételet (1838).

13. Raymond Pearl's formula for the total population of the United States, an application of Verhulst's law, takes the form:

$$N = \frac{197,273,000}{1 + e - .03134\,t'}$$

where the time t' is measured (in years) from April 1, 1914, and therefore takes a negative sign before this date.

14. D'Arcy W. Thompson gives many examples in his admirable book, *On Growth and Form* (Cambridge, Eng.: Cambridge University Press, 1942). He also discusses the curves of Gomperz, Backman, etc., which are related to the S-shaped curve of Verhulst.

15. I am using the word "saturation" in a loose sense.

16. For a comparison of calculated values and observed values for 1790 to 1910, see Alfred J. Lotka, *Elements of Mathematical Biology* (New York: Dover, 1956), p. 67 (originally published in 1924 as *Elements of Physical Biology*).

17. Raymond Pearl and L. J. Reed in *Proceedings of the National Academy of Sciences* (1920), VI, 275.

I think it is interesting to note that even though the S-shaped curve held good for the United States, the process was more complicated than Verhulst supposed. Figures prepared for Congress show that, if the "white" population is considered on its own, a total of 41.3 million can be attributed to the increase of the population present in 1790 (3.2 million), and a total of 53.5 million to the increase of the immigrant population arriving between 1790 and 1920 (26.5 million). See the United Nations' *The Determinants and Consequences of Population Trend* (New York, 1953), p. 139.

18. For instance, Pearl's formula for the United States given in Note 10 implies that the upper limit of the United States' population is 197,230,000.

19. R. Pearl, *The Biology of Population Growth* (New York, 1930) and *The Natural History of Population* (London, 1939).

20. W. S. Woytinsky and E. S. Woytinsky, *World Population and Production* (New York: *Twentieth Century Fund,* 1953), pp. 251 *ff.*

21. Warren S. Thompson and R. K. Whelpton, both men of great reputation.

22. Frank Notestein *et al., The Future Population of Europe and the Soviet Union: Population Projections* (Geneva: League of Nations, 1943).

23. "An exponential increase . . . is the natural law of the variation of a homogeneous phenomenon with time." (J. A. Ville, "Le rôle des mathématiques dans la formation de la pensée economique," *Cahiers de l'S.E.A.,* Suppl. 138 [June 1963].)

24. Some illusions surrounding compound interest are discussed in my paper "L'Epargne," *Étude SEDEIS* No. 669.

25. During the decade starting in 1949, the growth rate was 4.6 per cent annually. The forecasters' "projection" corresponds to an annual growth rate of 4.3 per cent.

26. A calculation performed by Deborah Paige *et al.,* in the *Étude SEDEIS* No. 804 (December 1, 1961) indicates that, in the period 1913–59 taken as a whole, the output per man-hour increased at an average rate of 1.5 per cent per year, which is the same as in 1855–1913.

27. Raymond W. Goldsmith has shown that this applies even in the relatively short economic history of the European population of America (*Étude SEDEIS,* No. 844 [February 10, 1963]). Taking the per capita Gross National Product, he argues that the "secular rate" he obtains for 1839–1959 could not have prevailed throughout the time of European settlement, since in that case the GNP would have amounted to less than $30 per head of population in 1679. This *reductio ad absurdum* gives progressively more striking results as one considers longer and longer periods. If the per capita GNP of France had increased at an annual rate of 1 per cent between 1500 and 1800, it would have been only one twentieth as large in 1500 as in 1800.

28. The most probing attempt to separate the causes is by E. F. Dennison in *The Sources of Economic Growth in the United States and the Alternatives before Us* (New York: Committee for Economic Development, January 1962).

29. For instance, "capital inputs" are obviously not autonomous in relation to technical change, which they are meant to "embody." It is hardly surprising to

find that, by themselves, capital inputs have contributed but little to the increase in production per worker; but, by using the very same method, i.e., the assumption that factors receive the value of their marginal products, one would prove that the contribution of inventors, in itself, has been insignificant. As these factors are fertile by their marriage, it is not unexpected to find their celibate contributions slight.

30. See Oskar Morgenstern's skeptical remarks in his paper "On the Accuracy of National Income and Growth Statistics," *Econometric Research Program No. 43* (Princeton, N.J.: Princeton University, August 1, 1962). I think his skepticism on this matter is excessive.

31. Condorcet, "Réflexions sur la méthode de déterminer la probabilité des evènements futurs, d'après l'observation des evènements passés," *Histoire de l'Académie des Sciences de Paris, pour l'Année 1783* (Paris, 1786), pp. 539, 583.

32. That is to say, the measurement of the Gross National Product is not invariant with respect to institutional changes. In this connection see the National Bureau of Economic Research's *A Critique of the U.S. Income and Product Accounts,* Vol. XXII of *Studies in Income and Wealth* (Princeton, N.J.: Princeton University Press, 1958), and George Jaszi, "The Measurement of Economic Growth," *The Review of Economics and Statistics,* XLII: 4 (November 1961). With regard to the per capita consumption see my article in *Étude SEDEIS* No. 74 (January 10, 1964).

33. We are well aware of this in the following statement by Quételet: "Population tends to increase by geometrical progression. The resistance, or sum of obstacles to its growth, varies, other things being equal, as the square of the speed with which the population tends to increase. . . . The obstacles to the growth of a population really operate, then, like the resistance which a medium opposes to the passage of bodies. This extension of a law of physics, which is most happily confirmed when we apply it to the documents supplied by society, provides a new example of the analogies which are found in many cases between the laws regulating material phenomena and the laws applying to man. So that, of the two principles which I take as the basis of the mathematical theory of population, the one is generally admitted by all economists and is hardly contestable, and the other has been verified in all applications in which a movement and continuously acting obstacles had to be considered." (A. Quételet, *Sur l'homme et le développement de ses facultés, ou Essai de physique sociale* [2 vols.; Paris, 1835], I, 277–8.)

34. The works to consult on this question are John Charnock, *An History of Naval Architecture* (3 vols.; London, 1800–02), and Robert G. Albion, *Forests and Sea Power* (Cambridge, Mass.: Harvard University Press, 1926). The latter is an admirable combination of economics, technology, politics, and strategy.

35. By M. Delapalme and Professor Aigrain at a meeting of the "Groupe de Travail 85."

36. D'Arcy W. Thompson, *op. cit.*, p. 27.

37. We find here a contrast noted in Chapter 2.

38. This very crude estimate refers to the United States.

39. Or an addition of two S-shaped curves.

40. Or an aggregation of a number of S-shaped curves.

16

Short-Term Economic
Forecasting

Forecasting in economics is an activity fully licenced both in the City of
Action and the City of Intellect. Sought and subsidized by executives in
government and business, it is also recognized and accredited by the uni-
versities. For it to attain so remarkable a status, two suspicions had to be
overcome: that of men of action about "the speculative views of intellectuals who lack any experience of reality"; and that, even stronger, of
men of learning about "intellectual adventurism which discredits science
by going beyond the established facts."

The young economist who is given the opportunity of studying actual
situations, and of forming prognostications and opinions capable of affecting their evolution, is a party to the "becoming of the future" in a way
that compares very favorably with the economist of yesterday and the
political scientist of today.

But though the role now allotted to economic forecasting is eminent, the
phenomenon is so recent that, to my knowledge, no history has yet been
written of its development, nor a manual of the most common methods
employed.[1] I obviously do not intend to fill these gaps; my ambition is
only to provide a few pointers; these may provoke others to produce the
missing works, but I am mainly concerned that they should be suggestive
when I come to consider forecasting in the other sciences of man.

Forecasting and Factual Data

In general, the art of forecasting consists of passing from *knowledge* about *present* conditions to *estimates* of *future* conditions. As we have previously noted, the Latin tongue aptly distinguishes things that have already happened, *facta,* from things that will be, *futura*—a forecast is a passage of the mind from *facta* to *futura.* The purpose of this reminder is to emphasize that every effort to forecast presupposes a search for the *facta.* In this respect, forecasting contrasts with theory. To take a simple illustration, it is a true theoretical proposition that if a road is never widened and the number of cars using it progressively rises, then a time will come when the average speed will drop as the number increases, however fast each individual car is designed to travel. But to forecast *when* the average speed will drop below a *certain* level, it is necessary to know the *number* of cars now using it, and to assume the *rate* of increase: here our concrete knowledge is of decisive importance.

Economic forecasting is very closely linked with statistics, a tool long neglected by economics, as was attested by the great economist W. Stanley Jevons in 1871:

> The private-account books, the great ledgers of merchants and bankers and public offices, the share lists, price lists, bank returns, monetary intelligence, Custom-house and other Government returns, are all full of the kind of numerical data required to render Economics an exact mathematical science. Thousands of folio volumes of statistical, parliamentary or other publications await the labor of the investigator.[2]

Jevons' assertion is of twofold interest: it shows that economists had until then paid no heed to actual data; yet if Jevons recommended employing the data, he did so only for "the scientific investigation of the natural law of Economics" and not for making forecasts.

It is, I think, paradoxical that a science whose subject was as earth-bound as any should long have displayed an Olympian disregard for practical needs. Traders could worry about the state of the market, and the Treasury about the yield of a tax, while the economist moved on a plane far above these mundane problems, content with the general precepts of his contemplative science.

A Theory of Order

Economists since Adam Smith have found their inspiration in an image of spontaneous order arising from the unintentional concurrence of men's actions in the pursuit of self-interest. If a multitude of animalcula happen to combine into a definite figure, an architectural form, before our eyes, we are at first struck with astonishment and admiration, and then want to explain the phenomenon: this feeling and this intention were the ingredients that made the economist. Thus the term "socialist" originally denoted the economist's antithesis, somebody who refused to see the order he described. No doubt, the economist let himself be carried away by certain dispositions natural to man: when we have discerned a figure in apparent chaos, our discovery assumes such value in our eyes that we can see only the figure, not anything jarring with it. We fasten on the factors producing it and on them alone, and after analyzing them, we use their mechanism in order to build a synthetic model of reality which exhibits in pure form the order we have perceived. This is the natural procedure in explanation, the way of forming any "representative" theory.[3]

Once launched on this Newtonian course, economic thought was to tend toward a Newtonian system of the economic universe. Schumpeter calls Léon Walras the greatest economist of all time for expounding this system[4] in 1874, approximately one century after Adam Smith. And Samuelson endorses this judgment:

> . . . There is but one system of the world and Newton was the one who found it. Similarly, there is but one grand system of general equilibrium and it was Walras who had the insight (and luck) to find it.[5]

But what lies beneath this comparison? As Schumpeter says:

> From the workshop of Walras the static theory of the economic universe emerged in the form of a large number of quantitative relations (equations) between economic elements or variables (prices and quantities of consumable and productive goods or services) that were conceived as simultaneously determining one another.[6]

Schumpeter speaks of the Walrasian theory as a "major exploit" and the "Magna Charta of exact economics," and Samuelson says:

Today there can be little doubt that most of the literary and mathematical economic theory appearing in our professional journals is more an offspring of Walras than of anyone else.[7]

However, a question comes to mind. Samuelson, that eminent economist, regularly issues forecasts: what does he owe to Walras in making them? Nothing at all, I think. This simple question helps to show that a certain distance separates theory and forecasting.

Invited by the best judges to regard the Walrasian system as a masterpiece of economic theory, we may well ask: "What is it good for?" Ely Devons' answer[8] to this is that it demonstrates the "interconnectedness of all economic phenomena," shows how innumerable interrelations can be consistent "without any central administrative direction," and indicates how price movements and the interaction of supply and demand bring about a "coordination between dispersed and decentralized decisions." As a didactic model, the system is a masterpiece, but it has no practical applications for a great number of reasons,[9] of which it suffices for me to mention unrealistic postulates[10] and the excessive number of equations.[11]

But far worse than that: the attraction so beautiful a model deserved to exercise and, as Samuelson attests, did exercise, helped to steer economic thought away from the practical need for forecasts.

The systems of equations of Walras or Pareto were not designed to be solved:[12] their function was illustrative rather than practical.

It is odd [says Morgenstern] that this situation—of professing an empirical theoretical science which in its highest form (as then understood) would forever remain inapplicable—has not given rise to either of the following: (a) profound dissatisfaction with this impasse or (b) an attempt to aggregate the variables and equations in such manner as to make at least a global system numerically applicable. (This was to come much later.) Instead, these authors appear to have been satisfied with the abstract description of the economic world their theory seemed to give without demanding any further application. The policy consequences they did draw were essentially affirmations of some basic principles which did or did not have any connection with the theory. The policies proposed were definitely not consequences of a detailed application of the theory to a concrete situation by means of computational evaluation of numerical data.[13]

Given the detachment of economic theory, it is not surprising that forecasting should have developed autonomously, according to the practical needs it was designed to meet and the factual data made available for it.

In the absence of any theory, one is reduced to naïve modes of prediction, which remain the same in all fields of application; these modes will be discussed below. To do any better,[14] one must have a view or conception of the system of interactions to which or within which the forecast applies. But the conception is of no practical use unless it is "aggregative,"[15] with only a limited number of qualities needing to be considered. The aggregates used to build models sufficiently rough to be workable were formed by statisticians and in particular the statisticians who attached themselves to the global and partial concepts of the "Gross National Product" family. These tractable models are the instruments of prediction and of modern theory, and thus prediction, a plebeian technology, has been wedded to patrician theory: an alliance contracted mainly under the impact of the Great Depression of the 1930's.

Naïve Procedures

We wish to estimate the future (*futura*), having knowledge only of the past (*facta*): how can we use this knowledge? Let us start with the simplest procedures, without fear of laboring the obvious.

We are interested in the future state, at a given time, of a certain phenomenon that lends itself to numerical expression (according to given conventions). What we want is a number representing the future state— in common parlance, this is the "value" to be estimated. To obtain such an estimate, the first means at hand is one of three naïve postulates.

1. *The postulate of constancy.* This assumption is that what we are interested in behaves, within the time span considered, like a constant. The consequence is that the future value sought is the same as the present value. The use of this postulate does not necessarily imply that what we are dealing with is a "natural constant" such as we encounter in the natural sciences. We may have no better reason to presume the stability of the value during a coming period than its having obtained during a past period, in which case the longer the past period of stability and the shorter the future envisaged, the more confident we feel about the maintenance of the same value. The postulate of stability is commonly used in forecasts and plans with a three- to five-year span, particularly for ratios, such as elasticities or other structural relationships, and sometimes with the insertion of a random element.

2. *The postulate of unchanging change.* This assumption is that the

value of the phenomenon will move in the same direction and at the same pace as during a past period. A simple projection into the future of the trend observed in the past allows us to read off the value for any moment of the future. This postulate is commonly applied to "productivity" (in the simple sense of production per worker) as a first, rough and ready method of estimation.

3. *The postulate of periodic variations.* This assumption is that the value will be subject to fluctuations following a pattern which has been observed in the past. This postulate is usually combined with the previous one, as for instance when we say that production will increase in the same proportion this year as last, while undergoing seasonal variations of the familiar pattern in the course of the year; or again when we "project" the growth of industrial production as a long-term *trend* varied by *cyclical fluctuations.*

In these naïve procedures of estimation, the "material" used for prediction simply consists of past values of the quantity we are interested in. Our utilization of the material is confined to carefully examining how the variable has behaved as a function of time, our postulate being that its behavior in the future will be the same as in the past.

The method does not bring in any explanatory theory; it is totally independent of all economic science. But though it is crude in its principle, its application cannot be so: the "best" measure of a past trend poses a problem of decision in statistics.

A reader unfamiliar with economic forecasts might ask why procedures so simple in their principle should be mentioned here, thinking they could have no place in a "nice" work of the intellect. But specialists know that these rude intellectual tools, however insufficient, have an important role in forecasting.[16]

A forecast that a movement will continue to conform to the same trend and to the same modalities rests either on the principle of inertia or on the "principle of insufficient reason." The quantities attracting most attention, as for instance the Gross National Product or productivity, are "aggregates" varying under the influence of innumerable causes. As a first step, it is not absurd to assume, for want of a sufficient reason, that a known movement will continue, provided one then looks for the sufficient reasons.[17]

Constant Relationships

How can we put our knowledge of the past to a more scientific use? The idea first suggesting itself is to look for stable relationships holding between variables in the past, in order to assume their continuing constancy in the future. A master of the subject, H. Theil, says:

> It can be maintained that predictions—at least expectations which fall under the scientific category—are generated by means of the assumption that something remains constant; the constancy of this "something" is the theory used in the formulation of the prediction.[18]

Theil then emphasizes that the nature of this "something constant" constitutes the whole difference between different methods of forecasting. If the national income is predicted by extrapolation, the "something constant" is the growth rate (assumption number 1 above). If the national income is predicted by means of an econometric model, the "something constant" is the whole array of coefficients for the system of equations (this amounts to sophisticated use of assumption number 2).

But we are not as yet discussing econometric models. For the present we are thinking only about a stable connection between one variable and another (or several others). The "something constant" we are looking for is a function of well-defined shape and with quantified parameters. Our search for correlations between time-series is by no means haphazard: it is guided by presuppositions—in other words, by theoretical hypotheses. Hence, statistical analysis is both a verification of a theoretical hypothesis and a fashioning of a tool for forecasting. That it should be both things at once is quite natural, but as we shall see, it is sometimes one thing rather than the other.

I shall explain the procedure quite simply. A priori I assume a relationship between y and x: taking y along the ordinate and x along the abscissa, I plot my statistical data as dots. On my scatter diagram I draw the curve which seems to best fit the data. I can regard my curve as a good representation of the relationship between the variables as long as I can explain any large deviations by special causes. But if I want to predict the next value of y, it is not good enough for me to give an *ex post* demonstration of the causes of a deviant y: I must say what y will be *before the event*.

If we are concerned to assert the "truth" of a theory, we try to verify it over a long period of time. If we want a predictive equation in order to pre-calculate "exact" values, we base the equation on a short period and use it only a short time, hoping the characteristics of the base period will be preserved during the period of use. And since the "predictive" equation is meant to "stick" close to the facts, it will be cumbersome and complex compared with the theoretical function, which we try to express in an elegant form.

The contrast between a theoretical function and a predictive equation can be illustrated by some well-known British studies of changes in wage rates. We may mention first A. W. Phillips' investigation of the hypothesis, conforming to the law of the market, that the change of wage rates depends on the percentage of unemployment.[19] Using data for the period 1861–1913, Phillips wrote a function conforming to his initial hypothesis [20] and which he thought "predicted the past" with sufficient accuracy to be worth retaining. This function was of an elegant form.[21] Applying it to his two other periods, 1913–48 and 1948–57, he found that it agreed with the facts well enough. In his opinion, the discrepancies between the values "predicted" by his function and the recorded values could be sufficiently explained by the intervention of particular causes, and thus his initial hypothesis was confirmed.

Next we should mention two teams of researchers who independently of one another tried to establish predictive equations for wage rates: on the one hand, L. A. Dicks-Mireaux and J. C. R. Dow,[22] and on the other, L. R. Klein and R. J. Ball.[23] The contrast between Phillips' elegant function and the cumbersome and complex predictive equations proposed by these two teams is very striking. The equations are too long to be written out here; it is sufficient to say that the wage rates depend on two variables (instead of one as in Phillips' function), several past values of these variables have to be substituted into the equations, and a large number of parameters as well as a so-called "dummy" variable are introduced.

The contrast is readily understood, for with the equations a "dead-on" prediction has to be made. Once the future events discussed in the original papers were past, R. J. Ball compared the predicted values with those actually observed, subjecting the predictive equations to a thorough review.[24] The most important forecasting error related to the rise of unemployment in 1959, both equations predicting a much stronger depressive effect on the wages than was in fact observed.[25]

With the scientific scrupulosity which increasingly becomes a duty, Ball compared the validity of certain naïve predictions and of the equations. One of the assumptions he let the naïve predictor make is as follows: the total change in wage rates in the current quarter will be the same as in the last.[26] As the movement of wage rates has very few turning points, men of experience will not be surprised to find that this prediction gives somewhat better results than the equations. A psycho-sociological interpretation can be put on the finding: *psychological expectations* based on past changes play a very big role in determining wage rates.

Verification and Prediction

It is important, of course, to avoid exaggerating the difference between the attempt to verify a theory and the attempt to construct a tool for prediction. The two are logically connected, and draw closer and closer together in practice as the same rigorous techniques of statistical science are increasingly used in both.[27] But though these techniques are now exploited for the verification of theoretical propositions, it does not seem they were devised for this purpose but rather to subserve prediction. Theory did not lend itself to such verification in its Walrasian guise; it had to start by becoming macro-economic, a transformation which took place under the impetus of practical needs.

Let me quote an author who says that prognostication has long been his main occupation, R. C. Tress:

Macro-economic analysis is essentially an empirical invention. While, in principle, it is possible for a theory of macro-economics to be built up by rigorous aggregation of the analyses of micro-economic behavior, such is not, in fact, the basis of the present achievement or the most promising source of further development. Partly, macro-economics is a product of a kind of intuitive aggregation, as in the case of the multiplier or the disputed accelerator. Increasingly, I would suggest, it is likely to be derived from hypotheses secured by the direct study of the aggregates themselves, as in the case of the lag elements in contemporary trade cycle theory to which I have already referred and of the "constancy propositions" relating to the capital/output ratio, the share of profit and the rate of profit which the researches, particularly of Professor Phelps-Brown and his associates, have lately presented to us. *These are not the products of deductive theory.*

Nor are they merely statistical checks on the validity of theory—though, as Mr. Kaldor has lately hinted with his new theory of economic growth, they can be turned to advantage in that way. Their main prospective value, or so it seems to me, is in the direct contribution they can make to the construction of macro-economic analysis itself, by giving it greater specification and thereby increasing *its practical efficiency.*[28]

Thus the contrast I drew between verification of a general proposition and preparation of a particular prediction is dissolving thanks to the adoption of the same methods, and even more significantly, thanks to the transformation modern theory has undergone under the growing interest in prognostication. The macroscopic concepts, which, it is well known, were formed by the marshalers of facts (such as Simon Kuznets and Colin Clark), have become citizens of theory through the work of Keynes, because he was concerned with a very real evil, unemployment.

Yet the contrast remains by no means negligible. Mark Schupack has this to say in an important study of the predictive accuracy of empirical demand analyses:

> The general consensus appears to be that empirical studies have been unable to conform to the rigid requirements which the theory stipulates. Stigler stated the case over twenty years ago, capping a decade and a half of strenuous discussion; Stone has recently reaffirmed this point of view. Until changes are made either in the theoretical structure or the available statistical data and methods, verification is unlikely to take place.
>
> Not all of the difficulty with theory verification lies with the empirical workers. The theory itself is not very fecund. First, the empirical implications do little to restrict or guide the empirical worker in his choice of demand functions. Second, the theory deliberately abstracts from the factors, both economic and non-economic, which can cause the demand curve to shift over time. The importance of these "dynamic" factors can be seen in Stone's work. For many of his markets the residual time trends are the most important explainers of the changes in quantity sold. Thus, the theory itself gives very little guidance for proper empirical work. One is left with the feeling that even if verification should be possible, the resulting verified theory would not be particularly interesting or useful.

Schupack's conclusion is that empirical demand studies are useful only from the standpoint of a search for a predictive tool:

No ties with demand theory need be maintained; the predictive accuracy of the derived demand equation is the only criterion against which the work is to be judged.[29]

The contrast between verification of a theory and prediction is of great importance in another respect. A proposition presented as a general law is able to make much more impact than a complex predictive equation. Professor Phillips' work, the subject of much discussion in Britain and America,[30] has helped to accredit the idea that the inflation of wages should be avoided by keeping unemployment above a certain level. If we accept Phillips' curve and assume prices will be stable only if the increase of wage rates is equal to the increase of productivity, we can determine the "necessary and sufficient level of unemployment" by finding where the "acceptable" rate of increase intersects his curve. Phillips himself says:

> Ignoring years in which import prices rise rapidly enough to initiate a wage-price spiral, which seem to occur very rarely except as a result of war, and assuming an increase in productivity of 2 per cent per year, it seems from the relation fitted to the data that if aggregate demand were kept at a value which would maintain a stable level of product prices the associated level of unemployment would be a little under 2½ percent.[31]

Although his curve shows that the "level of unemployment necessary for stability" drops as productivity climbs, the fall is much slower than the rise. Thus the theory can be interpreted as a recommendation to attain the highest possible productivity, but also, much more obviously, as a recommendation to maintain unemployment at the necessary level for price stability. And this seems to have influenced American and British policy-makers—an instance of the practical effects of a theory. If we wanted to, we could predict that this or that theoretical proposition will have such or such historical effects. But there is something else that needs to be said. Those who, like myself, are shocked by the idea of a "necessary level of unemployment," finding it inhuman, are driven by a strong emotional reaction to reject the theory: I can cite my own experience as evidence. This observation indicates that it is far more difficult to be neutral with regard to the sciences of man than with regard to the sciences of nature. On the other hand, nobody would hesitate to evaluate a predictive equation in terms of its degree of confirmation by the facts.

The Date of Exogenous Variables

A predictive equation is by definition a formula which contains variables and constant parameters and enables us to calculate the value of a variable y at a future date t. For simplicity, let us assume the formula contains only one variable x. By hypothesis, we can find the required value of y by substituting the value of x into the formula. Yes, but the value of x at what date? Suppose the formula was established in such a way that the value of y at time t is expressed as a function of x *also at time t: $y_t = f(x_t)$*.

In this case, I can calculate the value of a *futurum* y_t only from the value of another *futurum* x_t, a contemporary of y_t and, like y_t, unknown. I can of course try to "guess" the value of x_t and then insert it in the equation. But then any error in x_t will be reflected in y_t. And not only that.

Suppose my chances of error in guessing x_t are as great as in guessing y_t directly. It would be absurd to use the formula, for no formula is absolutely rigorous, unless it is a tautology and thus of no interest to us here. I have no interest in adding my chance of error in the formula to my chance of error in guessing x_t, and I am far better off if I guess y_t directly. A tighter way of making this point is as follows: it is worthwhile for me to use a formula which relates variables referring to the same date only if my chance of error in directly estimating x_t is sufficiently smaller than in directly estimating y_t to more than compensate for the chance of error inherent in the formula.

If the variable x in my formula refers to a much earlier date than y, there is, on the contrary, no difficulty. Suppose that x stands for a value coming twelve months before the value of *y: $y_t = f(x_{t-12})$*. In this case, I play on velvet. Assuming I need one month to find the value of x at $t = 0$ (i.e., my value of x is one month out of date), I can easily predict the value of y eleven months ahead:

$$y_{11} = f(x_{-1})$$

If predictive equations are to be mechanically used in deducing a future unknown from a present "known," the equations must have "time depth": that is to say, the values of the variables on the right-hand side of the equation need to refer to *dates as far in advance as possible* of the date for which y is predicted.

The time depth we are able to impress on our equations is by no means great. It should be remembered that all of classical economics was a static leading to *simultaneous* equations—relationships holding between states of variables at the same moment of time. And in our day, the idea of coherence, the idea that the states of variables at the same moment of time are compatible, continues to play an important and necessary role in our conceptions of the future. The idea of a general equilibrium prompts us to relate different variables at the same date, and practical observations of partial equilibriums suggest that the response of one variable to another is a rapid one. In particular, it is characteristic of price movements to manifest themselves with great rapidity.

To take a specific example, suppose that a number of industrial economists are invited to submit, by September 1, 1964, forecasts of automobile sales on the home market during October 1965, the author of the best forecast to be awarded an important job. In the summer of 1965, the organizers invite a second group of economists, of the same caliber as the first, to take part in the same competition, giving them up to September 15 to submit forecasts of automobile sales in the following October. The first group of economists, hearing of this, would feel very unjustly treated. "Where do you see the injustice?" the organizers would ask. "Like you, the second group had only one chance to make a prediction." To this the economists would retort, "Come, you are joking. You gave them their opportunity much closer to the event, and that makes a tremendous difference."

We feel intuitively that the immediate future can be guessed much better from things directly preceding it than from things coming a long time before. This feeling, such is its strength, manifests itself even when unfounded: players at roulette, it is said, often want to know what numbers have come up, even though the number to come up next is completely independent of the numbers preceding it. But in general the feeling is well founded: the data closest to the event are generally a better indicator than more remote ones, for they are more determining. The situation of consumers in the third quarter of 1965 has a greater effect on their purchases in October 1965 than does their situation in the third quarter of 1964.

To insist on this is superfluous. Accordingly, it is easy to conceive that the values needed for the independent variables in predictive equations correspond to dates quite close to the date for which the dependent variable is predicted. This remark is essential.

Thus a predictive equation for wage rates does not give us their numerical value in eighteen months' or a year's time. It yields us a prediction only when we are able to know the actual values of the independent variables. And if some of the required values are simultaneous with the wage rate instead of prior to it, we can obtain a prediction—in the commonly accepted sense of specifying a future value of a variable a reasonably long time in advance—only if we "guess" the as yet unobserved values of the independent variables. The importance of this point will be further emphasized in the sequel.

Econometric Models

In modern scientific speech, the word "model" has acquired a meaning opposite to its traditional one in the arts and in morality. Formerly, "model" designated an object of representation (the painter's model) or of imitation (a model of virtue). Now it designates something artificially constructed to represent or imitate some aspect of reality. Here, the word is used exclusively in the latter sense.

We know a structure completely only if we can "construct" it, materially or intellectually. Our knowledge of a structure in the external world is mediated by a model: how good our knowledge is depends on how faithfully the structure we have built simulates the structure in the world.[32] The important simulation is of function rather than of appearance—a distinction corresponding to the difference between the rational and the puerile mind. The idea that we acquire a physical power over a being possessing ourselves of its simulacrum is puerile:[33] the idea that we acquire knowledge of an existent by building an artificial and like-behaving system is rational.

Economists have always been very much aware that the economy is a complex system of interrelations, and Walras' chief title to fame is, as we have seen, his representation of this complexity by a system of equations. But we have also seen that his system remained an idea without possible application, based as it was on individual actors and their actions, which are now conventionally spoken of as "micro-elements." To arrive at a workable system, it was necessary to think in terms of "aggregates," or "macro-elements."

We have become so accustomed to thinking in terms of aggregates that the student who asks about the meaning of the word is surprised to find that it simply refers to global concepts such as total wages paid by the private sector of the economy or total sales of durable goods.

A model of the national economy is a system of equations expressing the relations that we believe hold between the important variables. The system is "econometric" if the parameters can be expressed as numbers. This is not to say that the system is solvable, for, as a matter of logical necessity, it has more variables than equations. The number of unknowns must be reduced by assuming the values of some of the variables. The variables treated as "given" are called *exogenous,* while those treated as unknown are called *endogenous.* These generally accepted terms give very good expression to the difference between the values that are "imported" into the system, and those deduced from it.

It is important to note that an *exogenous* variable sometimes appears with values referring to several different dates. All of them, including any referring to the same date as the unknowns, are regarded as "given."

Likewise, an endogenous variable sometimes appears with values referring to several different dates. In this case, only the latest one in order of time is treated as unknown: all the earlier ones are "given."

Thus the predetermined variables will include: 1. the parameters; 2. all the values of the exogenous variables, at all dates; and 3. all the values of the endogenous variables, with the exception of the latest one in date for each variable.

Since the quantities are aggregates, an econometric model has a minute number of equations compared with that, scarcely conceivable, required for the system of a Walras or a Pareto. The first econometric model to appear, J. Tinbergen's, contained only forty-eight equations, six of which were mere identities or definitions.[34] Later models contained even fewer equations. Any econometric model must include definitions, in order to avoid any ambiguity about the quantities employed. For example, if I have a definition saying: "Consumption plus Investment plus Government Expenditure plus Net Exports equals National Expenditure,"[35] I know that government investment must not be included in investment in this system, and that inventory accumulation is grouped with fixed investment.

It is a tautology that the definitions are rigorous equations. All the other equations hold only approximately. The econometrician postulates that they give rise to small and random errors, often represented by a stochastic variable: if systematic errors are observed in the predictions, the equations will be corrected.

Some of the chief names associated with the development of models are J. Tinbergen, L. R. Klein, and Richard Stone.[36] Their work is profoundly influenced by the work of Leontief, to whom we owe the representation of the economy in the form of the input-output matrix. Tinbergen produced a model of the American economy as early as 1939 and provided the chief inspiration for the model officially adopted in Holland in 1955 for economic forecasting and planning.[37] The forecasts of the Dutch model have been subjected to a masterly *ex post* analysis by H. Theil.[38]

Klein has produced several successive versions of an econometric model for the United States, the most recent ones in collaboration with Goldberger.[39] On the basis of his work, the Research Seminar in Quantitative Economics (RSQE) has developed a model used in forecasting, which has been successively revised since 1953.[40] Klein has also constructed a model for the United Kingdom, but the most important work on that country has been carried out by Richard Stone at Cambridge.[41]

The choice of the relations, the refined statistical techniques for estimating parameters, and the methods of calculation do not form part of my subject. My purpose is to describe the key ideas involved in forecasting, and consequently I have no cause to insist on the errors actually committed in forecasts:[42] but the principles of error are of interest. Wrong predictions may be due to defects in the structure of the system of equations, or to the substitution of wrong "given" values. For concision, I shall speak of these sources of error as "structural faults" and "bad insertions."

Fortunately, it is very easy to distinguish the two sorts of error. Suppose a prediction about some particular year went badly wrong. At the time the prediction was made, the value of the exogenous variables had to be guessed, but now their true values are known. Therefore, we can substitute the true values in the equations, and in so doing, we make what is known as an *ex post* prediction. The errors still remaining in this prediction are structural, whereas those removed from it were the result of bad insertions.

If defective predictions could be attributed to structural faults, we would be in a rather good position, for we can always hope to improve our formulation of a relationship. Vexation at a failure to obtain a perfect model is unworthy of the scientist, who should devote himself instead to the progressive improvement of his model. A relation he assumed to be linear is perhaps nonlinear after all, and he can always try and see.

Unfortunately, Theil's analysis of Dutch forecasting errors shows that by far the greater number of them disappears in an *ex post* prediction, and thus the wrong estimation of the "given" values is the great source of error. This finding, which redounds to the credit of Dutch economists, is fit to discourage the placing of exaggerated hopes on prediction by means of models.

But is this surprising? We wanted to "calculate" our unknowns instead of "guessing" them. Very well. However, we cannot calculate without inserting data, which are *futura* at the time and therefore have to be "guessed." The situation is basically the same as for our simple predictive equation, although it is somewhat better in one respect: the results we are looking for are part of a system and must be coherent, and thus if the results yielded by the "given" data seem a priori implausible, we can revise some of the "given" data. The method we use will possibly consist of successive approximations. But we must not be blind to the implications of such a method: our "guesses" of the results (or at any rate of their upper and lower limits) are used to "test" our "guesses" of the inserted data.

In short, even the finest model does not free us from the obligation of guessing. We would have nothing to guess only if all the data to be substituted were known far in advance.[43] One possibility suggests itself: all the exogenous variables could be determined far in advance by decisions made by a single agent and faithfully executed.[44] But the philosophical implications would be as follows: this agent, in knowing his own will, would know the whole future. Nothing could be more implausible. We feel therefore that a model completely absolving us from the necessity to guess would be wrong. There is always something to guess.

Presages

There is always something to guess. And to do so the mind falls back on the naïve modes of prediction described previously, and particularly on postulate number 1, a prolongation, in the imagination, of a movement now under way. This method is more common than any other. One psychological trait connected with its use should be noted: if the movement is a fairly pronounced one, we tend to predict that it will proceed in a rather less pronounced manner, as though we unconsciously calculated a weighted average of our two most natural assumptions—"No Change" and "Same Line of Change." The work of "composition" in the mind doubtless explains why, in a time of rapid expansion, producers significantly underestimate their future sales.[45]

But we also know very well that a tendency can be reversed. Our awareness of this possibility is naturally a function of our past experience: we contemplate the reversal of a tendency if we have several times or frequently seen it reversed, but not if we have never seen it reversed. Good forecasts of turning points are in practice much more important than good forecasts of rate of change. And it can be observed that, in forecasting turning points, we attach great value to precursory signs, which are properly called "presages."

Let W be the phenomenon whose turning points we wish to predict. If on numerous occasions we have seen a reversal of W preceded by a reversal of V, the reversal of V appears to us as a precursory sign. Our impression is strengthened if we are careful to observe all the reversals of W and all the reversals of V over a long period, and the chronological connection between the two is very frequent. The more frequently a reversal of V has been followed by a reversal of W, the more probably, to our minds, a reversal of V now means a reversal of W later.[46]

It is far more difficult than one might imagine to conduct a careful investigation. The National Bureau of Economic Research has spent more than forty years studying fluctuations of time series, in work guided by the idea of a business cycle (Juglar's contribution to economics[47]) and successively directed by Wesley C. Mitchell, Arthur F. Burns, and Geoffrey H. Moore. One of the results to emerge from this work is a set of "leading indicators":[48] series in which a turning point regularly precedes a turning point in the economic activity. These indicators are too well known to need any lengthy explanation. Two facts will suffice to bring out their importance—first, a survey of business economists in America at the end of 1961 indicated that the observation of National Bureau indicators was by far the most prevalent of the forecasting methods they employed;[49] second, since March 1962 the United States Department of Commerce has issued a periodical specially devoted to business-cycle indicators.[50]

In the indicator method, signs of a turning point in the series W are found by looking for antecedent turning points in some *other* series or set of series. The National Bureau has also developed another method, diffusion-index forecasting, in which the *internal* behavior of the series W is studied for signs of a turning point.[51] The series W is an aggregate consisting of a weighted average of small aggregates, and thus the movement of W in one direction (say upward) results from movements of its constituent aggregates; therefore, a successive decline in the proportion of upward-moving constituents is possibly a sign of a coming reversal of the upward movement of W.[52]

Leading indicators are not compelling as arguments—a point that bears emphasizing. In 1962 strong objections were heard about their having given a bad prediction; such complaints manifest a fundamental mis-understanding of the instrument, which is not at all of the same nature as an econometric model. An econometric model is a bad predictor if and only if the *ex post* substitution of true values for the exogeneous variables yields a wrong "prediction." What is asked of the model is to give a good transformation of data into results: it is meant to provide true relations between the data and the endogenous variables. In the method of leading indicators, the relations between the presages and the phenomena are not supposed to be necessary. All that is claimed is this: the reversal of V has been followed by the reversal of W with great frequency, so that if V occurs we can assign to W more chances of occurring than not, other things being equal. Other things may intervene to make us modify this judgment, which in any event is never more than a judgment of proba-bility. And indeed, to say that the case (a reversal of V followed by a reversal of W) is a frequent one implies that the forecaster who auto-matically asserts a reversal of W on seeing a reversal of V would be certain to go wrong in a certain proportion of cases.

The Pipeline

A new plant begins production, adding its capacity and output to those already existing in the industry. The fact is new but not unexpected. Before going into operation, the plant could be seen for quite some time as a new building to which equipment was delivered; before that, as a construction site; and before that, as a blueprint, with a schedule for the allocation of funds, jobs assigned to contractors, and orders placed with suppliers. From this stage on, the plant's "pre-existence" was sufficient for its future existence to be asserted (with a margin of error concerning the date) and for the *futurum* to be treated as a "fact with a future date."

We can foreknow this fact, and insert this *foreknown* in a picture of the future date, thus introducing an element of solidity into the future scene. "As true as the production capacity of the other plants of the company is now P, the production capacity in two years' time will be P plus the capacity of the new plant, which by then will have begun operation."

The foregoing statement about the future is not a mere assertion about a *project* formed by the company's directors, not a mere expression of a subjective certitude. A third party who has bothered to inform himself could make the statement, for the execution of the project has begun and the genesis of the fact is a process manifestly under way: steps are being taken toward the realization of the plant, and this advance cannot be back-stepped. The situation can be described by saying that the future existence of the plant has *entered into a "historical pipeline."*

Any fact which takes definite form only through visible physical operations stretched over time has a stage spent moving through a "historical pipeline" (this stage is a finite period of ordinary time). And therefore the mind can grasp such a fact quite a way "up the line," before the fact emerges.

This method of forecasting is an excellent one for constructed things. Is there any equivalent for events whose physical nature does not imply details of production?

Intentions

The problem just raised would have a simple and general solution if economic agents of every kind were good predictors of their own actions significantly far ahead of time. We could then simply ask all men what they will do in the coming year, and their answers would make known to us all actions, which we could then aggregate to find out the course of events.

Are men good self-predictors? And in particular, are they good self-predictors sufficiently far in advance for a compilation of their self-predictions to be of practical use? If before going to market today every housewife exactly predicts her expenditure, we are not given sufficient notice to put the self-predictions to use.

There is, I think, a great difference in nature between institutional agents (a large business or government agency) and individual agents. In an "institution," the executives generally have to know in advance what they will be doing in the coming year, for they must obtain the assent of a separate deciding body before they act. Thus the funds allocated to capital expenditure in business[53] and the sums voted to different government agencies can serve as good indicators, and so can the McGraw-Hill estimates of capital expenditure.[54]

The problem of self-prediction is seen in pure form in the case of consumers perfectly free not to do what they had intended, or if they have the means, to do what they had not thought of doing.

Studies of consumer intentions are now made in great number. I shall refer only to those conducted for more than fifteen years by George Katona and his collaborators at the Survey Research Center of the University of Michigan. There has been an ardent debate in the past few years between Katona and some eminent colleagues of his, such as James Tobin[55] and Arthur Okun,[56] regarding the usefulness of intention surveys. In Katona's opinion, an "index of consumer attitudes," derived from answers to a series of questions, is of greater use in forecasting than are announcements of intentions (self-predictions). His critics, rejecting his index, hold that self-predictions are the only valid part of the survey.

Let us consider one of the studies over which there has been disagreement.[57] Two surveys were made of the same sample of 1,159 people: in January–February 1961 each person was asked whether he intended to buy a car in the current year, and in January–February 1962 he was asked whether he had in fact bought a car in 1961. It was found that 52 per cent of the Yes-Intenders did in fact buy cars, and so did 21 per cent of the No-Intenders.[58] Thus, as Okun insists, a declaration of intention is statistically significant.[59]

But Katona persuades us to take another view of the matter. In the second survey, it was observed that only 22 per cent of the total number who bought cars had the intention to do so at the beginning of 1961. In 1960 the corresponding figure was 33 per cent.[60] Thus 67 per cent of the car buyers in 1960 and 78 per cent in 1961 had no intention of buying a car at the beginning of the year.

I think this is very important. If only a small proportion of the buyers were No-Intenders, it would be evidence that consumers generally do not improvise and that their actions are generally the result of projects formed some time in advance. From the standpoint of the reliability of self-prediction, I would like to find only a small number of improvisers among buyers,[61] but in actual fact they form a large majority.

Katona brings out the significance of this majority very fully. Among the No-Intenders who did in fact buy cars, not less than 56 per cent bought on the spur of a sudden decision or within a month of making a decision.[62] Furthermore, 31 per cent of the Yes-Intenders who bought cars did so immediately after or within a month of the first survey, so that their classification among the Plan-Aheaders was simply the result of the sampler happening on them just at the time when they had improvised a decision. Thus, for most people, even an action as important as buying a car is, at best, an object of very short-term self-prediction.

The idea of a "short horizon" receives further support from the fact that the Yes-Intenders bought proportionately more than the No-Intenders only during the quarter running concurrently with the inquiry and the quarter immediately following. As one might expect, the percentage of Yes-Intenders who bought cars is largely a function of income (61 per cent for those above $3,000, and 26 per cent for those below), so much so that the proportion of poor Yes-Intenders who bought cars is slightly smaller than the proportion of rich No-Intenders who did so: 26 per cent as opposed to 27 per cent (these figures are averages for the two years). Again not surprisingly, the percentage of Yes-Intenders who bought cars is related to changes in their personal circumstances: 63 per cent for those whose position improved, and 47 per cent for those whose position deteriorated.

This comparison of achievement with declared intention does not suggest that agents in the consumer category are good self-predictors. But is this really surprising?[63] And is it a bad thing in relation to forecasting? Surely not, if an analysis of the differences shows that they can be related to objective factors, thus enabling us to construct a behavior function.[64]

With regard to producers, Modigliani[65] claims that a thorough and systematic comparison of their behavior with their "anticipations" (a term including their self-predictions and their predictions about the environment) would eventually yield behavior functions enabling us to dispense altogether with further surveys of anticipations. But in my opinion, Modigliani goes much too far.

It is understandable that the economist in the pursuit of the intellectual ideal of the physical sciences should want to reduce the behavior of economic agents to a "legality" in order that he can deduce a future objective state from its predecessor, and treat all intervening decisions as epiphenomena. But to eliminate the inventive and creative decisions of producers is surely unrealistic.

Economic Budgets

My intention in this chapter was not, I repeat, to expound the methods employed in short-term economic forecasting, but to bring out some of the principles involved.[66] And since I wanted to insist on the guiding ideas, I have given econometric models, because of their clear design, more weight than they actually have in practice (except possibly in Holland). It is worth referring in this connection to the remarks of Lehman and Knowles about the contrast between Theil's econometric model and the methods used in America by the Council of Economic Advisors to the President and the Joint Congressional Committee on the Economic Report.[67] In rough outline, these methods involve a year-to-year comparison of the demands made on the system (by government, business, consumers, and foreign countries) with the capacity of the system (plus foreign contributions).

It is well known that in January of each year, the President of the United States is required by the Employment Act of 1946 to submit to Congress a report which describes the economic condition of the country during the preceding year and sets forth the foreseeable trends relating to certain specified general objectives. The Council of Economic Advisors was established under the Act to "assist and advise" the President in the preparation of the Report, and the Joint Committee has a team of experts to help it in studying the Report. In the United Kingdom, an Economic Survey is presented annually to Parliament.[68] And in France, an Economic Budget for the coming year is prepared by the S.E.E.F.[69] and presented to the Commission des Comptes de la Nation; in addition, the Commission de Conjoncture prepares semiannual forecasts for the Conseil Économique et Social.[70]

If my ambition had been other than to indicate a few of the key ideas of short-term economic forecasting, I should have had to study the work of these forecasting services. But this would be a major undertaking, far outside the scope of my book and difficult to conduct owing to the lack of literature on the methods employed. To my knowledge, there has not even been a systematic attempt to compare forecasts with actual results, with the exception of the very fine study by André Barjonet in France.[71]

Since World War II, work in forecasting has developed very rapidly in government agencies, and in France with particular vigor. The international literature on short-term forecasting does not reflect the true importance of French work at all adequately, largely because most of it is contained in documents for internal use in organizations and has not been disseminated.[72]

The French forecasts are situated within the framework of a four-year plan (the Fifth Plan, 1966–1967, is for a five-year period), which is in a sense a normative prediction, and the methods of approach used for them are profoundly influenced by this circumstance. In American forecasts, changes due to various motive causes are simply estimated in relation to the previous year, whereas the existence of a four-year plan implies that certain targets need to be reached within the current year.[73] And so, instead of seeking diverse and confused causes of progress, the forecaster looks for inhibiting causes that could prevent the objectives from being attained and produce a disequilibrium between demand adjusted to the plan and production unable to respond to demand, and that could thus result in higher imports (to fill the gap), rising prices (due to consumer pressure), and the diversion of resources from investment to consumption. In short, the forecast becomes a judgment of the chances that a previously formulated forecast will be fulfilled.

The French forecasts have, it seems to me, a *sui generis* character arising from their moral and institutional context. After the war, it became a principle of national policy that the physical growth of the economy should be as rapid as would be compatible with the sovereignty of the consumer, and each Plan is an *ad hoc* four-year outline. The French Plan, like any other, is subject to the requirement of coherence: each activity provides an outlet for other activities and generates them, serving as an *input* for other activities; but if a user requires a certain combination of inputs and one of them is scarcer than the others, the scarce input acts as a restraint on the others; and reciprocally, an input may find itself restrained if it cannot be utilized owing to the scarcity of some other input. But, in addition, the French Plan is subject to the requirement of psychological coherence. The sovereignty of the consumer means that consumer goods and services must be supplied in the desired proportions (and these change with time); furthermore, it is useless to increase the consumers' purchasing power in the hope that they will absorb easily supplied goods, as the result will only be to bid up the price of commodities in short supply. And it is obvious that a system paying less regard to consumer preferences could lead to greater statistical growth rates, but not of the same social significance.

From this brief sketch of the guiding principle and institutional character of the French system, we can see that the Plan comprises annual targets, remembering, however, that Pierre Massé has often stressed they are different in nature from the four-year objectives. The annual targets are signposts to which a man imbued with the Plan is naturally drawn. But as soon as this happens, the view of the coming year is quite different from what it is in an unplanned economy. In the case of the American economy, the experts look for various motive causes which could make this year's figures differ from last year's. In the case of the French economy, the experts are concerned about particular inhibiting causes which could prevent this year from showing the scheduled progress over last year. This difference in point of view is reflected in the ways of speaking: the American press will boast of a new record, where the French press may deplore the failure to reach a certain marker.

In short, since the Plan is a normative forecast, the annual forecasts of the S.E.E.F. are in a sense second-order forecasts: admonitory forecasts relating to the degree of implementation of the Plan. And the criticisms made by the Commission des Comptes de la Nation about the S.E.E.F. forecasts can be regarded as third-order forecasts: "We foresee that your forecast about this divergence from the normative forecast will go wrong in such and such a way."

At the end of this chapter there is an authoritative exposition of French Economic Budgets by Jacques-Daniel Mayer, which I am very pleased to be able to reproduce.

The Abundance of Resources

Although their work covers a wide range, we can make this generalization about the technicians: they try to give precise expression to sensed relationships, and to measure the degree of confidence to be placed in signs. And thus the practician has certain established relationships at his disposal, which he cannot apply unless he guesses certain values, but which enable him to put certain available signs to use.

An abundance of instruments enables the practician to adopt more than one intellectual itinerary: and not only can he do so, he must.[74] Any way of predicting which is used as a recipe one automatically follows will inevitably make the forecaster go wrong in a certain proportion of cases. And to look for a more and more complex system of equations or for the perfect recipe is not the solution: it may be of use for a better explanatory representation. For the purposes of forecasting, however, what is needed is to make different forecasts which are as independent of one another as possible and serve as cross-checks. To take the briefest of examples, an estimate of an aggregate obtained by some method should be compared with independent estimates of its components. The practician can be compared to the judge who summons many witnesses before making up his mind.

It is a fact that there are more or less reliable methods, and another that there are more or less lucky forecasters—so much so that it has even been suggested the forecasters themselves could be used as an instrument for measuring probabilities of future events: by questioning each forecaster separately and comparing the results, then questioning the forecasters again.[75] The underlying idea is evidently the one developed by Condorcet in the famous essay[76] in which he treated the probability of error of a majority decision in terms of the probability of error of the individual members of a tribunal, who are consulted one by one, without being allowed to communicate with one another. If there is a choice between only two decisions, and if one consults eleven experts who each have 95 chances in 100 of arriving at the right verdict, a simple calculation shows the odds are 1,000 to 1 that a simple majority will be in favor of the right choice.[77]

Let us leave this talk of probability. The point is simply that in economics, as in any other field, the forecaster must exercise his judgment. And who could be surprised at this? The whole difference between economic forecasting and other kinds of forecasting lies in the wealth of means available to the mind.

In this respect, there is rapid impoverishment as the term of the forecast recedes into the future: the signs disappear, and empirical relations based on a recent past are deformed.

APPENDIX

by Jacques-Daniel Mayer

1. The French Economic Budget is a projection of a complete system of accounts for the coming year. The French system of national accounting was specially designed to facilitate this projection and the utilization of

the accounts for checking whether decisions of economic policy are coherent and adapted to the whole body of economic targets.

2. In the methods of projection important use is made of the characteristic procedures of short-term economic forecasting, and in particular of the lags between a decision by an economic agent, the resulting action, and the results of this action. A knowledge of the decisions already taken provides information about economic variables in the coming year.

Once this information, which is partial in nature, has been gathered, it is used in the preparation of very detailed accounts. Thus the preparation always has to be a compromise between two conflicting tendencies—the utilization of economic relations between global variables, and the utilization of direct information about partial variables.

3. This compromise is effected in the following manner in France. A budget which is in the main global is prepared with the help of a simple mathematical model. Anything of use for short-term forecasting contained in the preparatory work for the Plan is also incorporated in this budget, which is then worked out into highly detailed national accounts.

The different accounts are then subjected to scrutiny by a vast network of experts in all the economic agencies of the government and in an increasing number of public and private organizations.

The information gathered from the experts is afterwards used in the preparation of the Final Economic Budget.

The advantage of this procedure is that most of the organs of administration involved in the preparation of economic decisions by the government take part in the preparation of the Budget. The procedure also helps to give the Budget greater internal coherence.

The procedure leads to a detailed Economic Budget which incorporates a forecast of inter-industrial flows, the accounts of the different sectors, and a picture of financial operations into a single system.

4. Mathematical tools are principally used for elements of the Budget related to the behavior of a large number of small decision-units (for example, household consumption). On the contrary, direct information is used for elements related to the behavior of a small number of individually important agents (for example, the investment of large companies, and variables determined by the state).

However, in each case, an attempt is made to compare the results of all the methods of information. Thus investigations of consumer intentions are analyzed, and direct information about plans for investment is compared with values of this variable yielded by econometric equations.

5. A comparison of the forecasts with the figures actually recorded is made every year. These comparisons indicate that:

a. On the whole, variations of output are forecast much better than variations of prices.

b. On the whole, internal variables are forecast much better than imports and exports.

c. On the whole, variations of consumption are forecast much better than variations of investment.

These three results can be easily explained. In the first place, the same output equilibrium can be obtained at different price levels, and the brakes which restrain a general increase of prices and incomes (monetary policy, foreign trade, budgetary restrictions) operate only after a fairly long period of time. In these conditions, it is very difficult to estimate the extent of a general skidding of prices without taking into account subtle psychological and political considerations.

The explanation of the second result is that the relative changes in exports and imports can be much larger than in internal variables because France has only a relatively small role in international trade. Exports and imports can vary by as much as 20 or 30 per cent, whereas such a variation in consumption is inconceivable. Moreover, the preparation of the Budget brings out the mutual interaction of agents in France (for example, a variation of production leads to a variation of incomes and this leads to a variation of consumption, which in turn must be compatible with the variation of production). In foreign trade, nothing corresponds to this, except to a certain extent in trade with the French Franc Area.

Finally, the forecasting of investments is difficult, and is not represented by many instances of success in the international literature on the subject. The behavior of entrepreneurs in investment is far more complex than that of consumers in consumption. In most cases, technical restraints play only a minor role. There is only a distant relationship between the production potential for a year and the investments that actually will be made in that year. Thus the situation with regard to investments is as follows: they are fairly easy to forecast because large companies have projects that are laid down in advance and related to the Plan, but the risk of error is considerable, for these same companies can modify their behavior fairly rapidly in the course of the ensuing year.

NOTES

1. The first work on the subject, which was produced in French, is Alfred Sauvy's *La Prévision economique* (Paris, 1943). Recently an abundant literature has developed. Especially useful, because they are written by practitioners, are C. W. McMahon, ed., *Techniques of Economic Forecasting* (Paris: OECD, 1955), and Bert G. Hickman, ed., *Quantitative Planning of Economic Policy* (Washington, D.C.: Brookings, 1965).

2. W. Stanley Jevons, *The Theory of Political Economy*, 4th ed. (London, 1911), p. 11.

3. The mind is at fault only when it becomes attached to its "construct" to the point of denying or obscuring aspects of the represented reality which jar with the "representing" model. When this happens, the "construct" becomes an idol of the mind, instead of its servant.

4. Léon Walras, *Eléments d'économie politique pure, ou Théorie de la richesse sociale* (Paris, 1874).

5. Paul A. Samuelson, in his speech as president of the American Economic Association, 74th Annual Meeting, December 27, 1961. Published in the *American Economic Review*, III:1 (March 1962), 3–4.

6. Joseph A. Schumpeter, *History of Economic Analysis* (New York, 1954), pp. 967–8.

7. Samuelson, *loc. cit.*

8. Ely Devons, "Applied Economics: The Application of What?" in *Essays in Economics* (London, 1961).

9. Judith B. Balderston, "Models of General Economic Equilibrium," in Oskar Morgenstern, ed., *Economic Activity Analysis* (New York, 1954).

10. Some unrealistic assumptions have to be made in order to construct a "pure" model. But according to Schumpeter, Walras not only postulates perfect competition, but he also postulates "that the quantities of productive services that enter into the unit of every product (coefficients of production) are constant technological data; that there is no such thing as fixed cost; that all firms in an industry produce the same kind of product, by the same method in equal quantities; that the productive process takes *no* time; that problems of location may be neglected." (Schumpeter, *op. cit.*, pp. 973–4.)

11. According to Judith Balderston, for 1,000 commodities and 100 factors of production, there would be 2,199 equations and unknowns to be solved in the system. (*Op. cit.*)

12. Pareto himself pointed out the practical impossibility of solving the equations owing to their excessive number (*Manuel d'économie politique*, p. 227). Morgenstern gives a better reason taken from statistics (Oskar Morgen-

stern, "Experiment and Computation," in Morgenstern, ed., *Economic Activity Analysis,* p. 491).

13. Morgenstern, ed., *loc. cit.*

14. In economics any estimate of a *futurum* is called a prediction; it is of course understood that a prediction can always be wrong.

15. For example, one considers the global production of a group of industries instead of the production of each individual firm.

16. J. Méraud, one of the best French forecasters, writes: "The first method is simple *extrapolation,* implicit or explicit, of recent tendencies. This method is sometimes called naïve. In fact, everyone who makes forecasts starts by using extrapolation to a greater or lesser extent, even if he thinks he is using more subtle methods. The more so as he must start by forecasting the present, as Alfred Sauvy once said. Statistical information is generally available only after a certain lag, and therefore the forecaster must start by estimating the present situation from data referring to a more or less recent past, and only then can he forecast what the situation will become." (J. Méraud, "Quelques méthodes de prévision à court terme," *Cahiers de l'Institut de science économique appliquée,* Suppl. 116, Series AK No. 1 [August 1961], p. 7.)

17. Thus Méraud justifies extrapolation as "the first stage of a short-term forecast." He goes on to say: "The role of the economist is to *reason* this extrapolation, that is to say, to *bend* the curves representing the recent past upward or downward according to the pointers of the other forecasting instruments in his possession." (Méraud, *loc. cit.*)

18. H. Theil, *Economic Forecasting and Policy,* 2nd ed. (Amsterdam, 1961), p. 18.

19. A. W. Phillips, "The Relations between Unemployment and the Rate of Change of Money Wages in the United Kingdom, 1861–1957," *Economica,* XXV: 100 (November 1958).

20. Phillips assumed that wage rates would be a function of the scarcity of labor, but not a linear one owing to the asymmetrical behavior of employers and workers—the former raise wage rates quite rapidly when unemployment is low, in order to attract labor, whereas the latter are reluctant to offer services below the prevailing rates when unemployment is high.

21. He gives the formula:
$$\log\,(y + 0.9000) = 0.984 - 1.394x$$
(*y* is the percentage change of wage rates and *x* is the percentage of unemployment).

22. L. A. Dicks-Mireaux and J. C. R. Dow, "Excess Demand for Labour," *Oxford Economic Papers* (January 1958), and by the same authors, "The Determinants of Wage Inflation 1946–1956," *Journal of the Royal Statistical Society,* Series A, Part 2 (1959).

23. L. R. Klein and R. J. Ball, "Some Econometrics of the Determination of Absolute Prices and Wages," *Economic Journal* (September 1958).

24. R. J. Ball, "The Prediction of Wage-Rate Changes in the United Kingdom Economy 1957–1960," *Economic Journal* (March 1962).

25. According to both equations, wage rates should have dropped at the levels of unemployment which occurred, but in fact there was only a slight slowing down.

26. This prediction must not be confused with the assumption of a constant trend. Here the predictor is supposed to know the total change over the last quarter, and assumes that the same change will take place in the current quarter. In practice, because of the time it takes to assemble statistics, a predictor is unable to know the exact change that took place last quarter until the present quarter is well under way.

27. Statistics, which is still thought of by the general public as a matter of counting, is increasingly becoming a general science for the testing of relationships, or, if one prefers, a science for measuring significances, a master science, and thus applicable to all disciplines. For a particularly simple and clear example of the use of statistical techniques to choose between several possible determinants of a given phenomenon, see the paper by John Meyer and Edwin Kuh, "Acceleration and Related Theories of Investment: An Empirical Inquiry," *The Review of Economics and Statistics,* XXXVII: 3 (August 1955).

28. R. C. Tress, "The Contribution of Economic Theory to Economic Prognostication," *Economica* (August 1959). (The italics in the quotation are mine.)

29. Mark B. Schupack, "The Predictive Accuracy of Empirical Demand Analyses," *Economic Journal* (September 1962).

30. Thus I owe to Professor Samuelson my acquaintance with Professor Phillips' work.

31. A. W. Phillips, "The Relations between Unemployment and the Rate of Change of Money Wages in the United Kingdom, 1861–1957," *Economica,* XXV: 100 (November 1958), 299.

32. On simulation in the social sciences in general, see Harold Gützkow, ed., *Simulation in Social Science: Readings* (Englewood Cliffs, N.J.: Prentice-Hall, 1962). On simulation in economics, see the symposium in the *American Economic Review* (December 1962), containing articles by G. H. Orcutt, Martin Shubik, and G. P. E. Clarkson, and H. A. Simon (the articles are accompanied by bibliographies).

33. An extreme example is in witchcraft, in which manipulations of an image are supposed to have an effect on the person represented. Of a similar type is the idea that one hurts a country by treading on its flag.

34. J. Tinbergen, *Statistical Testing of Business Cycle Theories: II. Business Cycles in the United States of America 1919–1932* (Geneva, 1939).

35. An example given by Carl F. Christ, "Aggregate Economic Models: A Review Article," *The American Economic Review,* XLVI: 3 (June 1956). It is an article of great clarity on the whole subject.

36. It is also necessary to mention Colin B. Clark, a pioneer in so many domains: "A System of Equations Explaining the U.S. Trade Cycle 1921–1941," *Econometrica* (April 1949).

37. *Centraal Economish Plan* (The Hague, 1955).

38. H. Theil, "Forecasting in Relation to Government Policy-Making," in an important publication by the National Bureau of Economic Research, *The Quality and Economic Significance of Anticipations Data* (Princeton, N.J., 1960), and by the same author, *Economic Forecasts and Policy,* 2nd edn. (Amsterdam, 1961).

39. For want of space to list Klein's numerous articles, let me mention L. R. Klein and A. S. Goldberger, *An Econometric Model of the United States 1929–1952* (Amsterdam, 1955).

40. Discussed by one of its chief authors in Daniel B. Suits, "Forecasting and Economic Analysis with an Econometric Model," *The American Economic Review* LII: 1 (March 1962).

41. L. R. Klein, R. J. Ball, A. Hazlewood, and P. Vandome, *An Econometric Model of the United Kingdom* (Oxford, 1961). See the review by Marc Nerlove, "A Quarterly Econometric Model for the United Kingdom," *The American Economic Review* LII: 1 (March 1962). The author of this review assumes a knowledge of Carl F. Christ's article, which because of its perfect clarity does indeed deserve to be treated as the fundamental work on the subject.

For the work of Richard Stone and his group, see the publications of the Department of Applied Economics of Cambridge University and, in particular, *A Computable Model of Economic Growth* (July 1962), *A Social Accounting Matrix for 1960* (October 1962), and *Input-Output Relationships 1954–1956* (May 1963)—all published in London by Chapman and Hall.

42. A comparison of predicted values and observed values is given in the article by Suits. The errors for 1955 and 1959 seem to me enormous. Thus in 1955 the increase of consumption (at constant prices) was forecast as 1.7 per cent but was in fact 7.2 per cent, i.e., four times as great as estimated. The error is grossly minimized by expressing it as a fraction of the total consumption!

43. This condition is satisfied by some variables. For example, the investment expenditures of large companies are fixed by decisions made quite far ahead of the actual expenditure and faithfully executed.

44. The state is the agent that first comes to mind. But the praiseworthy efforts of civil servants to program the actions of the government are upset by politicians changing policy. How many governments could predict their own actions correctly?

45. See H. Theil, *Economic Forecasts,* pp. 154–5, for a striking illustration and the following pages for an expert discussion.

46. A naïve yet frequent error is to start with the reversals of W and consider what proportion of them has been preceded by a reversal of V. Even if the proportion is large, the precursory value of a reversal of V will be very small if

V is reversed much more frequently than W, there being among the cases of reversals of V a majority of cases with no reversal of W. It is essential to start with the reversals of V, and, if they are followed by a reversal of W with great frequency, the sign is of significance as a presage.

47. The memoir by Clément Juglar, *Les Crises commerciales et leur retour périodique en France*, crowned by the Académie des Sciences Morales et Politiques in 1860, was published in 1862.

48. A bibliography of the subject would fill many pages. Geoffrey H. Moore has published two papers in the *Bulletin SEDEIS:* "L'appréciation de la conjecture," Suppl. No. 681A (September 1, 1951) and "La Vérification expérimentale des cycles," Suppl. 1, No. 841 (January 10, 1963).

49. This study was conducted by G. H. Matterdorf for the McGraw-Hill Economic Department and published in its bulletin of February 5, 1962.

50. *Business Cycle Developments*, a monthly publication of sixty-eight pages, for which Julius Shiskin, chief statistician of the Bureau of the Census, is responsible.

51. I have given a simple explanation of the method at the end of Moore's article in the *Bulletin SEDEIS* of September 1, 1957.

52. For a criticism of diffusion indexes, see S. S. Alexander, "Rate of Change Approaches to Forecasting: Diffusion Indexes and First Differences," *Economic Journal* (June 1958), and also Herman O. Stekler, "Diffusion Index and First Difference Forecasting," *Review of Economics and Statistics* (May 1961).

53. A compilation of these allocations is prepared by the National Industrial Conference Board.

54. These estimates have been regularly published for several years in the *Bulletin SEDEIS*.

55. James Tobin, "On the Predictive Value of Consumer Intentions and Attitudes," *Review of Economics and Statistics*, XLI: 1 (February 1959).

56. Arthur M. Okun, "The Value of Anticipations Data in Forecasting National Products," in a book brought out by the National Bureau of Economic Research, *The Quality and Economic Significance of Anticipations Data* (Princeton, N.J., 1961), which I will henceforth refer to as *Anticipations*.

57. George Katona, "Fifteen Years of Experience with Measurement of Consumer Expectations," *Proceedings (1962) of the Business and Statistics Section of the American Statistical Association.*

58. The division between Yes-Intenders and No-Intenders is a matter of definition. In the survey, the people were classified in four groups according to whether they announced they would 1. certainly buy; 2. probably buy; 3. possibly buy; or 4. had no intention of buying. The division between Yes-Intenders and No-Intenders was obtained by dividing group number 3 in half.

59. Okun gives a convenient formulation of this. Let p be proportion of Yes-Intenders in the sample, and $1 - p$ the proportion of No-Intenders. Further-

more, let r stand for the proportion of the sample consisting of Yes-Intenders who bought cars, and s stand for the proportion consisting of No-Intenders who bought cars. The proportion of car buyers in the sample will then be:

$$rp + s(1-p), \text{ or } s + (r-s)p$$

If the average value of r is greater than s over a long series of tests, a declaration of intention is significant.

60. The difference is partly explained by the downturn of the economy in 1960 and the upturn in 1961.

61. It would be relatively unimportant if the proportion of Yes-Intenders fluctuated considerably, for it is not surprising that changes in circumstances should discourage a variable proportion of Yes-Intenders.

62. This figure and the one immediately following apply to the two years taken together.

63. Any number of models can be constructed to explain this. The simplest model—not that I claim it is a good one—is based on the observation that consumers' expenditure on non-durable goods and services tends to increase more regularly than the disposable income. In the model, the remaining difference is treated as a residue available for savings or for purchases of durable goods, and it is assumed that the preference for one use rather than the other is a function of the size of the residue when the time comes to actually contract a purchase. Thus an error in predicting one's financial situation will be reflected in a modification of one's contemplated course of action. This model, however, is only one of a large number of possible explanations, which need to be tested by empirical observations.

64. For the prediction of car purchases, a "consumption function" would evidently not be sufficient. See Milton Friedman, *A Theory of the Consumption Function* (Princeton, N.J.: National Bureau of Economic Research, 1957), and for a clear survey see Sten A. O. Thore, *A Critique of the Theory of the Consumption Function* (Turin: Editions de l'Institut Universitaire d'Études Européenes, 1956). The number of car purchases is not connected to consumption expenditure (in real value) by a constant relationship. Regarding their fluctuations, see *Survey of Current Business* (September 1963), p. 24.

65. Franco Modigliani and Kalman J. Cohen, *The Role of Anticipations and Plans in Economic Behavior and Their Role in Economic Analysis and Forecasting* (Urbana, Ill., 1962).

66. Katona's analysis of consumer attitudes conforms to the tripartite model of solid, viscous, and volatile elements, several times presented in this book. Katona's classification comprises: 1. attitudes stable over a long period, corresponding to sociological norms acquired in childhood; 2. attitudes undergoing transformation, but at a sufficiently slow rate to be regarded as stable from one survey to the next; 3. attitudes highly sensitive to circumstances. (*Anticipations, op. cit.,* p. 61.)

67. *Anticipations, op. cit.,* pp. 44–51.

68. A curious feature of this document is that forecasts of the economy have played an increasingly less important part in it—a deficiency supplied by the forecasts of the National Institute of Economic and Social Research. It seems that Professor Stone's work at Cambridge on the elaboration of an econometric model is not much utilized.

69. Service des Études Economiques et Financières, founded by Claude Gruson.

70. This practice developed under Alfred Sauvy's tenure as president of the Commission: Jacques Dumontier is in charge of exposition and André Malterre of speculation.

71. *Étude des comptes de la nation* (*Comparaison des prévisions aux resultats pour les années 1953 à 1960*). A report presented on January 30, 1961, to the Conseil Économique et Social.

72. For instance, some old outline forecasts by Michel Vermot-Gauchy at the Division des Programmes, and the work of L. A. Vincent and others. But what is more, the S.E.E.F. has never, to my knowledge, published a methodological description of the way in which the Economic Budgets are prepared, although it has published a very complete one for the Accounts of the Nation.

73. I mean signposts guiding the mind. Pierre Massé has often stated that the four-year objectives do not imply that annual objectives forming a fixed proportion of the total must be attained.

74. The substance of the paragraph is derived from an excellent paper by Robert W. Adams in the *1962 Proceedings of the Business and Statistics Section of the American Statistical Association*, pp. 76–7.

75. Olaf Helmer and Nicholas Rescher, *On the Epistemology of the Inexact Sciences* (RAND Corporation, October 13, 1958). See also N. Dalkey and O. Helmer, *An Experimental Application of the Delphi Method to the Use of Experts* (RAND Corporation, 1962).

76. Condorcet, *Essai sur l'application de l'analyse à la probabilité des decisions rendues à la pluralité des voix* (Paris, 1785).

77. In 1960 I wrote a paper "On the Probability of Making the Right Decision" for my seminar at Berkeley.

17

Long-Term Economic
Forecasting and Its
Social Aspects

One of the chief tasks of economists in short-term economic forecasting is the preparation of estimates for the "coming year," a practice clearly deriving from the centuries-old routine of fiscal planning for a period of exactly one year. The origin of annual budgeting possibly goes back to yearly harvesting—but that is a matter of speculation outside the scope of our present inquiry. Economic forecasters, while paying tribute to the year as a unit for accounting, are too much aware of economic phenomena as "flows" to ignore how they will change from quarter to quarter or—if possible—from month to month: of especial importance is pinpointing the month when a now-accelerating flow will begin to decelerate, or vice versa.

Long-term forecasting (fifteen years or more) is quite a different exercise, with a different purpose, and this is the subject of the present chapter.

The reader may well ask: "Why have you skipped over medium-term planning (with a four- or five-year span)?" To this I could answer simply: "Planning is not forecasting." The objectives of a plan are "projects," in the precise and literal sense given to the word throughout this book—an object of desire cast by the imagination into a domain suited to receive it, the future. The dual nature of the future as a domain where we situate a "willed event" and where we make an inventory of "possibles" was sufficiently indicated in the opening chapters. In planning, we do not look for the most likely of the possibles but instead formulate what is wanted.

This answer is not fully satisfactory. Indeed, a plan is a forecast: it has to be. A plan is worthless unless it is feasible; it must lie within the field of "possible futures"; it is a "possible" that the mind singles out as the most valuable, and the probability of whose occurrence must be maximized. Thus a plan has a dual nature—it is both a "forecast" and a "project" (French experts like to speak of plans as "normative forecasts"). This fundamental ambiguity is of course what makes planning important; it differs from prevision in that it does not marshall possible futures according to their present likelihood but concentrates on one which is willfully chosen; it differs from wishful thinking in that the chosen future is feasible. It embodies the human struggle for an achievable best. But this also makes it a very intricate subject: anyone who has some experience with the planning process, and some capacity for self-criticism must admit that estimates of likelihoods are sensitive to personal preferences, which adds a complication to the technicalities of the subject.

Whatever theoretical arguments may be adduced for or against the inclusion of this subject, one overriding practical consideration demands its exclusion—planning is far too great a topic to be dealt with incidentally: if I tried to do so, I should be giving a pale echo of what has been said much better elsewhere.[1]

Besides, I must not dwell upon economic forecasting; it is admitted here on an auxiliary basis, and not as part of the main subject matter. Representing, as it does, the "advanced" sector of forecasting, it can supply us with ideas for the "underdeveloped" sectors forming our field of inquiry, that is, social and political forecasting. It was in this same spirit that the 1963 FUTURIBLES Symposium was entitled "From Economic Forecasting to Political Forecasting."[2]

The Recourse of the Economic Forecaster to Social Forecasting

The value of economic forecasting as a prototype must not be exaggerated. The "natural" conditions subscribing to the advance of forecasting in economics have been well identified by Pierre Massé:

We may say that it lies in the nature of things. Why? Because more than political life, economic life is subject to the combined forces of inertia and statistics.

Economic life has to do with the inertia of matter, the inertia of the transport and urban infrastructures: we are, as we can all see, prisoners of the rigidity of our cities. Economic life also has to do with the inertia of economic behavior. The behavior of men is modified very slowly; for example, the distribution of consumption expenditures between different goods and services unquestionably changes—but by evolution rather than by mutation. Furthermore, there is the inertia of economic laws. The economy obeys certain laws, and if one does not heed them, one has to pay the penalty, as, for example, with housing in France.

All these restraints create an environment giving economic life a certain continuity and conducive to the making of forecasts. In addition, economics —and I am thinking more particularly of those aspects related to planning —is primarily concerned with global variables: global production, global consumption, global investment. And as soon as global variables are studied, it can be observed that changes in them are governed by the law of large numbers. Moreover, the planner must take into account interrelationships that act as constraints limiting the freedom of his decisions and also the arbitrariness of his forecasts (the one goes with the other). This behavior of the planner is expressed by his use of projections. He makes projections into the future, and these are—to speak very schematically—extrapolations of tendencies observed in the past and corrected for factors that there is serious reason to believe will have a bending effect.[3]

But besides giving the conditions favorable for economic forecasting, Pierre Massé stressed that reliance on them is a fast-diminishing function of the time span envisaged: it is unsafe to project an observed trend far ahead, or to assume that structural relationships which have been found to obtain will hold for a long period. It is only in relation to a very near horizon that we can "predict" entirely on the basis of economic statistics, while if we wish to stretch our view further ahead, we must look for phenomena—in the realms of technology, politics, and psychological attitudes—that will impinge upon the economic system. Thus economic forecasting has, so to speak, a "short range of autonomy" beyond which an association with social and even political[4] forecasting becomes indispensable.

Economic Forecasting and Political Events

By speaking of the "range of autonomy" of economic forecasting, I mean that the economic forecaster is entitled to think about that space of time in terms of economic phenomena alone, but not, of course, that the economic future is itself autonomous within that period.

Economic forecasts, even if well reasoned within their own field, can prove quite wrong owing to the intervention of a political event: thus American forecasts for 1950 because of the Korean War; likewise French forecasts for 1950–51 (when the Korean boom led to growing exports, contracting imports, and wages shooting up). British, French, and American forecasts for 1957 went wrong because of the closure of the Suez Canal in October 1956. Indian forecasts for 1963 and 1964 were upset because the Chinese attack on the border in October 1962 caused the Delhi government, fearing a major renewal of this offensive, to divert part of its economic effort into military preparations. What is interesting about this last example is that the official experts went wrong through a change in the policy of their own (unchanged) government—a change which itself depended upon the inscription of a new possibility in the government's political forecast.

Also of great interest is the upsetting of French economic forecasts for 1962 and 1963, when the volume of private consumption suddenly outran the official estimates: the excess was in the same proportion as the sudden increase in population resulting from the mass flight of French settlers from Algeria to France. French economic experts had in fact foreseen this exodus, but, as it was government policy to deny that it would take place, they could not take its effect into account in their forecasts. Similar inhibitions are by no means rare in forecasting by civil servants; and this creates a problem because in most countries civil servants are the best-informed and best-qualified forecasters.[5] There is a general difficulty involved here, and the empirical rule to be followed is that the official economic expert is justified in treating a disturbance due to an extra-economic cause as an accident lying outside his province, unless he is specifically told to take that same cause into account.

On the contrary, in a long-term economic forecast, the expert must ponder the technological, social, and political changes able to deform the relations he employs.

A Simple Growth Model

In a long-term model of growth, reduced to its simplest form, the expert's "data" include: a hypothesis about the growth of population (giving him the number of parties involved in consumption); a related but different hypothesis about the growth of working population; a further hypothesis, related to the second, about the total number of man-hours worked; a hypothesis about the changing distribution of man-hours between the different sectors of the economy; and hypotheses about the output per man-hour in each sector. From these the expert obtains a hypothesis about the global growth of output. It is subject to criteria of coherence—each postulated output must be supplied with the needed inputs. The technological coefficients he uses in satisfying these criteria are functions of time; he would overestimate the fuel required for an estimated expenditure of energy if he did not allow for an improvement in the energy yield. Since the improvement is relatively continuous, the correction is not hard to make.

A major innovation such as the hovercraft is a different matter. The assumptions made about the probability and timing of its entry into regular use can have a considerable effect on estimates of how much a certain estimated growth in transport requirements will cost in infrastructures. The difference is particularly striking for countries where transport infrastructures are as yet little developed,[6] but is also significant for advanced countries.[7]

As to the social and political changes affecting production, the first thing to note is this: the expert cannot estimate the total man-hours to be supplied by the country's population at a future date[8] unless he makes social hypotheses about the reduction in the number of working hours in a year, and about the different rates of participation of men and women in the labor force in different age groups. In general, it can be assumed that a declining proportion of people under twenty will go to work because of more extensive schooling, and likewise a declining proportion of people over sixty because of better conditions for retirement, but such changes can vary considerably depending on political decisions.[9]

The conjectures about the work supplied by the indigenous population must be corrected to allow for immigration. The impact of the image of a "rich" life on poor countries will surely lead to much stronger flows of population as transport ceases to be a barrier. A great deal will depend, however, on the immigration policies of the advanced countries. The population of these countries will assume a different aspect according to whether they admit workers only on a temporary basis, or on a permanent basis, accompanied by their families.

The margin of doubt is much larger about the productivity than about the number of man-hours supplied. An output per man-hour rising at an annual rate of 4.25 per cent will double in seventeen years, whereas if its annual rate of increase is 2.5 per cent, it will increase by only one half over the same period. Thus the most essential hypothesis in a long-term forecast concerns the rate of increase in output per man-hour. On what does this increase depend? The first variable to which the expert turns is the growth of the capital investment per worker. Thus attention is drawn to the share of the Gross National Product representing capital formation: and hence to the social and political conditions tending to increase or decrease that share.[10] But a constant relationship between additions to the capital and additions to the output can by no means be assumed. This is intuitively obvious as soon as one thinks of the growth of national capital investment in terms of specific, discontinuous events, each corresponding to the introduction, into a different enterprise, of equipment which incorporates greater or smaller innovations, leads to more or less readily received changes in routines and requires more or less readily available talents.

The institutional structure may be such that the potential of certain enterprises will not be fully utilized because of the routines of enterprises above it and below it in the flow of production; L. A. Vincent has developed this point.[11] It can also happen that while technological progress changes the job structure the distribution of skills fails to respond, so that there will be a scarcity of some types of workers and a plethora of others. Such a disequilibrium is a barrier to the attainment of full employment.[12]

So far I have spoken only about production. Social forecasts are even more necessary in relation to consumption. It has become a habit among social scientists to use the questionable term "laws of consumption" when referring to what is known about the variation of household budgets as a function of income. By conducting a statistical study in a given year, it is possible to find how the percentage of the income reserved for a given expenditure shrinks or expands from one income level to the next; this percentage is called the "budgetary coefficient" of the expenditure. To find the elasticity of the expenditure, one calculates the ratio of the percentage change in the expenditure to the percentage difference in income. But we must ask whether results drawn from a study of average consumption expenditures at different income levels are applicable to changes taking place in time. Can static laws legitimately be treated as dynamic?[13] Are we to assume implicitly that families attaining a given income level in fifteen years' time will distribute their expenditures in the same way as families now at that level? And if we do not use "static elasticities," may we trust in "dynamic elasticities" observed in the past, and if so for how long? (A dynamic elasticity is the ratio between the percentage change in a given expenditure and the percentage increase in income over a period of time.)

A report submitted to the "Groupe 1985" of the French Plan[14] very sensibly says:

> The chief available statistical material consists of the time series of the national accounts. The series portray the effects of all factors that have influenced consumption. The factors generally cannot be isolated (because the series are too short and too imperfect, and at a deeper level, because the factors are too often interconnected, or in other words have too strong a collinearity). To make a projection under these conditions comes down, unavoidably, to the implicit admission that influences, following the same tendencies as in the past, will continue to exert themselves.

But simple projections suffice to raise great problems of social forecasting. For example, the foreseeable growth in the number of cars indicates that public expenditure attributable to traffic will have to expand enormously—the more so as the flow of vehicles is not the only problem to be solved. It is also necessary that children should play and workingmen sleep, and this will be impossible without extensive transformations, in which the slums now being built can have no place.

My only intention here was to indicate briefly how social forecasting is related to economic forecasting. The marriage of the two will perforce take place. We are witnessing no more than the first beginnings of long-term forecasting; therefore there is good reason to consider its first steps.

The First Steps

The first attempt at a long-term economic forecast[15] was probably that of Colin B. Clark,[16] whom one is not surprised to find yet again in the pioneering role he has played in so many ways. His attempt, undertaken entirely on his own initiative, remains the most daring in the field: what he aimed at was nothing less than a general picture of the world economy as it would be in 1960. Although Clark wrote his book during the war, his forecast covers, in effect, a period of twenty years, since he had to use prewar figures. His picture was based on the relationships of agriculture to industry and services.

Clark used an econometric model. Accordingly there was a risk of error in the structural equations, which a priori were not likely to remain invariant over a long period (particularly one marked by great upheavals from the very start). And there was also a risk of error in the exogenous variables, which included, it is worth noting, the rates of growth of productivity in agriculture, industry, and services. While it was impossible for his calculations to be correct, Clark's courageous venture affords us a precious means of comparing the prospects which seemed likely twenty years ago with the actual course of history.[17]

Clark rightly sensed the growth and spread of industrialization. Quite naturally, he inferred that the terms of trade of agricultural products would improve in relation to industrial products, but in actual fact the improvement has been far smaller than he anticipated.[18]

Clark deserves great credit for his very good forecast of the population explosion (at a time when others were so wide of the mark) and for his insight into postwar industrial expansion (when others expected a relapse into prewar stagnation). And in view of the scarcity of land, it is not surprising that he thought of agricultural output rising with greater difficulty to meet demand than industrial output; this explains why Clark expected so great an improvement in the terms of trade for agricultural products.

A similar sense of the pressure a growing and spreading industrial society exerts on natural resources provided the initial inspiration for the Paley Commission, only this time the natural resources concerned were raw materials and fuels. The commission was appointed by President Truman as a result of the boom in raw materials at the time of the

Korean War. The Paley Report, published in June 1952,[19] struck public opinion mainly through the graph on its first page, showing the annual per capita consumption of various primary products in the United States. At the time it was common knowledge that both Western and Eastern Europe aimed, in their different ways, to overtake the American standard of living, and there was increasing talk about the efforts of technically backward countries with vast growing populations to catch up. Thus the graph immediately brought to mind the enormous quantities of primary products that would be required as the average worldwide consumption rose toward the American level. The members of the Paley Commission did not abandon themselves to such fancies, however legitimate, and calculated as well as they could the foreseeable consumption up to 1975, finding that, on the whole, the required quantities could be obtained without difficulty and without increases in the unit cost. Professor Edward S. Mason, one of the members of the commission, has kindly given me this explanation of what was accomplished:

> You ask about projections of raw materials demands and supplies that were made at the time of the Report of the President's Materials Policy Commission. As a matter of fact, these projections for the most part have turned out to be not too far off the mark. There is, as you may know, an agency whose formation dates from the Report of the Commission, which does a good deal of work continuously on the raw materials situation. I refer to Resources for the Future, which has its offices in Washington. The Report of the Commission was concerned in its projections not only with prospective demand but also with availability of supplies. The examination of the supply situation turned pretty much on the question whether real costs per unit of output could be expected to change significantly. A good deal of work was done on the trend of real costs over the last few decades and these studies showed that with the exception of wood and timber products there has been very little, if any, increase in real cost per unit for raw materials despite the very rapid increase in demand. For a sizeable number of minerals the reserve position was also carefully studied in an attempt to foresee whether prospective declines in the grades of ores that might be available would lead to an increase in real costs per unit. Finally, we undertook a number of studies on the probable results of technological change on the supply and probable real costs of various minerals.[20]

The Paley Commission marked a date in the history of long-term forecasting: it was appointed by a public authority and had extensive means of investigation at its disposal. Its report was a pure forecast—a description of the probable trends—and differed in this respect from another document published in the same year, an introduction to India's first five-year plan,[21] in which a thirty-year period was considered in relation to an actively sought "possible."

Recent Efforts

Ten years lie between Colin Clark's book and the Paley Report; another ten went by before the inception of two major endeavors. One of them was initiated in June 1961 by the British Minister of Transport, Ernest Marples, who appointed a working group to consider the impact of the automobile upon towns in the long-term perspective. Their conclusions were published in the "Buchanan Report."[22] The other was initiated in November 1962 by the French Plan Commissioner, Pierre Massé, who picked eleven people—who were then formally appointed by the prime minister—to form the "Groupe 1985," giving them the widest possible terms of reference: namely, to consider the social promises and problems arising from the economic development expected from technological applications and productivity gains. I must confine myself here to a discussion of the Buchanan Report.*

The Buchanan Report

We cannot *fore*see the future in the same way that we see the present scene, with all its concrete details. But it is not too difficult for us to depict the deformations made in the scene by a strong current crossing it and regarded by us as a future datum. The growth in number and circulation of cars is a good example of such a current; it exerts a seeable and foreseeable pressure on towns—the scene of human existence. The visible pressure creates problems, but our response to them is in danger

---

*Translator's note: The author was a member of the Groupe 1985. Its labors were still in progress when he wrote the French version of this book, and he did not feel at liberty to discuss them. Nor could he deal with them now in the space of a few paragraphs.

of being inadequate if we neglect the future growth of traffic flows. Circulation in urban areas is a long-term problem.

The Buchanan Report accepts the increase in the number of motor vehicles as a material datum of the future: the number increased from 4.9 million (including 2.5 million cars) in 1952, to 10.5 million (including 6.5 million cars) in 1962; the prospective growth is by 7.5 million vehicles (including 5.7 million cars) between 1962 and 1970, and by 9 million vehicles (including 7 million cars) between 1970 and 1980. The working group peered ahead as far as the year 2010, when they think saturation will be reached: by that time, for a population of 74 million, there should be 30 million cars (against 6.5 million in 1962), 4 million motorcycles (against 1.9 million), and 6 million utility vehicles (against 2.1 million). These figures show just how important the individual's desire to own an automobile is. As the authors indicate very well, car-ownership is a manifest social will. Made up by the addition of individual autonomous wills, this social will is constant in a way that the majority will expressed in elections is not. It provides a basis on which forecasts can be made. Men want and will want to own cars and use them. Owning cars depends on the growth of incomes; using them is an entirely different matter.

Using automobiles in a structured environment not designed for them —there lies the difficulty. It leads to environment deterioration and traffic flow obstruction. Whatever the distribution of total road mileage between urban and rural areas, it is clear that more and more vehicle-hours are spent on roads in towns than on roads outside towns. Yet according to the Buchanan Report, the average speed of traffic in large cities is 11 mph— a figure slightly smaller than the average speed of horse-drawn vehicles in New York in 1907.[23] This fact indicates how absurd it is to build cars capable of attaining speeds drivers can use only on rare occasions, and too often with harm resulting. The improvement of the services performed by the motor vehicle does not require any further development in the machine[24] but a radical alteration of the roads open to traffic. The problem does not, however, come down to "making traffic move."

Cars wreck towns—at a time when towns provide the living environment of a rapidly growing majority of the population, they are losing their traditional virtues. Once children played in streets, friends and lovers strolled along them, old folk gossiped in them. None of these benefits subsists now that the automobile has taken over from man. These amenities have been lost without any equivalent being substituted (a loss not reflected in the national accounts). It is particularly shocking insofar as children are affected: most children now grow up in towns, but they are given nowhere to play. We should ask whether this is not a source of psychological disturbance.

While certain traditional functions of streets cannot be restored to them once they become a channel for the flow of vehicles, certain minimal conditions must still be satisfied if there are to be riparian inhabitants or workers. Men must not be irritated by vibrations, overcome by fumes, and dazed by noise. One has to distinguish between the traffic physically possible and the traffic psychologically bearable. This distinction is funda- mental in the Buchanan Report; it is not sufficient to consider the flow the road can be made to bear, without considering the pressure the en- vironment can take and the men living and working there tolerate.

The natural result of this useful distinction is to isolate, at one extreme of the spectrum, large traffic arteries that serve exclusively as distributors and are well separated from houses and offices, and at the other, environ- mental areas from which traffic is excluded and to which pedestrians alone are admitted. The report presents an appealing image of a "traffic architecture" in which accessways and buildings are treated together as part of a global conception—buildings are easy of access, while their amenities and aesthetic qualities are protected. The essential task, however, is the adaptation of the towns now existing, a problem the working group studied in terms of specific cases.

They took a small town, Newbury (assuming for it a population of 37,000 by 2010, with a hinterland population of roughly the same size); a large town, Leeds (assuming its population would remain at roughly 500,000); a historic town, Norwich, with important architectural sites needing to be preserved (with a population of 200,000 by 2010); and finally a commercial area in central London adjoining Oxford Street and covering an area of 148 acres (with 9,000 people now living in it and 50,- 000 people working there). In each case, the experts considered the present traffic and estimated the growth of traffic "desired" by 2010. They tried to solve the problem of accommodating this traffic while providing an acceptable environment for human beings. At the same time they stressed that the problem is urgent since the bulk of the traffic increase will take place before 1980. Specific redevelopment plans are offered for each town. In fact the experts give a fan of projects because they acknowledge that the most adequate project in each case might seem too ambitious. They accordingly consider various less costly alternatives, but warn that the smaller the scale of reconstruction, the more vehicle usage must be curtailed:

> The broad message of our report is that there are absolute limits to the amount of traffic that can be accepted in towns, depending upon their size and density, but up to these limits, provided a civilized environment is to be retained or created, the level of vehicular accessibility a town can have depends on its readiness to accept and pay for the physical changes required. The choice is society's. *But it will not be sensible, nor indeed for long be possible for society to go on investing apparently unlimited sums in the purchase and running of motor vehicles without investing equivalent sums in the proper accommodation of the traffic that results* [the italics are mine]. . . . There seems to be an issue here which society must face, for at present the two investments are getting further and further apart. All the indications are that to deal adequately with traffic in towns will require works and expenditure on a scale not yet contemplated.

While it is indispensable and urgent to cope with the growth of car-ownership by rearrangements that are very costly, the authors of the report believe it is no less important to contain the flood of cars while reconstruction proceeds. They considered a number of measures for restraining the use of private cars in towns, the simplest and most liberal of which is the levy of a high parking charge. They emphatically assert as a *principle* that the owner who stops his car on a public road is responsible for the inconvenience he causes and must be suitably taxed by the public authority. It is not the levy that is unjust but its absence. The use of road space is a concession: the public authority is entitled to charge for it by the hour or, on a subscription basis, by the month; differentiate the charges as it sees fit (with a monthly system of payment it could charge according to the size of the vehicle); and exempt whom it likes (for example doctors). The authors believe public transport must be encouraged, thinking it reasonable to subsidize public transportation, so as to attract users and warn about the danger (already apparent in California) of letting it deteriorate as the use of private cars grows—the only result of a cut in public transportation services is an even greater use of private cars.

The Buchanan Report introduces some interesting methods of technical study, but these do not form part of my subject. It is particularly interesting as a forecast because it is based on a future material development that is pre-formed in a psychological attitude treated, with good reason, as a persisting "force"—the wish to own a car. It forecasts the pressures resulting from this development and offers various ways of meeting them. One must choose between these ways; there is a problem of decision, or rather a multiplicity of particular problems of decision arising from the major decision about what general attitude to adopt.

Long-Term Global Forecasting

The Buchanan Report affords an example of a long-term forecast starting from a particular phenomenon whose growth is postulated. The "natural" effects of the phenomenon are looked for, and proximate problems of decision relating to effects more or less remote are posed. To try to represent the whole future scene is more ambitious: surely we are in danger of losing ourselves when we look for causes now present which will affect the future, and even more when we try to imagine what further causes will arise in the meantime. In the first rank of causes rising ahead, there must be a place for spontaneous reactions to the various future situations, as well as for actions deliberately taken to avoid an obstacle glimpsed on the horizon or to hasten progress toward a goal chosen on the horizon, or, more generally, to improve the social itinerary. Consequently, a long-term global forecast presupposes the analysis of all present factors and the self-prediction of future decisions taken distributively or collectively.

There seems to be only one way of making this problem manageable: that is, to start from a heavy tendency, as in the Buchanan Report, except the tendency must be much more general, and to assume that future decisions will be adapted to this tendency. In fact all long-term forecasts count on human societies having a growing technology at their disposal, and on a "general will" to utilize the available techniques. That is to say, they implicitly rest on one fundamental prediction: social and political decisions will be directed toward exploitation of the possibilities afforded by the sciences of nature.

Depending on how long a period the forecaster wishes to consider, he will confine himself to considering techniques which are already economically feasible, or also take into account those now in the laboratory stage of development, or go on to consider those whose development is now conceivable. In short, according to the horizon he has chosen, he will be content with an inventory of the techniques at hand, or he will guess at those which science may generate.[25] It is interesting to consider the various techniques which have traveled a greater or smaller distance toward acceptance inasmuch as individual techniques have specific social consequences. Forecasters often use a cruder approach; they content themselves with treating the "technological input" as a lump factor guaranteeing a certain rate of growth of labor productivity, provided that an adequate rate of capital investment permits the "embodiment" of the technological input. But even when the specific features of technological change are ignored, and it is treated merely as a quantitative factor, the anticipated growth of output still leads to forecasts of the associated structural and qualitative changes.

For example, consider the very likely hypothesis of a rapid growth of French agricultural productivity, disregarding the techniques responsible for this growth. The demand for products supplied by farmers[26] remains very inelastic as the per capita national income rises, and it is therefore reasonable to infer that the agrarian sector of the population will shrink considerably. A social group becoming a small minority after thousands of years as a strong majority is clearly a far-reaching change in the structure of society. As recently as the eighteenth century, labor was essentially linked with the soil (the meaning of *laboureur* in French is a survival of this), and there was no idea it could be otherwise. How significant are the delightful names given to the months in the Revolutionary calendar adopted by the National Convention in 1793! The intention was to make the calendar reflect the concerns of workingmen, and this meant "consecrating agriculture by means of the calendar." Among the many noted men of science who helped to prepare this reform, not one suspected that the working population was to be divorced from agriculture, that the majority would forsake the world of plants for a world of machines, moving from a peasant state subject to organic forces to a salaried state subject to organization. Surely this dwindling of the agrarian population is the most fundamental phenomenon in social history.

Alongside this contraction, we may consider the expansion of personnel in education and research—an expansion related to economic growth both as cause and as effect. If the economy is to grow rapidly, research must expand considerably,[27] and a vast teaching program must be set up so that workers' qualifications shall keep apace with techniques and equipment.[28] But, in return, society cannot put its growing wealth to better use than by devoting every care to cultivating the faculties of the rising generation: as the young look forward to more and more leisure, it is more and more important for them to have enough culture to spend their leisure well.[29] Therefore, it seems fairly likely that the "cultivators of minds" will be as numerous as the cultivators of the land. And we sense straight away how different a society with that demographic structure will be. Thus quantitative considerations are by themselves sufficient for us to derive structural forecasts. D'Arcy W. Thompson said:

> Every growing organism, and every part of such a growing organism, has its own specific rate of growth, referred to this or that particular direction; and it is by the ratio between these rates in different directions that we must account for the external forms of all save certain very minute organisms. This ratio may sometimes be of a *simple* kind, as when it results in the mathematically definable outline of a shell, or the smooth curve of the margin of a leaf. It may sometimes be a very *constant* ratio, in which case the organism while growing in bulk suffers little or no perceptible change in form; but such constancy seldom endures beyond a season, and when the ratios tend to alter, then we have the phenomenon of morphological "development," or steady and persistent alteration of form.[30]

I shall not develop these themes here, proposing to treat the forecasting of forms elsewhere. But I had to indicate that quantitative hypotheses of a very summary sort, such as the rate of growth of production per man or per man-hour, can entail forecasts of morphological modifications. One is led into forecasting changes in the structure of production, the administration of jobs, and the organization of education. Coherency constraints appear, but simultaneously choices offer themselves to us. For example, should we move our greatly expanded university population outside large towns, as is done in England and America? And how should we house families—by massing them together in large buildings or by dispersing them in small houses?

More generally, the needs man exhibits as society grows richer are to a decreasing extent natural ones, and to an increasing extent needs generated by the situation in which he is placed. Consequently, we may ask where the technological process is taking man in order to foresee his needs. But in considering the long term, we may also reverse the question and ask what needs, felt and gratified, will best contribute to man's fulfilling himself; in what situations should he be placed so that he shall feel these needs rather than others; and is it possible, and if so, how, to direct him toward the most fitting situations?

To put it quite simply, we are not reduced to merely asking where the technological process is taking us. We can also ask, and surely must ask, how we can best contrive the process for the flourishing of the *plant man.* Long-term forecasting is, naturally and even inevitably, normative.

NOTES

1. Pierre Massé's paper at the 1962 Congress of the International Economic Association in Vienna is worth singling out from an abundant literature. For a good discussion of procedures, see E. Betout-Mossé in *Études de comptabilité nationale,* No. 4 (1963).

2. The Symposium was held in Paris from July 6 to July 8, 1962; it was opened by Pierre Massé and Claude Gruson. A quotation from my foreword to the symposium is of some relevance here: "The intellectual moment of these names may give a wrong impression of the nature of our conference. Economic forecasting as such does not form part of our agenda. We have invited Pierre Massé and Claude Gruson in order to emphasize from the start the contrast forming the basis of our conference.

"Economic forecasting is a well-established discipline, regularly practiced by recognized experts, who have an enlightened audience and work with caution, as befits economic scientists. These experts use explicit methods, which have been much discussed at international gatherings and in an extensive literature.

"None of these traits is characteristic of social forecasting, and still less of political forecasting. The whole object of our conference is to reduce a little the enormous difference now existing between economic forecasting, an advanced technology, and social and political forecasting, both backward technologies.

"Can social forecasting and political forecasting become disciplines as well-established as economic forecasting, and if so, how? That is the point of our conference. Economic forecasting is meant to serve as an introduction both stimulating and suggestive. The experts who will speak to us about economic forecasting on Saturday morning will stimulate sociologists and political scientists to emulate them; they will show that the lack of social and political forecasting is a handicap in long-term economic forecasting; and they will indicate that the intellectual procedures used in economic forecasts provide many suggestions for the elaboration of methods of forecasting in the social and political domains."

3. Pierre Massé, "De l'incertitude économique à l'incertitude politique," the opening address at the 1963 FUTURIBLES Symposium, printed as *Futuribles,* No. 69, *Bulletin SEDEIS* (December 10, 1963).

4. Pierre Massé mentions the hypothesis of European political unity as an example.

5. We should note the difficult situation in which the government expert finds himself if his forecasts indicate a big price rise at a time when the government is trying to keep prices down. If the expert released his figures, he would be accused of helping to push prices up.

6. I spoke about this possibility at the Geneva Conference of 1962. An important article by Jean Bertin has since come to my attention. He says:

"In certain regions of the globe . . . there are virtually no roads or railways, and the high cost of building them is often boosted still higher by climatic conditions (such as heavy rains). To get transport going, the use of hovercraft traveling over rough running tracks or 'roads' is worth contemplating. In most cases, these 'roads' can be built with bulldozers, and an approximate leveling of irregularities (forests, rocks, and river edges) is all that is required. No tamping of road materials is necessary, and no bridges need be built since hovercraft can travel over water. Despite the weak consistency of the soil, high speeds (60 to 80 km/hr) can be attained with very little metal fatigue; this would not be the case with vehicles riding on wheels.

"The mobility and flexibility of such a system of transport could be of vital importance for the new countries. Only a very small investment of capital is required initially, and when roads and railways are eventually opened, they can be located along the true lines of force of the traffic. These can be studied over a sufficient period of time, without the growth of the economy being endangered by an absence of means of transport or by heavy expenditures on them" (J. Bertin, "Les Vehicules à coussin d'air," *Revue de l'X* [June 1963].)

7. For example, experiments on using hovercraft for Channel crossings may indicate that the traffic needs could be met by this means instead of a tunnel or a bridge. An enormous investment would be required for either of the latter projects, and this seems absurd when underground transport facilities for everyday journeys are lacking in most large towns in England and France.

8. The number of "natives" who will be old enough to work can be known long in advance by simply displacing the cohorts now in existence through time (and allowing for the number of deaths in each).

9. See Michel Vermot-Gauchy, "La Planification à long terme: vers de nouvelles méthodes d'études," in three parts: *Futuribles* No. 53 (April 10, 1963), *Futuribles* No. 54 (April 20, 1963), and *Futuribles* No. 55 (May 1, 1963). Vermot-Gauchy believes that the population of France will increase by more than 14 per cent between 1959 and 1975, but that, depending on the hypothesis, the total number of man-hours devoted to production will decrease by 6 to 18 per cent.

10. Regarding the underdeveloped countries, see my paper, "Aspects sociaux et politiques du développement économique," *Futuribles,* No. 28 (April 20, 1962).

11. L. A. Vincent discusses this in his important paper of February 1960: "La Prévision économique à long terme: essai sur la méthode" (INSEE).

12. In America this imbalance now obtains in many skilled jobs.

13. M. Fournier, "Lois de consommation statistiques et dynamiques," *Études de comptabilité nationale*, No. 2 (S.E.E.F.).

14. By J. Delors.

15. So unquantified a prediction as the one by Edmond Théry in the preface to his *La Transformation économique de la Russie* (1912) does not count: "If, in the great European nations, things continue in the same way from 1912 to 1950 as they have from 1900 to 1912, then by the middle of the century Russia will dominate Europe politically, economically, and financially."

16. Colin B. Clark, *The Economics of 1960* (London: Macmillan, 1942).

17. There is a sketch, much too brief, of such a comparison in K. C. Kogiku, "The Economics of 1960 Revisited," *Review of Economics and Statistics* XLII: 4 (November 1960). The tone of this paper is much too critical, for my liking, of an enterprise whose daring commands respect. But one of Kogiku's criticisms is, I think, of major importance for the philosophy of the subject: "The main difficulty seems to be that Clark's model is static; its structural equations do not contain time, and theoretically his model is to hold at any point in time as well as in 1960. . . . His static model does not accommodate [his] dynamics of growth." In other words, the relations set forth in the structural equations are supposed to be invariant, which they are not.

18. The question of the terms of trade was extensively discussed at the 1962 Vienna Conference of the International Economic Association.

19. *The President's Report on Raw Materials* (5 vols.; Washington, D.C., 1952).

20. Personal letter from Edward S. Mason to the author, dated Harvard, June 19, 1962.

21. *India's First Five-Year Plan* (New Delhi, November 1952).

22. *Traffic in Towns: A Study of the Long-Term Problem of Traffic in Urban Areas* (London: H. M. Stationery Office, 1963).

23. The fact about New York is taken from Lewis Mumford, *The City in History* (New York: 1947), p. 550.

24. Car races have become absurd, for the qualities that count in them have little to do with cars for the general public, which are the only cars that matter. It is indefensible to subsidize the manufacture of racing cars instead of spending the money on sport.

25. On techniques that science may in time generate, see T. J. Gordon and Olaf Helmer's *Report on a Long-Range Forecasting Study* issued by RAND Corporation.

26. This must not be confused with consumers' expenditure on food products. The consumption of food products remains highly elastic at high levels of per

capita national income, but as Kuznets has shown for the United States, this is a result of the growing importance of processing, handling, and transport. The demand for the food products in their primary state has a very low elasticity. References are given in *Étude SEDEIS*, No. 874, Suppl. 1 (January 10, 1964).

27. See Abraham Moles, "La Cité scientifique en 1972," *Futuribles*, No. 41 (October 20, 1962) and P. C. Mahalanobis, "Les bases scientifiques du développement économique," *Futuribles*, No. 57 (May 20, 1963).

28. Some very reliable American experts regard the lag in technical training as a determining factor of present unemployment in the United States.

29. Of all the waking hours facing a youth of seventeen, he can now count on spending 25 per cent of them at work, with the remaining 75 per cent free (except for time spent commuting). A rough calculation for the United States, in "Toward a Political Theory of Education," an essay contributed by the present author to *Humanistic Education and Western Civilization*, ed. A. A. Cohen (New York, 1964).

30. D'Arcy W. Thompson, *On Growth and Form* (Cambridge, Eng., 1942), p. 82.

Part V

TOWARD THE
SURMISING FORUM

18

The Political Order
and Foreseeability

Society and economics determine one another. Economic forecasting and social forecasting provide each other mutual help, and in certain respects, it seems, merge into one. Political forecasting is quite another matter. Men think it is easy insofar as they think political change follows of necessity from social change, particularly since the latter, a slow and heavy process, lends itself to forecasting. Is it here perhaps that the way of overcoming the difficulty men have always encountered in political forecasting is to be found? Not according to Hume:

> It affords a violent prejudice against every science, that no prudent man, however sure of his principles, dares prophesy concerning any event, or *foretell* the remote consequences of things. A physician will not venture to pronounce concerning the condition of his patient a fortnight or a month after. And still less dares a politician foretell the structure of political affairs a few years hence. HARRINGTON thought himself so sure of his general principle, *that the balance of power depends on that of property*, that he ventured to pronounce it impossible ever to re-establish monarchy in ENGLAND: but his book was scarcely published when the king was restored. . . .[1]

A hundred years later, at the time of the Second Empire, Prévost-Paradol asserted that the democratization of society was an ineluctable, irreversible process, however it might unfold. But for a society to be or become democratic was one thing, and for its government to be or become democratic was another. A democratic society with an undemocratic government was perfectly possible, and the irreversible course observed in social transformation was by no means observed in political transformation:

> But whether the transformation of an aristocratic into a democratic society be slow or prompt, violent or peaceful, this transformation is nonetheless inevitable and, once accomplished, irrevocable. More than once a society may pass through all the extremes of anarchy and servitude, abolish thrones then raise them up only to abolish them again, effect abrupt revolutions in dress and language, affect in turn republican austerity or the servile flabbiness of the Eastern Roman Empire; but a river would sooner flow back to its source than a democratic society revert to aristocracy.[2]

Throughout his book, Prévost-Paradol linked the idea of continuity in the social system with the idea of unstable equilibrium in the political regime.

I would not, of course, claim to adequately treat an important subject simply by quoting two authors, but wish only to stress that a political forecast is not given to us as a bonus once we have completed an economic and social forecast to the best of our ability. It is worth returning to an example I have already discussed so that this point shall be better grasped.

In 1932 the United States and Germany, two great industrial powers, were affected in like measure by an economic crisis so acute that nearly one worker in three was jobless, the youngest being particularly hard hit. The governments, powerless to remedy these intolerable social situations, were clearly condemned, and great political changes were called for. These political changes were, largely, foreseeable, given the social necessity, which was identical in both countries. Men had to be put back to work, and for this a policy actively pursued by the state was urgently required. The obstacles in 1932 were neither ill-will nor vested interests (which, on the contrary, were endangered by the situation) but convictions nurtured by academic orthodoxy and honestly held by political and economic leaders as well as by men in high administrative positions. In this state of paralysis by conviction, there could be no energetic action without a new and heretical personnel, animated by determination if not by doctrine. In taking bold measures, this personnel would come into conflict with existing institutions and would be unable to carry through their measures without strengthened executive powers. It was easy to foresee that in these two countries—both possessed of federal constitutions—the federal government, the source of effort, would acquire powers to the detriment of the rights of the individual states.

This much of the political order was foreseeable from the social order. In a word, what could be foreseen was what Rooseveltism and Hitlerism had *in common.* Surely nobody would regard the difference between the two as insignificant. In relation to social economy, Hitlerism bore an initial similarity to Roosevelt's New Deal, and were it not for Hitler's passion-ruled policies, clearly the history of the world would be far different and far better. Why did Germany not have a German Roosevelt in 1933 instead of Hitler? I very much doubt that even an *ex post* social forecast can answer this question.

Think of the social characteristics of the two men in relation to the social characteristics of their respective countries at that particular time. One of the men belonged to a patrician and consular family of wealth and renown whose forebears were founders of the nation. The other, a nobody (*Homo novissimus*), was not even native-born. The former had received an excellent education, the latter was virtually self-taught.

I know I have already given this example[3] but I have no hesitation in using it again, for it shows how imprudent it is to derive a political prediction from social vision alone. Had we predicted a "Roosevelt-like" government when in fact a Hitler came to power, we would have little grounds for satisfaction with our prediction.[4]

Such an intellectual procedure is dangerous, for it is imbued with systematic optimism. It leads us into thinking that events in the political order fit the needs of the social economy, and since these needs can be grasped by rational analysis, we end up assuming that politics is the rational adjuvant of social change—an assumption which unfortunately is without foundation. Anti-Semitism in no way corresponded to the social needs of Germany, was irrelevant to its economic crisis, and with regard to diplomatic and military relations with foreign powers, was harmful to the national interests of the Reich and the special interests of the Nazi regime. Without this frenzied policy, it is not certain Germany would have been at war with the United States, and it is possible Germany would have been the first power to possess the atom bomb.

Nor is it necessary to refer to the past in order to see political passions causing a diversion from the course of things that might be foreseen from social economy alone. The Arab countries of the Middle East have a great lack of scientific and technical experts, of whom there is a great abundance in the neighboring state of Israel. By using these available talents, the Arab countries would save several years of economic growth, but for political reasons such a move is unthinkable.

"Politics has its own reasons which do not pertain to social economy." To ignore them or weigh them insufficiently is to condemn oneself to grave errors of judgment and forecasting. Hence it seems that political forecasting demands a large degree of intellectual autonomy: political history is not pre-formed in the material transformations of society. The proliferation of Caesarism in a multitude of states with very different social situations serves to confirm this impression.[5]

I fear that what is said here may be misconstrued, for the terms "political" and "social" are ambiguous. The "social forecasting" discussed here is the forecasting of big, slow changes in society, connected with economic and technological changes. I am warning against a simple deduction of political regimes or policies from these structural changes. This is not to say that such changes do not affect politics, but that our knowledge or forecasts of such changes do not entail necessary political forecasts. Our forecasts based on the growth and exploitation of technology do not lead to certainty about the political domain and do not entitle us to treat political change as an epiphenomenon.

I do not propose to tackle here the subject of political forecasting as such[6] but rather to turn it upside down: instead of discussing the forecasting of political change, I will stress that it is a main function of the political order to afford conditions favorable to the making of nonpolitical forecasts. Any sort of forecasting relies upon a presumed foreknowledge of some aspects of the future—the public authorities provide us with such foreknowledge in that their control of society aims at securing certain aspects of the future; thereby the public authorities serve us as guarantors of foreseeability.

There are many traits of the future for which the authorities stand surety, whether by implicit underwriting (the old way) or by explicit promise (the new way). The enumeration of these traits for a given government at a given time is as good a way as any of describing its character; one will find very different mixtures of traits to be preserved and traits to be achieved (targets). Now consider forward speculation on behalf of any discrete part of society, be it a family, a firm, or a social group. Every guaranteed trait of the future affords a support for intellectual speculation, but also constitutes a constraint upon the group's prospects. It follows that while a foreknown always has positive value, as information, it may, in the eyes of a given group, have such negative value as a constraint that the group is willing to trade that item of information against more hope. A prudent government will be responsive to pressures arising on that score, and this will induce the authorities not to multiply the foreknowns it guarantees beyond necessity.

But it may also happen that pressure develops against a guaranteed trait of the future which the rulers believe plays a key role in the whole structure of information they provide, in which case the pressure may result in a conflict whose first consequences is to topple the whole set of assurances. A brutal political discontinuity brings a period of utter uncertainty. These summary remarks may suggest that this view of government as an aid to forecasting by members of society could lead us back to the means of forecasting the fate of a particular government. But this is not our present concern.

Men would dispense with political power if they could, because of the harm it is capable of wreaking. But they can do so only in small and primitive societies.[7] Authority must become greater as society grows in size and complexity.[8] There is a reason for this, and it is relevant to our subject: in a small, traditional society, a man meets no one he does not know; men are linked to one another by familiar customs. This is not so in a large, mixed society. The more the society is mixed, the more a man needs to know what to expect of the unlike-seeming stranger. He needs a security for and against the behavior of "another." The more the society is changing, the greater is the number of innovations in men's behavior, and the more definitions of legitimate expectations are needed.[9] The government assumes responsibility; this is why we may call it a "guarantor for foreseeability"—a role which in our age we have seen extended into new domains (social security and full employment).

We have no need to base the whole order on authority, in the manner of Hobbes, in order to recognize that authority is conservative. Conservative of what?—of an order which is changing and into which Authority introduces changes. The nature of the "social guarantee"[10] given by the state for our legitimate expectations continues in principle unchanged, while the content of these expectations changes. And since we know that their content will change, without knowing the how or when of it, uncertainty prevails. In other words, the state, which is the guarantor of certainties, is also the instigator of uncertainty. Generally speaking, if it seems likely the future will differ from the past, we think it is desirable that this future should be a foreknown of which we are warned, rather than an unknown "something or other." Accordingly, we are that much more inclined to grant the state powers of dominating this future; but these powers can only be powers over us, and the greater these powers, the more public decisions matter to us. A public decision projects uncertainty until it is known. And this uncertainty is, in a sense, drained from society and gathered up in the state, attaching to all its decisions.

Let us put things somewhat differently. Any power is a power over the future, a capacity for action affecting the future. In consequence, compelled as we are to conjecture the future so that we may make deliberate use of the minute power belonging to us individually, we must foresee the use that will be made of other powers, and pay particular attention to concentrated and weighty powers, rather than to powers on our own scale of action. An unpredictable authority is therefore worse than no authority at all.

A Regular Political System

For the above reasons, a regular state may be defined by this characteristic: its decisions are known a long time in advance. This condition obtains if, between their proposition and their promulgation, decisions pass slowly and openly through a long process of public discussion. Suddenly announced decisions are the infallible mark of an arbitrary state. The only occasion for a sudden decision in a regular state is peril from abroad. Except in such an event, decisions must never be published unexpectedly, and must be formed ostensibly rather than occultly. Where declarations of a head of state or leader of the government are awaited as revelations, there—indubitably—the system is despotic rather than regular.

This criterion for distinguishing between a regular system and an arbitrary one presents two advantages: it is easy to apply; and it gives an empirical justification for why our preference ought to go to a regular rather than an arbitrary system. If authority—the guarantor of foresee-ability—is itself unforeseeable, it is the author of an evil that it should be preventing.

Political uncertainty is uncertainty about public decisions, and about the use authority will make of the ways and means at its disposal. Political uncertainty is small in England, where most of what there is of mystery attaches to one object—the red dispatch box the Chancellor of the Exchequer carries with him into Commons on the day of the Budget Speech. It is worth noting that in this speech the Chancellor speaks in the first person singular: and indeed, on this occasion, he has taken his decisions in secret, as in a system of personal power. But his decisions—kept secret for financial reasons—produce nothing more than marginal changes. If the Chancellor wished to make a radical change, as for instance, the introduction of a tax on wealth, he would prepare public opinion for it (as the last "Shadow Chancellor" started to do while still of the Opposition party) and would set up a Royal Commission, which after examining the pros and cons would eventually publish a Blue Book containing a majority report and possibly a minority report as well.

There is only one important uncertainty in the British political order, and that is a systematic uncertainty to do with general elections. But consider how small that uncertainty is. It concerns a simple alternative: either this same party will remain in power, or it will be the turn of that party sitting in the benches on the opposite side of the House. The Opposition is almost as well known as the government:[11] its program is public, the changes it has promised are known. Nor is the alternative to the present government all that is known, since by studying opinion polls and the results of by-elections and local elections psephologists can predict the results of general elections with good chances of success.

The Conditions of Political Foreseeability

Let us try to single out some definitive characteristics of the British system. First, *procedures are sacred*—whether in the exercise of justice, or in judiciary appointments, or in the making and execution of decisions. As more rules are observed, so is the system better defined and the guarantees it affords more numerous. It is a great and dangerous madness to think that an abstract principle can define a system and afford guarantees. Sovereignty of the people assorts with sauces of all kinds, as Benjamin Constant noted long ago, and his observation is still true today.

Secondly, there is an *intention common to all active participants in political life* to faithfully maintain the accepted procedures. There can be no question of acceding to power by illegal means, nor of exercising power by other than known procedures. People often talk about "observing the rules of the game": this long-familiar expression has acquired added force now that we are acquainted with game theory. As I noted in a previous chapter, game theory presupposes a universe in which possible actions are well defined, but ordinary life does not satisfy this condition. In a regular system, men deliberately enclose themselves in a universe with restricted possibilities. And this entails a greatly improved foreseeability.

Thirdly, *the stakes are limited.* The participants accept from the very start that they will not make all the changes they would like, even if they can make them by regular procedures. This "minimalism" is an indispensable condition for preservation of the system, because if one party was to set about doing everything it wanted by the regular ways and means, it would drive the other into reacting by irregular means. In pushing one's opponent to the limit, one motivates his acts of despair and so becomes partly responsible for them.

Under conditions of a maximalist use of power, rules might nonetheless remain inviolate, and parties might succeed one another in regular alternation. But in such a situation there would be great swing-abouts of policy, reflected, in the long run, in the tottering course of affairs of state.

The little I have said suffices to show how very "artificial" a regular system is—which is in fact a tribute to the system. "Natural" politics consists of doing just what one likes to the full extent of one's capacity. In other words, "natural" politics is arbitrariness unlimited save by the world of fact. An "artificial" system is fragile: always present is the danger of a conquering band of maximalists brutally simplifying the system. By way of analogy, we may think of two (or more) tribes which are accustomed to jockey with one another for the positions of command, displaying neither violence nor spite, when, suddenly, they are swept away by a warlike tribe, which to gain its ends has contracted alliances with various peaceful tribes and then treats its allies no better than the others.

Men Have Always Sought Political Foreseeability

"But your model is simply the British system once again. For the past two hundred years you and your likes seem to have been unable to dish up anything better." The reason for this is that for two centuries and more England has offered a system better regulated, more resistant, and more flexible than any other.

Before the British system there was another model of a regular system —the French monarchy. Foreseeability was assured by the principle of legitimacy, which comes down to this idea: "Long ours, and hence rightfully ours." Long-standing possession of power constituted a right to power, transmitted through the male line according to the system of primogeniture. It would be wrong to underrate the guarantee of civil peace afforded by this regular succession, which spared France from internal wars such as divided England, and from subjugation—the fate of the elective monarchies of Hungary, Bohemia, and Poland. But the principle of legitimacy was of far wider application: it governed the whole social order. If one could show that a piece of land or an office had long been in one's possession, it could not be taken away. The generalized principle of legitimacy I am describing will seem familiar to the welfare economist of today, for it embodies one of his main concerns— that change should bring improvements to some and harm to none, or, at any rate, adequate compensation where harm is done. It is obvious that such a principle rigorously applied acts as a brake on change—sometimes too much so. But it is also clear that by this principle subjects enjoy the same rights in their order as the sovereign in his. According to a very telling story, the miller of Sans-Souci once refused to sell his mill to Frederick II, saying he had the same right to his mill as the king to his crown. Yes, the same right! The rights, more or less extensive and exalted, are of like solidity, and the sovereign right cannot break the private right. The picture of the *ancien régime* sketched in revolutionary legends gives no inkling of this. Men have been mistaken about the vices of the *ancien régime:* the major failing was not arbitrariness, but the incapacity to promote necessary change.

The ancient French monarchy was guilty of acts as frightful as the massacre of St. Bartholomew's Day and the revocation of the Edict of Nantes, but only when confronted with utterly disconcerting situations, since its system of thought had no place for the Protestant phenomenon. It was undone not by these acts, but by the powerlessness of "New Deal" officials to drive necessary reforms through the parliament—the custodian of acquired rights. The parliament conceived its charge as that of reminding the king he was the guarantor of foreseeability, and of acting, itself, as such a guarantor. This can be seen in a careful reading of the remonstrances of the parliament of Paris upon Turgot's edicts suppressing the *corvées* and the *jurandes*.

These remonstrances are of great interest because their substance is shocking. The reforms proposed by Turgot were quite necessary and mild enough. Their rejection by parliament served nothing but established interests, and that for a short time: these were soon to be swept brutally away. The instance therefore illustrates the proposition that attention to the preservation of known rights, while in principle functional to the purpose of foreseeability, may easily become dysfunctional. To my mind, it is only by looking forward that we can judge which of the established assurances deserve to be maintained.

The ambiguous attitude of the ancient monarchic government toward change was manifested conspicuously and most disastrously in the decisions relating to the representation of the Third Estate at the States-General of 1789. The increased importance of the Third Estate in the life of the nation had to be recognized; and so its representation was doubled. But established positions had to be protected; and so each of the Estates was to deliberate and vote separately. Thus the Third Estate would not weigh in proportion to its just recognized importance. The latter decision could not be accepted by the Third Estate, and this was the beginning of conflict. Mirabeau warned the queen that the throne was now opposing a transformation the king had once supported—a transformation in the king's own interest. All in vain. The king was bound to the idea of maintaining acquired rights, taking this to be an essential duty of his office.

This glimpse at the past—cursory and therefore necessarily simplified —is justified by the need for emphasizing two points: foreseeability has always been the responsibility of the sovereign; and this responsibility can be so interpreted as to make for conflict with inevitable or desirable changes.

Major political crises are characterized by the sudden loss of many or most social certainties. As is well known, these are often brought on by reluctance, or powerlessness, to liquidate outworn certainties, and this not only in the realm of private rights but also of political institutions, without exception of the most hallowed. It behooves us to recognize that we live in an age of precipitate change in processes, a tempo productive of rapid obsolescence for material equipment. Obsolescence is communicated to institutions themselves. Therefore we can far less than at other periods guarantee that what is established shall endure. This involves for members of Society a loss of information which must somehow be recouped.

Information about the Future

Information about the future, as I see it, has the social and moral function of overcoming the contradiction between change and foreknowledge. It is wrong not to recognize that conservatism expresses a fundamental human need; we would be lost and helpless without the many landmarks we have memorized, and therefore we cling to the maintenance of the familiar to the eventual detriment of what might be. This conservative propensity is not specific to the most favored, some of whom indeed are emboldened by their good fortune; anxiety is most natural in those who are aware of holding their own only thanks to a daily effort, and nothing is more understandable than workers' fear of automation and attachment to work rules. In all walks of life, men have cause to defend present certainties failing alternative assurances. To such defensiveness, it is at least a necessary answer—not always a sufficient one—to offer reasonable prospects.

The term "reasonable" is stressed; nothing is more dangerous for psychological equilibrium than the launching of heady promises incapable of implementation. It is one of the tasks of those who envisage the future to zone off the unattainable. Many pleasing prospects are irreconcilable with likely human behavior; the sociologists and the political scientist must here weed out the improbable, just as the economist must cut down, in view of their investment costs, some of the technological forecasters visions.

The second and even more important duty of the social forecaster and strategist is to combat the general feeling of uncertainty which the rapidity of change sheds indistinctly over all institutions. The more change there is, the more valuable are some fixed points; which structural certainties should be tied down and placed beyond doubt? This is no small or easy subject, but it forms an essential contribution to foreseeability.

In between the unachievable and the unchanging stands the ample zone of feasible futures. It is the social strategist's concern to recommend plausible procedures for moving ahead in that zone, procedures favoring change and procuring some sufficient degree of foreknowledge.

The social scientist can not hesitate to reject both as a nightmare and as a myth the supposed combination of maximum change with perfect foreseeability by means of total Government control; firstly such complete control is effectively impossible, secondly however far it be carried the fruits announced cannot be guaranteed; thirdly it is for the exercise of our liberty that we require foreseeability, and therefore the model is absurd. This is not to say that we can afford to be heedless of its seduction.

Turning to more acceptable prospects, how can we devise the reconciliation sought between freedom and foreknowledge? To set forth the means thereto is easy, but to execute them is not. Suppose all agents are required to declare their intentions as to future actions. It will then be possible to discuss what mutual accommodations will be required if their intentions are to be coapted to one another. Men's intentions must be inflected. It is obvious that to operate on actions by issuing commands is of far less moral worth than to operate on intentions by rational persuasion. In the liberal regime of the future, an important position should be allotted to anticipatory discussion of intentions, and a reduced position to authoritarian prescriptions. This will be possible only if men honestly state their intentions[12] and are open to persuasion on the need of modifying their declared intentions. Although such a system can never be perfect—for no perfection is ever attained in reality—we can strive to approach it. Discussions of the kind held for the French Plan and at the Conseil Économique et Social are a prefiguring of what is to come.

Declarations of intent coming from powerful sources are particularly interesting. Large public agencies, large companies, large trade unions must be induced to speak. The discussions of intentions must be based on the representation of real forces. And since intentions must be adapted to one another, it is clear that the task of calculation and persuasion must devolve upon men of recognized prudence, who do not represent particular sectional interests. Thus in practice the discussion will lie between the *mighty* and the *prudent*.

Only a raving optimist would suppose that the prudent will succeed in conciliating all of the mighty. There will be passionate divisions over certain questions—and these residual questions will have to be treated as subjects of political contention.

Nothing should be settled by a simple weighing of wishes if it can be settled by rational argument. Cournot said that the science (I would say the art) of social economy is mainly concerned with sectional interests, whereas politics deals for the most part with human passions.[13] He went on to explain that in practice the two are intermingled because "interest engenders passion." But if we were to succeed in using reason to settle everything that is justiciable, the realm of the political would shrink to that remnant which is not justiciable, and conflict would be dulled because men will want to safeguard the harmony established in other domains.

I am not so great an optimist as to think that passionate divisions of opinion will cease once good solutions are found for all material problems. But it is evident that such divisions thrive where material problems are left untended or are only partially solved.

NOTES

1. David Hume, *Essays and Treatises on Several Subjects* (2 vols.; London, 1767), I, 43. Hume is referring to Harrington's celebrated work, *Oceana*, published in 1656 and dedicated to Cromwell. The restoration of Charles II took place in 1660.

2. Prévost-Paradol, *La France nouvelle* (Paris, 1868), p. 17.

3. See Chapter 11.

4. And it is worth repeating that a careful consideration of the *social* traits differentiating Germany from the United States could not have enabled anyone to foresee the *political* difference between Hitler and Roosevelt. For if we look at the characteristic *social* traits of each of these men, they are surprisingly different from the social traits of the two peoples that elected them. The Americans elected a man descended from an old and distinguished family, who had been educated at the best schools and was a member of the social elite. The Germans adopted a self-taught and foreign-born character of obscure origins—a *déraciné*. This in a country far more traditional than America; a country scarcely yet emancipated from the *ancien régime*—from which Germany had been cut off more by foreign traumatism than by any internal reaction; a country whose people were renowned for the respect they paid to culture, particularly in its academic forms.

5. This phenomenon had been rightly announced by Lord Bryce in his great work, *Modern Democracies* (London: Macmillan, 1921), when other authors were celebrating the spreading triumph of parliamentary government. See my article "The Principate," in *The Political Quarterly* (London), 36:1.

6. See my article entitled "Political Science and Prevision," in *The American Political Science Review*, LIX:1 (March 1965).

7. "Acephalous" societies. See Lucy Mair, "La Politique en Afrique nouvelle," *Futuribles* No. 29 *Bulletin SEDEIS* (October 1, 1964).

8. This is what Rousseau has explained. See my article "Théorie des formes du gouvernement chez Rousseau," in the periodical *Le Contrat social* VI:6.

9. The notion of "expectation" has been admirably discussed by Emmanuel Lévy in *Les fondements du droit* (1939).

10. The term "social guarantee" appears in several "Declarations" of the rights of man issued during the French Revolutionary period.

11. This system, like the system of hereditary monarch, satisfies man's need to know who is the successor. A parallel might be drawn between the deaths of two beloved and awaited heirs—Mr. Gaitskell and the Duke of Burgundy (Louis XIV's grandson).

12. This is an extension of Montaigne's principle that all human intercourse rests on speech. The more such intercourse extends into a distant future, the more it involves declarations of intent.

13. Cournot, *L'Enchaînement des idées fondamentales* (1911 edn.), §460, p. 525.

19

The Forecasting
of Ideas

The word "idea" is used throughout this chapter in its generally accepted meaning. We may say: "We have different ideas on the subject" or, equally well: "We have different ways of seeing the subject." The latter is a revealing substitution, with the suggestion that our mind "sees" by means of ideas. Similarly, in speaking about a historical event, we may equally well say: "We have different opinions about it" or "We see it through different eyes." The latter expression is probably the more telling, for what happens in such cases is not so much that we apply different criteria of value to "the same facts" as that we see different facts. Our different angles of vision bring out different facts. Our value-judgment is not so much subsequent to our reading of the facts, as it is immanent in the ideas we use in reading the facts.

Because Augustin Thierry regarded history as a progress toward constitutional government, he considered the French Revolution of 1848 a "catastrophe,"[1] and for the same reason, Renan spoke of the *fatal écroulement de février* leading to the *funeste solution de décembre* [1851].[2] Because Marx regarded history as a class struggle, the revolution of 1848 was in his eyes no more than a parody of the French Revolution of 1789, with nothing of value save the workers' insurrection of the June days.[3] Marx was incomparably harsh in his pronouncements on what he called a farcical re-enactment of a tragedy, a masquerade whose names, watchwords, and costumes had been borrowed from the past. On the contrary, those who looked at history in terms of the growth of national aware- ness saw in this same revolution a signal given to the idea of nationalism prevalent throughout Europe. Our perception of the facts depends on our ideas: it is through our ideas that we know reality.

This is so in everyday life. A schoolboy who says: "My idea of a job is to be an electronics engineer" is speaking about an intention provoked by an idea. The child has no experience with the job of an electronics en- gineer; he does not really know what it is, nor could he qualify for the job now; he must first acquire the necessary knowledge. "Electronics en- gineer" is therefore an idea in his mind—and an idea necessarily inade- quate to reality. This is what we non-philosophers ordinarily mean by "idea"—this, and not, to be sure, knowing the essence of a thing.

A man who calls for nationalization or self-rule in a country where such things are unknown is just like the schoolboy. The ideas in his mind cannot adequately cover the forms corresponding to them if and when they will be put into effect. The same holds true for the man who attacks the ideas before they are put into effect.

But the reason for the inadequacy of an idea is not simply that it is antecedent to the fact, as in the just-mentioned examples. The statistician who says: "The French standard of living rose by 50 per cent from 1949 to 1961" states an important established fact. But without a whole corpus of ideas used by us in measuring, that "fact" would not be. This is an ex- treme case—but a useful one for indicating that we can agree on a fact *only* if we have come to an implicit or explicit agreement on ideas.

Scientific Language and Ordinary Speech

Information theory has reminded us that a message from one person to another can be understood only insofar as they share a common language. Scientific information of great moment is often—indeed more and more often—expressed in a very few pages whose meaning is perfectly clear and unambiguous to scientists specialized in the appropriate discipline, though incomprehensible to scientists in other disciplines, as well as to laymen. The explanation for this is that the author draws on a store of ideas that he holds in common with his audience of specialists.

Sir George Thomson's description of the conditions that enable us to make scientific statements can, I think, hardly be improved:

All science . . . depends on its *concepts*. These are the ideas that are given names. They determine the questions one asks and the answers one can get. They are more fundamental than the theories, which are stated in terms of them. Examples are motion, mass, energy, electric charge, magnetic poles, temperatures, waves, particles.[4]

While reality as "being" is independent of our concepts, our awareness of reality and our expression of this awareness both depend on them. In any established science there is a set of unambiguous concepts with which successive theories are built. The structure of a theory can be added to or adjusted, and at times the adjustments are so fundamental as to require a recasting of the concepts themselves. Concepts and theories form a system of ideas held in common by men engaged in the same discipline. To take an easy example, when two economists speak about the "growth of productivity," what they have in common is not a knowledge of figures but an intelligence of relationships between different entities, of definitions of these entities, and of conventions of measurement. What they have in common is, in a word, ideas.

Whatever external use a science is put to, its inner life is characterized by the progress of ideas. We naturally speak of the branches of a discipline: a scientist at work on a new branch supports himself on the existing limbs. Sometimes a branch dies out; sometimes important new shoots grow from the trunk.[5]

This whole process of growth is subject to "artificial selection." As the chemist and philosopher Michael Polanyi has shown in a series of fascinating studies,[6] each proposition that is suggested forms the object of a minute inquisition—in the proper sense of the word—conducted by the specialists of the branch. No unfounded propositions are let through by this inquisition, but often well-founded propositions are also kept out— sometimes because they are disturbing to prevailing ideas, at other times because they do not point in the direction in which scientific enthusiasm just then happens to be channeled.[7] While this process of artificial selection is by no means infallible, it affords maximum guarantees.

The progress of scientific ideas is not my subject, and I have spoken about it only because I want to draw a distinction between scientific ideas and ideas in general circulation—the ideas appearing in our conversations and controversies. In the latter case the concepts employed are equivocal— so much so that the same word may bear quite different meanings.[8] Instead of scientific theories, we find assertions of relationships: but these are ambiguous because the terms are imprecise and the assertions are unverifiable, or are not tested. Unlike what happens in the sciences, an assertion is put forward without being subjected to a systematic inquisition by qualified judges. Each individual member of society accepts or rejects the assertion: there is a free trade in ideas, and in this state of laissez faire the diffusion of ideas in society depends on the individual choices of "consumers." The members of society, unlike adepts in a particular scientific discipline, do not share a single coherent corpus of ideas, which after artificial selection have the same meaning for each and every one and are accepted by all. Consequently, we may speak of the ideas *of* science, but should speak of the ideas *in* society: for convenience, I wish to speak of the latter as "social ideas." This means—I would like it to be quite clear—all ideas circulating in society, and not simply those ideas relating to the organization of society.

I drew the above contrast in the interest of clarity: my intention was not to condemn social ideas for failing to measure up to scientific ideas. The difference is part of the nature of things. It would not, I think, be feasible to impart a scientific character to social ideas, and any attempt to make society accept a coherent corpus of ideas vetted by examiners would be very dangerous.

In speaking about the commerce of social ideas, I borrowed a term from the history of economic ideas—*laissez faire.* It would be interesting to consider whether the reception of this principle in the economic order was anticipated and abetted by its reception in the intellectual order—but that would be a digression.

The Ecology of Social Ideas

Suppose that a census of the ideas existing in a given society at a given time could be made. Before taking this census, we would want to classify ideas by order, kind, species, and variety. The actual census would consist of counting the number of heads containing a given idea. If an idea is found in a million heads, we may say that this idea has one million bearers or that there are one million examples of this idea in our society. But the word "examples" seems somewhat unsuitable, for it is extremely doubtful that exactly the same idea is present in any two heads. It is tempting to speak like this: in any two heads, the "same idea" presents the degree of likeness and unlikeness which is characteristic of two individuals belonging to the same variety. Thus we come to treat this idea as a "population" of one million individuals.

In other words, I am suggesting that a human population should be regarded as an "environment" inhabited by various, greater or smaller populations of ideas. I do not claim that this way of looking at the question is the correct one, but simply that it is suggestive and well suited to my purpose.

The population metaphor accords very well with certain commonly used expressions. We say that an idea is "gaining ground" when its population is increasing, and that it is "losing ground" when its population is declining. We also say that an idea has been "set aside": which is not to say that the idea has disappeared, but that it has been relegated to a relatively insignificant region of the social space.

The discipline dealing with the distribution and development of all the different species living together in a given environment is known as "synecology." These different populations form an "ecosystem," within which there are relations of dependence and of competition. The same holds true for ideas: some ideas compound with one another, others are at war. It is even true of certain ideas, as of certain predatory species, that they can subsist only as long as the species of idea on which they prey subsists in sufficient number.

An ecosystem has periods of stability as well as periods of rapid change set off by a change in the environment or by the intrusion of new species. In these alternative causes of change we may see a fitting analogy to the two causes—material and intellectual—over which there has been so much dispute between historians of ideas.

This analogy is intended to make the notion of "a movement of ideas" more concrete. "But," the reader objects, "it is improper to treat ideas which are not even 'concrete objects' as though they were plants and animals." To this my reply is as follows: "Any intellectual representation of a reality is fundamentally and necessarily inadequate, but it is essential for us to 'represent' things in order to speak about them. The more concrete the representation is made, the easier it becomes to speak about them."

The representation used above suggests that the "natural selection" of ideas in the social field must be set against the "artificial selection" of ideas in the scientific domain. Clearly, natural selection does not afford the same guarantees of progress as artificial selection. The value of this

analogy can be brought out by the following observation: through artificial selection of plants, a gardener can produce varieties of a rare excellence, which propagate themselves only in much cruder forms and so
cannot maintain themselves in nature. Does not the same hold true for
ideas? And surely it is true that ideas flourishing in one environment
languish or take rather different forms when transported to another—
English political ideas are an obvious example.

I think therefore the image used here lends itself very well to my
purpose, which is the forecasting of social ideas. Which of the ideas now
known—for how can we speak of ideas as yet unknown—will make
progress in society? In what forms will they be established? And what
will be the changes in the ecosystem of social ideas?

"But your intention is perfectly simple," the reader might say. "Why
bring in all this talk about ecology?" I think it was important to do so
in order to emphasize that an idea does not occur in isolation but within
a partly hostile, partly propitious environment of ideas, which it helps to
modify. Obviously, we must not be prisoners of this image, but must
correct it by that other image—the movement of ideas—which serves to
emphasize that ideas are disseminated through acts of individual choice by
individual minds.

The Importance of Forecasting Ideas

The forecasting of ideas is of the greatest importance. On the assumption that changes in society are the result of changes in ideas, we cannot
forecast the former without forecasting the latter: this will be my first
point. On the opposite assumption, the forecasting of ideas is nonetheless
of major importance: that will be my second point.

The *philosophes* of the eighteenth century regarded ideas as all-power-
ful: false ideas (called "superstitions") were the root of evil, while the
advance of true ideas ("enlightenment") was the source of all progress.
This excessive view of theirs was turned against them when, in reaction to
the French Revolution, the atrocities committed in it were laid at the door
of the *philosophes!* It is natural that their exaggeration should have
provoked a recoil to the opposite extreme, but whatever may have been
said in the heat of controversy, I cannot believe any author ever truly held
that ideas have no concrete effects. From asserting that situations affect

the genesis of ideas, there is a very great gap to denying that the formulation and propaganda of ideas can have any effect at all. Marx, in particular, was, I think, very far from such a denial.

But suppose that in social and political forecasting we could entirely dispense with the forecasting of ideas—this either because we believe ideas have virtually no practical efficacy (which seems most unreasonable) or because we believe ideas are no more than intermediate products, so that the forecasting of situations is sufficient (that is to say, the transition from one situation to another is predetermined; ideas arising in a particular situation are determined by that situation; any part played by such ideas in the transition to the next situation is a purely necessary one).

Even if we were to take this attitude, it would still be fascinating to forecast the thoughts of our descendants, because of our interest in men as thinking, sentient beings. Suppose some man were given the opportunity to spend an hour in the year 2003: even if he tended as a rule to play down the causal effects of ideas, he would, I think, prefer to spend that hour talking to a man of the age, rather than spend it looking over the world as it will then appear.

In our time, it is worth noting, the role of ideas has been newly recognized. Keynes's opinion on this question is well known,[9] and the influence of his own thought serves to support his thesis.

Forecasts and Preferences

Idea forecasts matter to us, but there is a danger our preferences will run away with our forecasts.

We speak of "embracing an idea," and this is a very apt expression. The embraced idea becomes the mistress of our inner life: we value other ideas in relation to it, and feel in the wrong if our behavior should betray it. We are in love with the idea, and this is a most important point. This emotional attitude of ours governs our political ideas, and even applies to scientific ideas. A scientific idea is often portrayed as a robot-slave, of purely instrumental value, that is scrapped as soon as another, seemingly more effective one is proposed. But human nature contains far more sensibility than this account would allow, and the history of science shows that, in this domain too, ideas can inspire love, and men courageously defend ideas to which they are attached. Even science has its champions of lost causes, who sometimes play poignant roles.

But once we are enamoured of an idea, how can we help wishing that others will recognize its merits. A sense of duty to the idea and to mankind demands that we work for this recognition. And though our success may be small, how can we help feeling that sooner or later the qualities captivating us will be acknowledged? In short, the stronger our attachment to the idea, the greater is our confidence in its future acceptance by society. Thus, through our attachment to the idea, we are led, by a spontaneous movement, into predicting its social success.

This relationship between evaluation and prediction which holds for ideas is the reverse of that which obtains on the stock exchange. Before buying a stock, a man considers how other buyers will rate various stocks. On the basis of this prognostication of future popularity, he forms his present evaluation of the best buy. Keynes suggested that this mode of evaluation is analogous to a newspaper competition in which each entrant is asked to list the members of some class—say film stars—in the order he thinks the majority of entrants will give, rather than in his own order of preference. Here the prediction determines the evaluation. Such an attitude in any part of the intellectual and moral order would be ignoble: evaluation is the primary fact, independent of all prediction.

But our natural inclination is to pass from evaluation to prediction. We must beware of abandoning ourselves to this inclination, however natural, for if we did so, the problem of idea forecasts would disappear and our present preferences would be tantamount to predictions! The best way of guarding against this unconscious propensity is to face it openly, stating: "What I think today, everybody will think tomorrow." We see how absurdly fatuous this statement is and are well warned that preference is not the same as prediction.

The Social Career of Ideas

What I mean by the forecasting of ideas is forecasting their social career: that is to say, their diffusion, deformations, and applications. It is accordingly natural that we should look at the past social careers of ideas: for if we can find elements enabling us to trace the social progress of an idea—in its diffusion, deformations, and applications—we can learn something about the process of natural selection.

The *social* history of ideas, as it is understood here, arises out of an interest in forecasting and differs from other historical studies of ideas. First of all, it is in no way concerned with the formation of an idea in its author's mind.[10] Nor is it concerned with the revivals, cross-fertilization, and enrichment of ideas as they pass from one great thinker to another: that is, I think, what is commonly meant by "history of ideas." What matters here is the dissemination of ideas in the crowd.

We may speak of an idea as "reigning" if it is constantly expressed or referred to: the ways of speaking about it are evidence of the form it has taken; the sorts of occasion on which it is referred to tell us about its fields of application (which are susceptible of changing); a reference to it not only shows that the speaker is conversant with it, but also that he can assume many other people are conversant with it.

No contribution can be made to the social history of ideas without a careful exploration—such as I have not undertaken—and without an adequate method—such as I do not possess. Thus I am faced with an unfortunate dilemma, for I must give a specific illustration at the same time that I know it can only be a crude caricature of what needs to be said. With this warning I shall venture forth.

Never was so widespread a social scandal caused by a scientific book as when Darwin's *Origin of Species* appeared in 1859. Darwin's ideas provide us with a fit subject for the study of social acceptance: in the first place, because we can exactly date their dissemination into the public at large; in the second, because social selection affected their acceptance in a very striking way.

What the general public first seized upon was the concept of transformism—the idea that superior organisms develop from inferior organisms by evolution. Darwin was not the original author of this idea, as he noted with exquisite modesty in his preface, and scientific and intellectual circles were well acquainted with it. Proposed at the beginning of the century both by Lamarck and Goethe, it formed the subject of a great debate in 1830 between the transformist Geoffroy St. Hilaire and the fixist Cuvier, extending over six months of sessions at the Academy of Sciences of Paris. A famous story is told about this dispute: when news of the July Revolution in Paris reached Weimar, Eckermann, deeply moved, went to see Goethe in order to discuss the great event with him. He found

Goethe deeply moved like himself, but there was a misunderstanding about the "great event"—because, for Goethe, it was the session of July 19 at the Institut de France, at which he thought transformism had been vindicated. Goethe was wrong: scientific opinion came down on the side of Cuvier, largely because Geoffroy St. Hilaire could not indicate a plausible process of transformism.

On the other hand, Darwin supplied decisive reinforcements to the cause of transformism and established it in scientific opinion largely by suggesting a plausible process. This process was clearly indicated in the title of his epic work, which is rarely given in its complete form: *On the Origin of Species by Means of Natural Selection or: The Preservation of Favoured Races in the Struggle for Life*. Darwin shows in the first half of his title that he proposes to explain how transformism is effected: namely, by means of natural selection. That was his basic idea, and it was his very own. But consider the second half of the title—*The Preservation of Favoured Species in the Struggle for Life*.[11] It is tempting to ask "favored by whom?"—but Darwin's thought lies along another line: he really means "the fittest" instead of "the favored." But immediately we are troubled by a question: it is a tautology that the fittest for survival have a greater likelihood of surviving, yet it is not certain that the fittest for survival are in all respects the best. We all know the fragility of excellence. But we must leave this talk. The main point is that the struggle for life, ensuring the survival of the fittest and the elimination of the unfittest, is the way, discovered by Darwin, in which transformism is effected. And since this is Darwin's most specific contribution, let us look at its social repercussions,[12] remembering that Sir Julian Huxley tells us now that the applications of Darwinian ideas to human affairs were wrongly conceived.

We shall see how different was the social fate of the general idea of transformism and the particular idea of natural selection: and this is the example of social selection I wish to discuss. Darwin's ideas caused so much furor because it was immediately assumed that man was included in the proposed scheme, as Darwin expressly set forth in his subsequent books. *The Origin of Species* appeared at a time when science and faith lived in very poor accord, and was at once adopted as a pronouncement of science disproving a pronouncement of the Bible[13]—this historical fact is well known. But a deeper and better reason for the social acceptance of transformism was well put by Broca:

For my part, I find more glory in mounting than in going down, and if I allowed sentiment to intrude into science, I should prefer to be a risen monkey rather than a fallen Adam. Yes, if I was shown that my ancestors were mere animals stooping to the ground, herbivorous arboriculturalists, brothers or cousins to the monkey's own ancestors, far from feeling ashamed that my species should have such a genealogy and such relations, I would take pride in the evolution it has undergone, its continuous ascent taking it to the foremost rank, and its successive triumphs culminating in such superiority to all other species.[14]

The consonance of the idea of transformism with the spirit of the time was well expressed by Broca. For the past few generations, men had boasted of the progress of society instead of faithful adherence to ancestral customs. Taking less and less pride in illustrious origins, they adopted the stance of self-made men. Fouquet's motto, *Quo non ascendam?*, became every man's motto for self and society. To men of this cast, the news that their origins were far lower than they suspected could only give them confidence that they would go much further than they once expected. Some drew the inference: "Yesterday from monkey to man, tomorrow from man to superman." And thus transformism seemed to be a "scientific promise" that the present on which men were congratulating themselves[15] was not one of those happy but transient phases through which every civilization has passed, but a step in a grand progress, the splendid prospect of which was opening up.

But what was the mainspring of this grand progress? As Darwin indicated in his title, the progress was actuated by natural selection. But this idea is far less attractive than the notion of transformism; it is even positively repugnant.

Characteristics tend to diverge within a species: some of the individuals in a generation are bearers of more favorable characteristics than others —and success is the sign of this endowment. If the process of reproduction is dominated by the better-endowed individuals, their characteristics will be present in a greater proportion of individuals in the succeeding generation. In the struggle for life, the better endowed achieve such a position of predominance by pushing the less equipped down into positions unfavorable for existence and reproduction. This view is readily acceptable when applied to simple organisms, which do not elicit our sympathy, but it is heart-chilling when applied to man. It links biological progress to moral regression: for surely we know that the strong must help the weak, giving them, too, a place in the sun.

Yet such is the essence of "social Darwinism"—a doctrine put forward by Herbert Spencer even before *The Origin of Species* was published.[16] Ernst Haeckel, Darwin's great champion, said: "Darwinism is anything but socialistic. If a definite political tendency be attributed to this English theory—which is, indeed, possible—this tendency can only be aristocratic, certainly not democratic, and least of all socialistic."[17] To be sure, there would be no need to keep down the less fit if the fittest could impart aptitudes to them by instruction. But as Darwin stated and August Weissmann later showed,[18] aptitudes thus acquired cannot be transmitted. After Weissmann's investigations, Karl Pearson, the founder of biometrics, wrote:

> The suspension of that process of natural selection which in an earlier struggle for existence crushed out feeble and degenerate stocks, may be a real danger to society, if society relies solely on changed environment for converting its inherited bad into an inheritable good. If society is to shape its own future—if we are to replace the stern processes of natural law, which have raised us to our present high standard of civilization, by milder methods of eliminating the unfit—then we must be peculiarly cautious that in following our strong social instincts we do not at the same time weaken society by rendering the propagation of bad stock more and more easy.[19]

I have said enough. In the century that has elapsed since Darwin—the century that was sometimes spoken of as "the century of Darwin"—social ideas and practices have not developed with natural selection as a guideline, for this idea, unlike transformism, has not won social acceptance. Take this example: in a country where, as in France, the state pays regular allowances to families with children, we would be deeply shocked by the suggestion that allowances should be denied to parents whose ancestors might have hereditary defects and increased for parents whose ancestors were seemingly—in view of services rendered to science —endowed with hereditary virtues.

Neither the idea of natural selection nor the subsequent ideas of genetics[20] has been received in the social field.[21] The powerful surge of moral ideas has swept them aside. This is, I think, a clear example of the social selection of ideas.

The Force of Moral Ideas

It seems that moral ideas in particular lend themselves to widespread acceptance: and in this phenomenon we may see the strongest argument for democracy. The attitude of our mind to an assertion of the form "It is good that . . ." differs from its attitude to an assertion of the form "It is true that. . . ." A general relationship given to us as true is not accepted by us as such without preliminary examination of its implications and applications. To take an example germane to our concerns, suppose somebody asserts that "civic liberties are safeguarded wherever there is a written constitution." We then consider all countries with a written constitution one by one, trying to ascertain whether in each there is a state corresponding to our notion of "the safeguarding of individual liberties." Even if we start out with countries for which the proposition holds true, we eventually find countries for which it does not, and thereupon reject it.

Depending on whom a general proposition is given to as true, the initial examination is more or less intense and rigorous. The scientist makes a vocation of rigor, which is very necessary since he assumes the responsibility for certifying a proposition that I myself cannot check. For my part, I accept the proposition on trust from scientific authority. But whether I am a good or a poor examiner, it is always understood that the truth of a proposition cannot be accepted until its implications and applications have been checked. There is an open trial of the proposition during which a variety of experiments are produced to bear witness to the implications which the proposition contains. If its contents are defective, the proposition is unacceptable. If the proposition is accepted but defects in its contents are later found, it will be rejected or amended depending on how serious they are.

Nothing, it seems, corresponds to this process when the proposition is of a normative kind—the proposition is accepted or rejected by an immediate judgment. I do not mean to say that no consideration of its applications comes into this judgment, but between the mere intervention of some application or other, and the exploration of as many applications as possible, there is a great difference. For example, when the idea of equality was proclaimed in eighteenth-century France, the abolition of the privileges of the nobility was certainly contemplated—that is to say, a seemingly good practical consequence was contemplated in a seemingly good idea. That the wish for this practical consequence served to invigorate this idea, nobody can deny, but it is, I think, a cynical error to hold that the wish for this practical consequence made up the whole force of the idea. The error of so thinking is demonstrable, for if the whole force of the idea came from the wish to abolish aristocratic privilege, the idea would have had no force for those who did not want this result, so that the people who advocated equality would have had nothing to gain from invoking the idea of equality. But in actual fact, its opponents had a bad conscience, and its upholders a clear one, and this proves the idea had a force of its own.

However much an application deemed good may reinforce and invigorate a moral idea, I do not think the wish for that application is the reason for which the idea is adopted. But whatever role a presently contemplated application may have, the essential point is this: we do not look for other applications of the idea, and our acceptance of it does not depend on its realizable contents.

Let us draw a simile between a general proposition and an envelope. When we are concerned with truth, we do not accept the envelope until, in principle, we have exhaustively perused its contents. But we do not carry out such an examination preliminary to accepting a moral proposition. When we accept an idea as true, our exploration of its contents lies in the past. When we accept an idea as good, our exploration of its contents lies, for the most part, in the future. This contrast opens up certain important avenues for forecasting.

The assertion that a moral idea has been accepted without an exhaustive exploration of its contents means that there now exist particular propositions which are logically included in the general proposition but which, unlike the general proposition, have not been formulated or accepted. These propositions may be called "dormant." The discovery of these "dormant" propositions does not amount to "prevision" since they are given in the general proposition. But the search for these propositions leads straight to the problem of forecasting when they will be roused and what will then happen to them.

Consider that famous assertion in the American Declaration of Independence: "We hold these truths to be self-evident; that all men are created equal; that they are endowed by their creator with certain unalienable rights; that among these are life, liberty, and the pursuit of happiness." This assertion undeniably contains a condemnation of slavery, and this implication was seen by Thomas Jefferson, the drafter of the Declaration, but not by the slaveowners, who accepted and repeated his words. The psychological activation of this content was, as we know, slow in coming: it was not fully enacted in practice until nearly ninety years after the Declaration of Independence.

Abolition, when it eventually came, was a necessary condition for satisfying the foregoing general principle, and at the same time—according to the concept of equality then prevailing—a sufficient condition. It is largely because the concept of equality has evolved so much over the past century that the question of equal rights for Negroes has risen once again, one hundred years after the Civil War. And hence, we must note that an idea can make headway through the enrichment of its meaning, as well as through the activation of implications derivable from the very start.

Reigning Ideas and Their Rule

The phrase "reigning idea" is aptly a commonplace, for it suggests that an idea can very well "reign" without necessarily "ruling." Or, to pursue the metaphor, the idea can reign over the whole of society but at the same time rule nothing more than a "royal domain" of very limited extent, outside of which the only attribute of its reign is a certain formal respect manifested for it—more often than not, in words rather than in deeds.

Consider by way of example this political idea, which suggests itself because of its affinity with the foregoing political metaphor: "There is no legitimate right to command a group of men and speak in their name other than that conferred in an election by a majority of the group." This is—no doubt about it—a reigning idea: so much so, that tyrants do not forgo legitimizing their position by elections. But for all that this is a reigning idea, it governs very few things. We would not think of electing our generals and our ambassadors in the manner of the Greeks. The election of judges, introduced during the French Revolution, was abandoned almost immediately. And it is to be remarked that even in a country such as the United States, where a federal and democratic tradition leaves many questions to be decided by the direct vote of the electorate, people are generally made to vote for all sorts of things at the same time, and therefore tend to vote straight party tickets, instead of considering each question on its merits. In France it was suggested not long ago that parliamentary elections should be held at the same time as elections for the head of state. The effects of such a measure would be to make the voters' choice of members of parliament psychologically subordinate to their choice of a particular man for the presidency: everything would be reduced to an imperial election.

It is not part of my present subject to discuss the universal tendency of our age toward Caesarism, with elections playing a greater or smaller role. The resemblance with the practices of imperial Rome is sufficiently obvious—in some countries, emperors are changed by the praetorians; in others, a designated heir is groomed for the succession by a kind of adoption. But even where this process is least advanced, we see that offices are filled by the monarchic method of nomination from above, or by the oligarchic method of co-optation. And thus it is permissible to say that election is an idea which reigns but does not rule.

In contrast, the idea of social solidarity has exerted an increasingly strong sway during the past fifty years. It has been embodied in many important institutions, which, once established, were not challenged—and that is noteworthy. The expansion of this idea does not seem to be at an end; it is even spreading to the international scene, which presents one of the most important problems in the forecasting of ideas.

Foreign Aid to Developing Nations

The idea of foreign aid to underdeveloped nations was launched not so very long ago by President Truman, in the aftermath of American aid to Europe following World War II. Aid to Europe was, as we know, an idea reigning among individual Americans and governing their actions—the enormous number of CARE parcels sent by them is sufficient evidence of that. On the basis of those individual dispositions, the Marshall Plan was founded, instituting public aid from one state to another for a limited period of years. It was a far greater step to move from this to the principle of foreign aid without a definite time limit, yet this step was taken with the greatest of ease. While American aid to European countries led to aid to underdeveloped nations, the latter was of far greater significance. The former was of much greater extent and far more systematic than the help that might have been given to a country struck by a natural disaster, but did not establish or imply a new principle, whereas help was given to underdeveloped nations because of the tremendous difference in situation between donors and receivers. And this was clearly a principle of striking novelty—social solidarity transferred to the international field.

Some Americans regarded this type of foreign aid as a mere political device, but many others saw it as the cornerstone of international social solidarity. And since the politicians helped to create a precedent, their motives are, in the last analysis, of no importance. The consequences of this idea form a major object of conjecture.

It is, I think, highly significant that the advanced countries are discussing the criteria for a just distribution of the burden of foreign aid. If I give something to somebody, I do not concern myself with whether my neighbor too will make a gift; and if he makes a gift, I do not seek to compare my gift with his, or my reasons with his. I am sole judge of my liberality, and he is sole judge of his. There must be an obligation to give before it becomes legitimate to compare how we each acquit ourselves. Once this condition obtains, the question of the relation between contribution paid and ability to pay becomes a normal topic of discussion; the gift is turned into a tax. I think that the talk about sharing the burden of foreign aid contains the germ of the idea that aid is a tax paid by rich nations to poor.[22] And this presents us with a problem for forecasting: will this idea establish itself? Will such a tax become an institution? And if this should happen, what should the principle of distribution between beneficiaries be? According to need? or according to the countries' efforts at self-help?

But we may put aside this idea of a tax, for it is too specific, and besides it raises great difficulties of a practical nature.[23] Let us keep to the more general idea of a certain measure of international social solidarity. The spreading of this idea implies a complete reversal of the psychological status of the "masses" in Western countries. In a national context the masses are rightly seen as "disinherited" men: they make the darlings of chance feel guilty. But taking a broader view so as to include the masses from other countries as well, we find that compared with the disinherited millions in non-Western countries, the masses in Western countries should be counted among the fortunate.

To be sure, Western workers who are taking some particular attitude in a certain national context have no reason to take into account their relative superiority over workers in underdeveloped nations; they would rightly laugh if, in a wage dispute, they were told they were lucky to have what they have. But there would be no grounds for laughter if the idea of international social solidarity began to be so interpreted as to imply that the wealthy countries should take in the oversupply of workers from poor countries. Population transfers of this kind would be a rapid means of making some improvement in the situation of poor countries: but at the same time the instinctive reaction of workers in wealthy countries against such immigration would be perfectly natural and justified.

The effects of immigration from a poor country upon the salary scale in a rich country can easily be described. If most of the immigrants are unskilled workers, the salary scale will be spread over a wider range. But suppose the intellectual elite of the poor country tend to settle in the rich country. So far the total number to have done so is small, but the hypothesis is not absurd; young men coming from a poor country to complete their education are often inclined to remain in the rich country, thus swelling the number of intellectuals there. As more intellectuals stay on in the rich country, the salary scale in that country contracts, but of course the progress of the poor country is held back. Its progress will be accelerated—other things being equal—if surplus unskilled workers go from the poor country to the rich one, while highly trained technical assistants go from the rich country to the poor, but the effect of these population movements, as they become larger, is to spread the salary scale in the rich country wider.

Thus as the idea of international social solidarity is put into effect, it may well lead to certain national problems. There is of course a big difference between a flight of the imagination and a systematic attempt to forecast, but my only intention was to show how important a forecast about the development of ideas could be.

Empirical Relations between Ideas

I spoke above about an "ecosystem" of ideas, wishing to suggest by this that between ideas belonging to different species there are continual relationships of conflict, compromise, symbiosis, etc. I shall call these relationships "empirical"—which is perhaps not a very good term—so that they may be distinguished from the logical relationship between a principal idea and its implications. We may grant that a sufficiently accepted idea tends to extend and diversify the domain over which it rules by filling in the "outlines" of its logical consequences, but at the same time we must admit that this tendency meets with obstacles in other ideas—ideas which are not necessarily contradictory to it.

Let me take a simple example: capital punishment. For a long time men thought it was right and just to kill a murderer. The crime had to be avenged, the criminal had to expiate his act. That notion of punishment has been replaced by another, whose moral superiority we would acknowledge without hesitation—namely, to inflict death as a punishment is horrible. It is an undeniable fact that this new and better moral idea is socially dominant. But although this idea has a constantly growing influence on men's attitudes toward common criminals, the monstrous assassination in Dallas, which seemed a "crime against humanity," aroused once again—in that exceptional case—our primitive idea of vengeance. It is to be observed that the resurgence of this idea has contributed somewhat to a rebirth of popularity of the idea that political assassinations, even in less frightful circumstances, should be punished with death.

But I shall confine myself to common criminals, regarding whom the idea reigning in society is clear: "It is wrong to impose the death sentence." For the purposes of my argument, I am going to make a purely hypothetical assumption: namely, that sociometricians have counted violent crimes over a period of time and found that the fewer death sentences are imposed, the more violent crimes are committed. After eliminating as best they could the influence of other factors, our imaginary sociometricians thought they could safely assert as a true proposition: "As the chances of the death penalty being imposed on a murderer diminish, so is the risk of an innocent member of society being assassinated augmented." A man who believes that capital punishment is in itself wicked will find himself in some difficulty—not that, to my mind, our sociometricians have shown that capital punishment is "good" but merely that it is "useful," i.e., "good as a means."[24] And so our man will be torn between an immediate judgment of "goodness" and a judgment of "utility" established by sociological investigation.

I have chosen such an unpleasant example simply because it makes the conflict between the good and the useful particularly striking. In this particular example, the "utility" was imaginary, but the conflict between the two does in fact present itself in less dramatic cases and is common in the

field of economic and social arrangements. Montesquieu's vigorous condemnation of the proliferation of charitable institutions (which he designates by the genetic name of "hospitals") in the Papal States is worth
quoting:

> At Rome, the hospitals place everyone at ease except those who labor, those
> who are industrious, those who cultivate the arts, those who have land, and
> those who are engaged in trade.[25]

How now, surely it is right to relieve the poor! Yet Montesquieu argued
in this manner:

> When the nation is poor, private poverty arises from the general adversity,
> and is, so to speak, the general adversity itself. All the hospitals in the
> world cannot cure this private poverty; on the contrary, the spirit of in-
> dolence, which they inspire, increases the general and hence the private
> misery. . . .
>   Aurengzebe, being asked why he did not build hospitals, said: "I will
> make my empire so rich that there shall be no need for hospitals." He
> ought to have said: "I will begin by making my empire rich, and then I
> will build hospitals."

Let us translate this into modern terms—first there must be economic
development, and then welfare and social security measures proportioned
to the national wealth can be introduced. If this language seems very
tough-minded, it is worth remembering that in India economists of every
shade of opinion agree that economic development has the priority.

But economic growth is itself a source of conflict with regard to the
distribution of earnings. The distribution which seems a priori the most
desirable gives way, as we have seen in the Soviet Union, to one which
consorts better with maximization of the Gross National Product. Conflict between a form to which the mind first gives its preference and a
form which it later recognizes as operational is extraordinarily frequent,
and there is a continuous tension, leading to continual compromises between these judgments of the mind. The compromise adopted on earnings in Western European countries consists of starting with a primary
distribution designed to maximize output, and then superimposing a
redistribution satisfying the principle of social solidarity.

Again, first there must be economic development, then welfare and social security measures can be introduced as the growing national wealth makes the means for them available. Montesquieu's principle may seem harsh,[26] but there is not a single economist today—wherever he lives and whatever his doctrine—who does not regard the maximization of the over-all economic output as a precondition for relief of the poor. However much value he may attach to the target of public welfare, chronologically he will give it the second place because his social values cannot be embodied without an operational order different from his social ideal. Everywhere maximization of the product calls for an appropriate income structure, and pinned onto this operational distribution we see a secondary distribution, humanitarian and solidary, which is of great importance in the wealthy nations, but cannot be very significant in a state of general poverty of the kind found in India.[27]

The discordance between the structure spontaneously "elected" by the mind and that which is later found to be preferable in terms of results occurs over and over again. We seem to have an innate liking for figures that are simple, regular, and symmetrical, which we look for in nature and in society. But the history of scientific progress tells us of complex organizations found precisely where we looked for simple order. It should be a great lesson to us that our appetite for order is satisfied when we consider a crystal of copper, which is dead matter, and thwarted when we face the chromosome or its constituent genes: if the human mind had devised the world, it would be a dead world. The ancient belief that a "philosophy of nature" could be constructed by a simple effort of the reasoning faculty was, as it turned out, naïve—our understanding could never have imagined the fantastic complexity of the structures that sustained experimentation has taught us to draw.[28] Research on the "natural" frameworks of our thought is of great importance in this connection.[29]

In science the ideas best able to account for successively pursued experiments drive initial ideas away from the field. In the field of social ideas there is a continuous dialogue between ideas rooted in sentiment and ideas that have borne fruit in results. A moral idea can govern only through the intermediary of an operational idea, which is a master-servant, so that between this ruler and this vizier there is a constantly renewed tension.

It seems likely, therefore, that the most fruitful direction to follow in the forecasting of ideas is to consider what "ministers" (or operational ideas) will be proposed and accepted as servants of the ideas that it seems will reign. All sorts of other concurrently reigning ideas will exert pressure in favor of this or that "minister," and the force of the princely notion will very rarely be perceived so clearly as to provide binding criteria for all. Thus the fashion of certain intellectual notions at certain times will result in their acceptance as "ministers" in various domains: for instance, representation two hundred years ago, competition a hundred years ago, and integration today.

Operational concepts pass from one field into another. Market studies and intention polls have been taken over from business into politics.

I ought to speak about how new ways of thinking can give a new turn to certain ancient ideas, and also about the agreements and conflicts between the evolution of ideas and the evolution of structures—for, just as it is undeniable that there is a reciprocal influence between the two, so is it indefensible to assume a regular correspondence between them. I ought to point out how the tribute paid to certain ideas is but lip service, good for Sundays but not for weekdays. I have not begun to treat the subject—but then my purpose was not to treat the subject, but simply to indicate that here lies a topic for forecasting.

NOTES

1. Augustin Thierry, *Du Tiers État* (Paris, 1853), p. x.

2. Ernest Renan, "Lettre à Marcelin Berthelot," *Dialogues philosophiques,* 4th edn. (Paris, 1895), p. 11.

3. Karl Marx, *Le 18 Brumaire de Louis Bonaparte* (Paris: Édition Marcel Ollivier, 1928), p. 23.

4. Sir George Thomson, *The Inspiration of Science* (London, 1961), p. 4.

5. This is strikingly described by Gerald Holton in "Scientific Research and Scholarship: Notes toward the Design of Proper Scales," *Daedalus* (*Proceedings of the American Academy of Arts and Sciences*) 91:2 (Spring 1962).

6. Among Polanyi's studies are: *Science, Faith and Society* (Oxford, 1946); *The Logic of Liberty* (London: Routledge and Kegan Paul, 1951); *Personal Knowledge* (London: Routledge and Kegan Paul, 1958).

7. Michael Polanyi mentions the theory of adsorption as an example. The theory was well received at its inception in 1914, but was set aside when the importance of cohesive electric forces was discovered, because, by analogy, it was thought that they could also account for adsorption. Now, after more than forty years, the theory is an accepted part of the curriculum in schools (see *Science* [September 13, 1963]).

8. T. D. Weldon has shown this for political words, in *The Vocabulary of Politics* (London: Penguin Books, 1953).

9. So well known is Keynes's viewpoint that it seems superfluous to quote the two last pages of *The General Theory of Employment, Interest and Money*.

10. Incidentally, I do not think the formation of an idea can be explained. Anybody attempting to "take to pieces" the formation of an idea in a great author's mind is in no way wasting his time, for he is keeping company with a man of superior intelligence—and that is a delightful experience. But when he has analyzed all the conditions under which the thought was uttered and all the elements entering into its composition, he still has not explained how and why it sprang into being.

11. In the French translation of the book Clémence Royer changed Darwin's subtitle to *Ou des Lois de transformation des êtres organisés* (The Laws of Transformation of Organized Beings). This substitution strikes me as a sign of Royer's philanthropic repugnance to propounding the struggle for life, but whether or not we share his feeling we must recognize that he has betrayed the author's thought.

12. Once again, I am not concerned with the subsequent evolution of this idea in different scientific disciplines.

13. The antireligious aspect was important at the time but no longer. Today it would be thought strange that many defenders of transformism should have been convinced they had succeeded in "expelling Providence." For what could be more providential than a universe in which the superior always grows out of the inferior? Laws of progress reflect just as much glory on their Author as laws of stability, and cannot upset the Christian, who knows he was made of dust.

14. Broca, *Mémoires d'anthropologie*, III, 146, and quoted in Mathias Duval, *Le Darwinisme* (Paris, 1886), p. 425.

15. A few years earlier, Porter had published *The Progress of Nations*, a panegyric of industrial civilization in England.

16. In April 1852 the *Westminster Review* published an article in which Spencer said: "Que l'inévitables surabondance numérique des hommes (. . .) rend nécessaire l'élimination continuelle de ceux chez lesquels est moindre la faculté de conservation; et que, par le fait que tous sont soumis à la nécessité toujours croissante de gagner leur vie—nécessité qui provient d'un excès de fécondité—cette élimination entraîne un progrès; car, avec le temps, il ne survit que ceux qui, dans de semblables conditions, vont s'améliorant sans cesse."

17. Ernst Haeckel, *Freie Wissenschaft und freie Lehre,* quoted in Karl Pearson, *The Grammar of Science* (Everyman Edition), p. 73.

18. It is well known that Weissmann's work was accepted in the scientific world before Mendel's, which did not attract attention until after 1900 although it had been published as early as 1865.

19. Karl Pearson, *The Grammar of Science* (Everyman Edition), p. 28. (The

original edition appeared in London in 1892.) On the same page there is a foot-note whose social implications are so harsh that I will not reproduce it.

20. Recent genetics has seriously considered the possibility that nonselective or antiselective reproduction may lead to deterioration of the human race. H. J. Muller believes that in the very long run every single man may have so many defects of different kinds as to be a medical case.

21. To suggest Hitler is ridiculous. If he had accepted these ideas, he would have been compelled in all logic to respect and cherish the Jews.

22. This idea emerges in an article by Irving B. Kravis and Michael W. S. Davenport, "The Political Arithmetic of International Burden-Sharing," *The Journal of Political Economy* (August 1963).

23. Particularly it raises the very difficult problem of the balance of payments, which can be avoided only by deliveries in kind.

24. Goodness is not the same as utility. For a good treatment of this question, see Arthur N. Prior, *Logic and the Basis of Ethics* (Oxford, 1949).

25. *L'esprit des Lois,* Book XXIII, Chap. 29.

26. The *Notebooks* of this great man do not suggest that compassion figured prominently among his many amiable qualities.

27. The Planning Commission of India is forced to acknowledge this, for all the great social concern by which its work is inspired.

28. I have discussed this subject in a paper called "Order versus Organization," published in *On Freedom and Free Enterprise,* ed. Mary Sennholz (Princeton, N.J.: Van Nostrand, 1956).

29. See, for example, George A. Miller, "The Magical Number Seven, Plus or Minus Two: Some Limits on Our Capacity for Processing Information," *The Psychological Review,* LIII:2 (March 1956).

20

The Surmising Forum

It would be naïve to think that over-all progress automatically leads to progress in our knowledge of the future. On the contrary, the future state of society would be perfectly known only in a perfectly static society—a society whose structure would always be identical and whose "Map of the Present" would remain valid for all time! All the traits of such a society at any future time could be foreknown. But as soon as a society is in movement, its familiar traits are perishable: they disappear, some more rapidly than others—though we cannot date their disappearance in advance—while new traits appear—traits not "given" beforehand to our minds. To say the movement is accelerating is to say that the length of time for which our Map of the Present remains more or less valid grows shorter. Thus our knowledge of the future is inversely proportional to the rate of progress.

So that this may be understood more readily, let us consider a specific example: a father is thinking about the career of his thirteen-year-old son, which will extend at least as far as the year 2010. For this father, the career of his son is a path plotted on a map which will undergo successive deformations: it is a journey into increasingly unknown territory. The father probably assumes that the landscape will be more pleasant and its climate more beneficent than on his own journey, but this over-all optimism does not satisfy his psychological need to see something of what is to be, nor his very practical need to know for what—and therefore, how—he is to equip his son. And this individual concern of the father is the same as the collective concern of educators. The nonsatisfaction of this need to see from a distance is possibly a source of that anxiety which, as we saw, paradoxically coexists with an increasing number of promises about the future.

Now let us consider public decisions. Suppose change is accelerating: that is to say, an increasing number of new problems arises in each unit of time (a year or a legislative session), and questions calling for decisions are exerting increasing pressure on the responsible men. It seems natural and even reasonable in such a case to take the questions in order of urgency—but the results show that this is a vicious practice. No problem is put on the agenda until it is a "burning" issue, when things are at such a pass that our hand is forced. No longer is any choice possible between different determining acts designed to shape a still-flexible situation. There is only one possible response, only one way out of the problem hemming us in. The powers that happen to be submit to this necessity, and will justify themselves after the event by saying they had no choice to decide otherwise. What is actually true is that they *no longer* had any choice, which is something quite different: for if they cannot be blamed for a decision that was in fact inevitable, they can hardly escape censure for letting the situation go until they had no freedom to choose. The proof of improvidence lies in falling under the empire of necessity. The means of avoiding this lies in acquainting oneself with emerging situations while they can still be molded, before they have become imperatively compelling. In other words, without forecasting, there is effectively no freedom of decision.

Thus the decision-makers must look to forecasters for help. It can be wagered that every center of important decisions will eventually have its special staff of forecasters. But if the work of each special staff is confidential for its head, the decision-makers will have information about the future that the public does not. The decision-makers—demanding, as always, blind confidence in their decisions—will be able to gain it the more readily by assuring the public that they have consulted the augurs and taken the auspices. In so doing they would be resurrecting a very ancient political artifice in a modern guise.

It is so very easy to pretend that a certain decision is dictated by a valid forecast as long as this forecast is kept secret, so that public opinion can neither criticize the forecast, nor consider whether the decision is appropriate to the forecast. A forecast used for decisions that are "public" (in the sense of "governmental") must be "public" (in the sense of "publicly expounded"). In this way alone will the intellectual procedure of forming reasoned opinions about the future not be given as a "magic" operation.

Hence, a "surmising forum" is required where "advanced" (or "forward-looking") opinions about what may be and about what can be done will be put forward. And since the passage of time brings new situations and sows new seeds, clearly this forum must be in continuous operation. It is not a matter of foreseeing the future once and for all, but of discussing the future continuously. The surmising forum must be thought of as a true institution, to which experts from very different fields will bring special forecasts so that they may be combined into more general forecasts.

A Task of the Social Sciences

All this has been repeated here to ensure that the work of forecasting may be clearly seen as a necessary response to a growing demand for forecasts. The reason why we give forecasts is not that we know how to predict: decision-makers mislead the public if they suggest to it, or even so much as allow it to think, that this is so. We do not make forecasts out of presumption, but because we recognize that they are a necessity of modern society. And for my part, I would willingly say that forecasting would be an absurd enterprise were it not inevitable. We have to make wagers about the future; we have no choice in the matter.

We are forever making forecasts—with scanty data, no awareness of method, no criticism, and no cooperation. It is urgent that we make this natural and individual activity into a cooperative and organic endeavor, subject to greater exigencies of intellectual rigor.

Who will fulfill this social function? It is naturally incumbent on those whose object of study is society, or better still man in society. They have been dispersed into the different disciplines referred to, in turn, as the "moral sciences," "social sciences," or "sciences of man." I will not bother to describe the present separation of the disciplines, which is a result of the historical circumstances in which each arose. Instead I wish to emphasize that the common task of forecasting will cause them to converge again. None of these human disciplines, each fixed on one aspect of human behavior and relations, can make forecasts in its field without drawing support from the other disciplines. As data are compiled and methods compared, each discipline will undergo an internal transformation arising from the new orientation toward forecasting. In each, research capable of shedding light on the dynamics of change will be of primary importance, and we shall see fewer talents devoted to pure erudition (that which cannot conceivably affect our decisions).[1] Inspired by social utility, this conversion has already gone a long way in economics, enhancing the status of this science and contributing a great deal to its growth. This same conversion will bear identical fruit in all of the human sciences.

Soon men will wonder that growth in the "arts of advice" should have been so slow in following the vast expansion in means (technology). No doubt this lag will be rectified during what is left of the century.

How urgent it is for the moral sciences to engage in forecasting is seen more clearly if one considers that otherwise the social need in this area will be satisfied by an extension of technology; that is to say, a way of seeing developed for "objects" will be extended to "subjects," who, it will be thought, are to be manipulated in the same way as things.[2]

Thus an immense task lies before the sciences of man: and it would be quite unrealistic to think that we are well equipped for it.[3] In this book I have stressed the natural disposition of our mind to think the future described the naïve modes of forethought, and showed on how fragile a foundation they rest. Instead of a "Handbook for the Perfect Forecaster" I have written a refutation of the facile optimism[4] we find in men who think of progress as a gradual journey toward a given "destination." Were this the nature of progress, the terminus, "Future" seen from very far by the wise men, would reveal its features more and more clearly in the course of our journey. This way of thinking, denounced by Raymond Aron and Karl Popper, is patently contradictory to experience; as we travel through time we see new principles of change appearing, some of them expected, most of them utterly unexpected. And our society seems to be adding to its stock of principles of change, "charging" itself with new possibilities.[5] In short, an attempt to predict approaching stages by arguing back from a supposedly known endpoint is an intellectual short-cut with disastrous results.

The Technological Source

Everybody agrees that the great acceleration of change is a result of technological progress.

The most striking difference between our civilization and past civilizations is the tremendous increase in physical mobility of men, objects, and messages, with respect to both mass and speed. It is tempting to look at this multiplication of the quantity of movement as a *heating* of the receptacle "earth" (particularly as this change requires a very big input of energy).[6] This metaphor immediately suggests a diminishing solidity of structures—a "liquefaction"—but we must not be carried away by this image, and should simply recognize that technical progress is the source of a multitude of structural changes. The most fundamental of these is without doubt the successive shrinking of the peasant world, which traditionally accounted for a large majority of the population; the obverse of this fact is urban congestion, causing towns to burst out as cities and leading to the conurbations[7] of our century. Technical progress does not conserve the forms it engenders; from being scattered about in fields, workers were gathered together in vast iron-and-glass workshops, only to be piled high in office buildings. The operation of any machine is uniform—whether it be a "power machine" used in a factory or an "intelligence machine" of the kind now finding application in office work—and this suggests that men will be successively pushed out of successively routinized jobs, jobs made fit for the machine, but not, as some fear, into unemployment, rather toward jobs fit for men, that is, into jobs where their natural versatility can be utilized, and also that jobs will become increasingly diverse[8] and their over-all structure increasingly mobile.

Nobody will deny the influence of technical progress on education. The example of the United States, where unemployment is inversely proportional to education,[9] tells us that the job structure is undergoing a continuous transformation in the direction of a growing need for highly trained minds and a decreasing need for inadequately trained minds. However unfortunate the immediate effects of this tendency, they show that those who predicted machines would leave the majority of mankind with tasks hardly better than a beast's were far too pessimistic. On the contrary, technical progress requires the development of every man's intellectual faculties. And to say it once again: this development must take place for the sake of greater production, but, besides, it ought to take place for the better use of leisure.

It is clear that the inequality of living conditions is being worn down by the effects of technical progress. Even if the incomes structure should remain the same while the average rises,[10] this rise will of itself iron out the essential inequality: the vital difference between $25 a month and $250 a month is far greater than between $250 a month and $2,500 a month. Once men begin to satisfy their less elementary needs, the difference between their means of satisfying them is less harshly felt. If one man can afford only a Volkswagen while another can buy a Rolls-Royce, we are far less shocked at the disparity than if one cannot afford a coat when another has whole closets filled with coats. The mere fact of progress entails a decrease in material inequality (quite apart from any political measures for reducing inequality, which lie outside the present discussion), but it seems the same cannot be said for the inequality of status.

All socialist thinkers whose ideas were formed during the first half of the nineteenth century were struck by the brutal contrast between owner-employers and salaried proletariat: the "hands" were in the power of a "master." Since that time the proprietary boss has disappeared into anonymity, but companies as they grow larger are characterized by a more and more exalted pyramid of command. It makes no difference whether the company is in private or public ownership: the number of hierarchical levels is a function of the size of the organization, and the social distance between two men is a function of the number of levels between them. For a population integrated to an increasing extent into large organizations, it is natural that the echeloning of ranks should be reflected in society. Besides, attitudes fostered among men with powers of decision must be very different from those fostered among men with no such powers.

It is surely necessary for technical progress that no child's capability should fail to be utilized because of his parents' poverty. Thus technical progress leads toward democracy. It is quite possible that the interests of society and the concern for equality will conspire so that students shall receive a salary after reaching a certain stage in their education, and shall continue to do so as long as they can benefit from further education. This will ensure that everyone receives as much education as he can benefit from, and will lead in each age group to a hierarchy corresponding to the organizational pyramid. But this is the road to meritocracy rather than equality.[11]

Will this model inspired by Mandarin China[12] be taken to an extreme? We may think this will not be so, that there will be a place for qualities unsuited to academic consecration.

The Exploration of Technological Sources

I have spoken about some of the actual or currently accepted consequences of technological progress. Volumes could be, and indeed are increasingly, written on the subject. The most immediate, obvious task of the forecaster in the social sciences is to speculate about the consequences of technological progress: this is very necessary, but shortly I shall indicate how *insufficient* this would be. For the present I will confine myself to the necessity of the task, discussing where the forecaster can latch onto technology.

Let us consider two extreme cases. If the horizon of the forecast is so near that the technological input consists entirely of applications of already existing techniques, a forecaster making a quantitative estimate of economic growth is satisfied with supposing that the technological input will suffice to ensure that capital investments will have the required efficiency.[13] If, on the contrary, the horizon is very remote, the forecaster, concerning himself now with qualitative changes, will want to look at the "scientific perspective."

The "scientific perspective" is a self-prediction from the City of Science[14] indicating what scientific innovations will be scattered onto the social field, and when (dates can be given only with an error of several years). Thanks to this prediction, sociologists can base their speculations on "anticipated data." The self-predictions of science quite naturally consist of promises that solutions will be found for problems on which the work of different researchers is converging: for instance, the self-predictions can tell us that birth control by means of pills is virtually a fact, and that before the end of the century it will be possible to delay the onset of senility. These two predictions are of striking importance. In connection with the former, it is worth noting that in the poor countries of Africa and Asia there are nearly twice as many children per adult as in European countries,[15] and that this growth of population is a barrier to raising the standard of life. The second prediction suggests that the idea of retirement at sixty may not apply to the rising generation.

Occasionally, the scientific perspective informs us of a new fact associated with manifold consequences. The most fascinating I have heard of is the storage of solar energy on plastic films by means of a chemical transformation which absorbs energy and can later be reversed so that energy is emitted. This way of storing energy is similar to that used by plants, and the source of energy is inexhaustible, whereas other energy sources such as coal, oil, and uranium are not. But the most important point is, I think, that this technique would place us upon a more benign path than we have hitherto followed. Our civilization was able to take a great leap forward only because of a tremendous increase in the output of energy. But this energy is obtained by destroying naturally synthesized products—which are particularly elaborate in the case of oil and would be better used as a base for yet more complicated syntheses. In short, we have set about procuring energy much as soldiers in winter might obtain heat by burning a wooden house. And since there is always some kinship between our ways of thinking in different fields, we are subconsciously corrupted by this technique of violent demolition. If we could begin to obtain energy by imitating the gentle, constructive methods of plants, I am convinced that the good effects would radiate into other fields.

It would of course be logically absurd to expect the scientific perspective to inform us of unforeseen discoveries! It did not, for instance, announce the discovery of X rays. But more than that: it cannot tell us what paths research will follow. The physicist Gerald Holton has pointed out, in a very interesting article,[16] that science does not advance by continuing ever further in a direction which has already proved fruitful. The tree of science does not grow by sending out new shoots from the same branch—but by a new branch shooting out. Or think of this image: when a large catch of fish is obtained in a certain pond, fishermen will flock to it and catch many more fish; but though the fishing will continue good for a while, the catches will grow smaller, and it is in another pond, which nobody has thought of yet, that a new large catch will be made.

Finally, it must be observed that the technological innovations with the greatest social consequences will not necessarily arise from advances at the frontiers of science. It is arguable that the technical factor with the greatest effect on society has been the automobile. Yet the development of the automobile did not depend on any major progress in the upper reaches of science: and this remark applies even to the gasoline engine.

The *Grande Encyclopédie*,[17] published at the beginning of the century under the supervision of eminent men of science, has this to say under the entry "Motor": "The first engine burning gasoline was built by Lenoir in 1863. His automobile was driven by internal combustion. . . ." But this cannot have been regarded as a great scientific discovery, for the biographical entry of twenty lines devoted to Lenoir speaks of him as "a French inventor of Belgian origin" who, on arriving in France in 1838, had "no resources, no education, and no trade" and started out as a "garçon de café." It goes on to list various of his inventions, but does not so much as mention the automobile engine!

It is a safe bet that a "scientific perspective" drawn up soon before or after Lenoir's invention would not have mentioned the automobile. At that time there undoubtedly was a greater separation between scientists and inventors than nowadays, but—at a date closer to us—is it likely that a scientific perspective would have mentioned household appliances? And why should it have done so, since these goods did not put any new principles to use.

The popular confusion between science and technology has certain important social advantages, as was wittily noted by Abraham Moles. Since public opinion rightly hungers for technical progress, it is prone to encourage scientists—men devoting themselves to pure research. To be sure, an effort is being made to tie scientists to technological objectives (as for instance in the distressing field of armaments), while on the other hand the likelihood that empirical workers will make practical inventions is growing smaller. The once loose connection between progress in science and progress in technology may become close, but in social forecasting— the subject concerning us here—each of them matters to us separately and for quite different reasons: the progress of science because it is reflected strongly even if crudely in our current ideas (about such things as the size of the universe or the age of our planet), and the progress of technology because it introduces new material facts.

It takes time for conceptions reigning among scientists to become popular. If, therefore, we acquaint ourselves with the present state of science, we obtain quite a large breathing space for forecasting. It also takes time for a technological innovation to be diffused, and therefore a knowledge of innovations now in the operational stage (as for example the hovercraft) also gives forecasters a certain breathing space.

This simplifies the social scientists' necessary task of taking into account scientific and technological contributions. Their work will be increasingly facilitated by journals of scientific and technological information, whose level must be geared to their readers. The level will be so much the higher if social scientists can form a large audience with a good scientific education.

Should Forecasts Be Based on Technological Sources Alone?

Scientific and technological progress has so great an influence on our society that we must speculate about its possible social consequences, looking at progress as many individual movements, rather than as one overall movement.[18] But what I want to discuss here is whether forecasting in the social sciences should be concentrated on this object to the exclusion of all others.

By concentrating in this way, we can all consider the same flux of causes, which is, in some manner, "given" to us by outside informants. We can each use our own knowledge about a given country or environment in order to forecast different effects, and if we keep each other informed of the results, we can correct our first estimate of a given effect by considering the repercussion of all the other predicted effects on it. When we prognosticate the effects of such and such a cause in such and such an environment, we can consider the effects its introduction led to in some other country—provided we take into account the difference in environment.[19]

The advantages of concentration on this object are striking, as is borne out by the tendency of all of us who are engaged in forecasting to concern ourselves with this one question.

But rather than stress the advantages, I wish to show that we have no right to so confine ourselves. Take this very simple example—the life of a German family since 1913. Would we say that what has principally affected it are changes resulting from technological progress? Surely it was far more affected by World War I, the ensuing inflation, the Great Depression, the advent of Hitler, World War II, the division of the country, and a protracted crisis of conscience. This is an extreme case, but for most European countries, starting with France, it is also true that what has affected them most is not technology.

"Quite so. But you are taking a time of great tragedy." Very well. I will pass from the tragic to the trivial—from, say, Wagner, to Noel Coward. The way of life of the middle classes has been fundamentally altered in a brief space by the disappearance of servants. This fact is by now so accepted that we have ceased to wonder at it, until we travel to the underdeveloped countries, where suddenly we are struck by the number of servants found even in families living in modest circumstances. We then remember that throughout history, in all societies, there were servants. Alexandre Dumas is there to remind us that D'Artagnan—scamp that he was—had his own manservant. From the point of view of social equality, their disappearance is a major change. Even the smallest middle-class house once had two entrances, corresponding to the fundamental division of society. All this has vanished, and the wiping out of the distinction between "masters" and "servants" is one of the greatest changes imaginable. But is this a result of technological progress? Not at all. How could equipment designed to save manpower in industry and agriculture cause a shortage of household servants! The change was produced by a deliberate policy of full employment, which policy of itself generated more social change than all the social reforms together. But then if full employment does not prevail, will the jobless go back to being servants? Nothing of the sort is observed in the United States: men do not want that kind of work. This is a new psychological attitude, which exists thanks to political measures that give people the alternative of receiving unemployment benefits. Hence, this very important social phenomenon of everyday life owes nothing to technological progress; it is a result of political economy, psychological evolution, and social policy. If a social forecaster in 1913 had been presented with the "datum" of all the technological evolution to take place in the ensuing half century, he never would have inferred from it the disappearance of servants.

Technology Provides Opportunities for Change

However great the influence of technological progress, we grossly exaggerate its role if we believe that changes associated with it are caused by it alone and can therefore be foreseen from it alone. It is true that the form of messages has become more succinct due to the influence of telegrams, and that this may have affected style more generally. But the content of the messages does not depend on the instrument. While radio and television provide unheard-of possibilities for the dissemination of sounds, words, and images, the composition of the programs is not determined by the instrument, but chiefly by the dispositions of the public, to which the men generally responsible for the broadcasts adjust as best they can. If the instrument is used at the transmitting end by certain people who want to find the widest possible audience for certain messages, they will take care to envelop them in programs capable of drawing such an audience. Radio and television have raised singers as well as athletes to the top rank of social prestige, but how can this upheaval be attributed to the new instruments alone when amphitheaters led to a similar result in Rome and Byzantium? The instrument has simply given form to a latent social possibility; and we may note with satisfaction the contrast between popular taste in our day and the brutal and cruel tastes of the Romans. Nobody will deny that the instrument can be used for educational uses, but the problem of effective use is an intellectual and psychological question which is for the most part independent of the medium.

A technological innovation has necessary effects, but it does not follow that all the effects for which it provides an opportunity have the innovation as a unique and profound cause. Television does definitely tend to "personalize" politics. The advantage it gives to the personality in power does not, however, depend on the nature of television, but on the way in which the medium is used: it is well known that on television Vice-President Nixon came off much worse than his challenger John F. Kennedy. And as to the phenomenon itself—the personalization of politics—is this a new fact resulting from a new instrument, or an old fact which the instrument has revived? When Thucydides describes a political conflict in Athens, it is a true duel between personalities, as for instance between Alcibiades and Nicias. During my youth in France, politics took the form of a duel between personalities within each constituency—a unit in which the electorate was of roughly the same size as the body of citizens in Athens. At the national level, politics were far less personal, and it was considered important to keep them that way. "Beware of individuals," Henri Brisson used to say. Since then the situation has been altered conspicuously, but we may ask whether radio and television were the cause of this change. I would prefer to say that radio and television provided a way of activating a latent disposition.

Lest we attribute too much to radio and television, let us note that the

increased prominence of the individual leader was quite definitely foretold by Lord Bryce in 1921, and in even stronger terms by Gabriel Tarde
in 1899:

> We can predict with complete assurance that we shall see in the future
> personifications of authority and power, such that these new figures will
> cast into the shadow the chief despots of the past, a Caesar, a Louis XIV,
> a Napoleon. Our society is capable of building up prestige more pro-
> nounced if not as durable as that of past ages, and when a famous statesman
> will be uplifted by such prestige, it will be open to him to fulfill political
> and indeed social programs beyond even the boldness of a Bismarck.[20]

In short, some of the changes accompanying technological progress are
a necessary and direct result of it, but many others are fundamentally
distinct principles, which owe to it nothing more than their activation.
Still other changes have no connection at all with technological progress:
how could technological effects explain the changes in the political map
of our planet in the course of this century?

Hence, the forecaster must regard technological change as only one of
several factors of change. This answer seems evident as soon as we ask
what is the role of technological progress. "Why then have you taken
so many pains to expound a truism?" My answer to this is that the
truism is seen only when the question is asked. Technological progress
is a very new principle of change, or at any rate has only recently become
so important a principle of change—and it is a natural and pleasant
inclination that leads a forecaster of reasonable and philanthropic tem-
perament to concentrate on changes arising from optimal utilization of
this progress. While his concentration on such changes may start out
as a matter of preference, it can become exclusive without for that reason
becoming illegitimate: there is a great deal of merit in devoting one's
attention to what is, in some sense, an "optimal" line of the future.[21] For
my part, I think it is a healthy exercise for those who do it, and may
possibly have good effects on public opinion. But this exercise is a "project" rather than a "forecast": the mind attaches itself to one "elected"
blade of the fan of may-be's, without considering what is likely to be.

A healthy foresight requires that we consider the most probable combinations of the different orders of causes. We can do this yet keep our
normative intention—we are simply postponing it. We start by looking
where we are likely to go, and this entitles us to look for ways of modi-

fying our path. The task of "compounding" different causes is of great difficulty, and so we are encouraged to look for methods capable of making good our feeble argumentation.

Simulation

Even in the physical sciences, where we are concerned with "legal objects" (see Chapter 10), the number of combinations at times lies beyond the possibilities of calculation. In such a case it is worthwhile to reproduce in miniature the system whose evolution we wish to foresee.

Dennis Gabor has discussed an old and very interesting example of simulation:

> Around 1910 a silt bar about seven miles wide was building up across the entrance to the Rangoon River, the entrance to the port of Rangoon. By 1931 the depth was only 12 feet, and it was still decreasing. The Commissioners of the Port of Rangoon, justifiably worried, approached the great civil engineer Sir Alexander Gibb. He built a model of the river and of the gulf which measured 40 feet by 60 feet on a scale of one inch to 16 feet, reproducing the state of the river and sea bed as it was in 1875. Plungers reproduced the tidal movements, with such a speed that one year was represented by 15 hours' operation of the model. By the time the model had caught up with year 1932 the conditions proved sufficiently similar to the actual ones to encourage predictive runs up to the year 1982. On the basis of these, in 1935, Alexander Gibb gave the advice to do *nothing*. The growth of the silt bar was about to cease around 1937, and thereafter it would disappear as spontaneously as it had come. The port authorities (probably after some scratching of heads) accepted the advice, and they were right: the model has correctly predicted the future to this day![22]

The example discussed by Gabor[23] is very instructive. For the "model"[24] to be of practical value, its organic structure had to simulate reality, while it was clearly unnecessary for its appearance to do so. In terms of the purpose of the model, it made no difference whether the engineer's children could float little boats on the model of the port, or whether the model was so abstract as to be solvable by an electronic computer—a method used for the economic system and, in a few rare cases, the social system. We may wonder whether the failures, or "disconveniences," of computer models are simply to be expected in a stage when we are still groping, or whether they have some more profound cause: it is worth noting, in this connection, that the systems which are simulated are open,[25] and that in the models human behavior is represented by rigid behavior equations, whose only justification lies in statistical observations. An attempt to get away from this difficulty has been made in the RAND operational games, the underlying idea of which is that men should be represented by men.

There is a profound affinity between the idea of an open system—a system having a fan of possible futures rather than a predictable line of the future—and the idea of having this future "played" by men who decide each of their moves. Since the system is open, different games starting from the same initial data will unfold in different ways: thus none of the games will serve as a "prediction" of the actual course of the system, but—to the extent that the games are played under proper conditions—each of them is a journey in the field of present possibilities. Derived from the classical war game and first applied to a political cold-war game, this technique[26] also lends itself to more pleasant uses. Olaf Helmer believes that the planners of a developing country could discover certain future tensions by setting up a game with players assigned to each sector of the economy.[27] For my part, I can more readily conceive of a game in which the different social and professional groups and initiating institutions would be represented by qualified players. By acting out future social conflicts "for a laugh," perhaps men could manage to avoid them altogether or to tone them down.

The great drawback of this suggestion is that it would hardly be taken seriously. One can hear the cackles of derision with which *Le Canard Enchaîné* would greet any attempt by the members of the Conseil Économique et Social to spend a month or so acting out the working of the five-year plan. Any exercise entrusted to an electronic computer would be regarded as scientific, but an exercise entrusted to prominent men would be thought damaging to their prestige and this psychological datum must be taken into account. However, a game of simulation by men would probably win acceptance as an exercise for students.

It may seem paradoxical that simulation by human agents should be revived at a time when we are in possession of that extraordinary instrument for simulation—the electronic computer. Clearly, the one cannot rival the other: it takes about as many weeks for men to play a game as a computer takes minutes to complete its calculations. But the two are complementary. In simulation with a computer, behaviors are assumed; in simulation by human agents, the players discover their own reactions to situations. For the players this serves as a training, while an observer has an opportunity to vary the hypotheses about behavior he uses in programming the computer. Because of the difficulty of making calculations before computers were developed, hypotheses underwent a rigorous process of selection, whereas nowadays the astonishing instruments at our disposal serve to encourage us to try out a large number of various hypotheses. In looking for a model that accounted for the facts, we once thought ourselves lucky if we could find a single one, whereas now we regard a model as merely one of a "population" of models all capable of accounting for the facts. I do not wish to dwell on this, and shall not consider the question of whether our traditional preference for the simplest explanatory model should be maintained now that we have ways of testing complex models, confining myself to this one remark: the famous assertion that nature is simple is perhaps anthropocentric. That, however, is not my subject. It is quite possible that in models used for forecasting, haphazard shocks can set off different courses of things, depending on whether a shock attains this or that element of the system. Think for instance of shocks hitting chromosomes at different places! But I will now stop, for these questions are too difficult.

Simulation and Forms

Instead I wish to emphasize how useful simulation is in adding to our understanding of forms, and particularly of their dynamics. The subject is vast, and I must confine myself to indicating three questions, or classes of questions, that are tractable to simulation.

1. *The problem of operational form* or, in other words, of efficient organization. Suppose an organization has a well-defined task in some given context. By hypothesis, this organization is liable to one and only one criterion of efficiency: its value is purely instrumental. The organization is evaluated according to whether the sequence of results it obtains or will obtain in the course of time seems better or worse in relation to some unchallenged measure. The organization is designed to provide an optimal sequence of results in the context of given constraints, and therefore, in this respect, the organization should be optimal. The internal

structure best suited to its purpose must be found: this is a problem concerning the division of labor, the distribution of functions, the setting up of lines of communication, and the assignment of responsibility for decisions. This problem faces industrial firms,[28] and any public service or department of state with a sufficiently defined task. Marshak has suggested a useful approach to the formulation of this problem, which arises at all levels.[29] Simulation techniques can be helpful here because the problem is a matter of operational research applied to structures. It is worth noting that even the simplest statement of the problem, particularly for administrative structures, helps to show at what point in the history of the organization its purpose may have been forgotten, and modifications made under the influence of quite different considerations. Thus we are led into asking, whether, in an organization justifying itself by its results, senescence sets in when modifications are made without regard to efficiency.

2. *The problem of a preferred form* or, in other words, of the likely fate of an imposed form. We are not concerned here with choosing a form: it has already been chosen. Say, my boss wants it, or else I have seen it used in some other country, and find that it fits my principles or suits my feelings. But in whatever way it has been chosen, the essential fact is that this form is desired. Very well. But once it is instituted, will it be conserved or will it degenerate? Is it stable or not? If unstable, what are the chances of conserving it? And if it appears likely to degenerate, what are the forms into which it will be debased—forms far less desirable than some rustic form that could be instituted straight away? This is a fundamental problem when we are dealing with "willed" institutions. For example: will the political map of Europe set up at the Paris Conference in 1919 be a stable form? Or the British two-party system in the English-speaking countries of Africa? And what about self-rule?

The problem of a form's resistance to pressures and tensions has been known and discussed ever since men began to build houses. In our days, we cannot imagine any sort of construction without a great deal of scientific attention to the problem—and this is the domain where simulation most naturally suggests itself as a technique. It seems absurd that the problem should be ignored when it comes to institutional structures. This gross omission, which counts few exceptions, can be explained only by a psychological disposition: men ardently desiring a particular form refuse to consider its vulnerability. And not only that: the champions and advocates of a form treat whomsoever denounces its frailty as an enemy; they refuse to allow that he may have a liking for the form while having some doubts about its vitality. If he has displayed any signs of affection for the form, his estimate of its poor chances of success is treated as a betrayal. This is a very big obstacle to the progress of the political sciences in general, and of forecasting in particular. These psychological phenomena are, I think, the only possible explanation of our failure to apply simulation techniques to the future history of desired forms. Yet sooner or later we shall have to come to it.

3. *The problem of an observed form* or, in other words, of the processes accounting for observed distributions. Any collection whose members exhibit a certain measurable characteristic, but exhibit it in various degrees, can be distributed into classes according to the intensity of the characteristic. The simplest way of ordering the individual cases is to array them according to the degree of deviation from the average value of the characteristic for the collection as a whole. It is significant that we specially favor those distributions in nature and society that have the same shape as the distribution of human measurements of the value of some given quantity; we call such distributions "normal," thus revealing that we regard the failures of our human efforts to measure a quantity as somehow identical with the failures of "nature," which we assume actually "intended" to assign the same quality in the same degree to each individual in the collection but met with no more success in this than we ourselves in obtaining identical measurements of a quantity which in fact has one definite value. Yet there are many domains where we regularly find distributions which are not "normal." As early as 1879, Galton spoke of the lognormal distribution, and said that we should expect to find it in many domains.[30] In 1897, Pareto announced that a special distribution—known to us as "Paretian"—could be observed,[31] and much more recently, Gerald Zipf has assembled an extraordinary collection of Paretian distributions from very different fields. Zipf's daring and blunders were an obstacle to the recognition of his findings,[32] but his line of investigation has been taken up again, in a far more rigorous manner, by Benoît Mandelbrot.[33] A recent article by Madame Petruszewicz[34] has some important things to say about the mode of formation of a Paretian distribution. Simulation techniques using electronic computers have an obvious role to play here, because they enable us to determine what distributions are produced by different processes.[35] Un-

derstanding how the observed distributions are formed will obviously be of major utility. Once we are possessed of this knowledge, we shall no longer be surprised at finding this or that distribution, and—to borrow the language of Comte—we shall know whether a configuration is "unmodifiable," or whether, on the contrary, we can change it—particularly if we find it shocking to our moral sense—by injecting exogenous causes so that the course of the process may be altered. In situations that can be so modified, we find once again the duality of process and action that was discussed at length in this book. An understanding of the processes accounting for the observable forms is, it seems, an essential "common ground" of knowledge for all who are engaged in forecasting.

NOTES

1. A forecast, not a condemnation!

2. A danger indicated by C. S. Lewis in *The Abolition of Man* (London: Oxford University Press, 1946).

3. As Michel Massenet has clearly shown, the same causes that make forecasting more necessary also make it more difficult. ("Introduction à une sociologie de la prévision," *Futuribles*, No. 60 [June 20, 1963].)

4. For an attack on misguided optimism, see Jean Meynaud, "A propos des spéculations sur l'Avenir," *Revue Française de Science Politique* XIII: 3 (September 1963).

5. A major aspect of this growing wealth is neatly summed up in Robert Oppenheimer's famous saying: "Nine tenths of mankind's scientists are now alive."

6. It would be interesting to quantify the amount of energy spent on movement.

7. This term was introduced at the beginning of the century by Patrick Geddes, whose views are set forth in *Cities in Evolution* (London: Williams and Norgate, 1915).

8. Ronald Brech thinks this will lead to a growth in the number of small trade unions, particularly in the professions. (*Britain 1984, Unilever's Forecast, an Experiment in the Economic History of the Future* [London: Darton, Longman, and Todd, 1963].)

9. Figures are given in my "Conjoncture américaine," *Bulletin SEDEIS* (January 1, 1964).

10. I mean of course the distribution of incomes *before* tax, for I am speaking here about the effects of technical progress independently of redistributive politi-

cal measures. The alteration of the incomes structure due to economic progress alone is, it seems, a significant but small effect. Opinions are divided over this important subject.

11. The term "meritocracy" was coined by Michael Young in his very suggestive book, *The Rise of the Meritocracy* (London, 1958; Penguin edition, 1962).

12. Cournot, some fifty years ago, saw China as a model of what Europe would become.

13. In a society with stationary technological knowledge, the Gross National Product moves up along an S-shaped curve as the total capital investment is increased, and thus eventually reaches a maximum, corresponding to optimal equipment. All that remains to do is to maintain the equipment in good order. A nondecreasing efficiency of capital investment can be assumed only if technological innovations are introduced.

14. On the City of Science, see Abraham Moles, "La Cité scientifique en 1972," *Futuribles,* No. 41 (October 20, 1962).

15. See *The Future Growth of World Population* (New York: United Nations, 1958), Table 20.

16. Gerald Holton, "Scientific Research and Scholarship: Notes Toward the Design of Proper Scales," *Daedalus* (*Proceedings of the American Academy of Arts and Sciences*), XCI:91 (Spring 1962).

17. In my opinion, it is a model of its kind. It is still the most convenient to consult, for it is put together in the form of a dictionary, and it contains an extraordinary wealth of information.

18. According to Daniel Bell, certain American sociologists believe progress should be treated as a global factor. (See Bell's valuable analysis of forecasting in social science, "Douze modes de prévision en science sociale," *Futuribles,* No 64 [September 20, 1963].)

19. This is something quite different from treating different countries as though they were all undergoing the same evolution, with greater or smaller lags (the "railway postulate" discussed in Chapter 8). It is perfectly legitimate to adopt some criterion for measurement (such as the energy consumption per head of population) and then to determine the "gaps" separating different societies from the society "in the lead." But it is, I think, indefensible to regard the societies we have thus spaced on a graduated scale as embryos of the same species at different stages of growth, as though each society were destined to pass through the same forms as the societies lying ahead of it. Although certain phenomena lend substance to this view, they are more often the result of imitation than of intussuception. Besides, even a cursory examination shows that certain traits of the most advanced society appear in many other societies that have not yet reached the corresponding position on the graduated scale.

20. The work of Lord Bryce referred to is *Modern Democracies* (London: Macmillan, 1921). The quotation is from Gabriel Tarde, *Les Transformations du pouvoir* (Paris: Alcan, 1899), p. 219.

21. What makes it "optimal" depends on the "values" of the forecaster. But when the only values considered relate to the exploitation of technology, disagreements are confined to a relatively narrow field—or such at least is the impression I have gained from discussions.

22. Dennis Gabor, "Predicting Machines," published in the journal *Cambridge Opinion*, No. 27 (*Prediction*).

23. Gabor is, we may note, the author of *Inventing the Future* (New York: Alfred A. Knopf, 1961).

24. Concerning the meaning of "model," see May Brodbeck, "Models, Meanings, and Theories," in Dorothy Willner, ed., *Decisions, Values and Groups* (London and New York, 1960).

25. For a theoretical discussion, see Sidney Schoeffler, *The Failures of Economics* (Cambridge, Mass.: Harvard University Press, 1955).

26. The history of this technique was discussed by Herbert Goldhamer and Hans Speier in "Some Observations on Political Gaming," *World Politics*, XII:1 (October 1959), in which an account is given of four games played at the RAND Corporation, each lasting approximately one month and involving a dozen or more players.

27. Olaf Helmer and E. S. Quade, *An Approach to the Study of a Developing Economy by Operational Gaming* (RAND Corporation, March 1963).

28. See, for example, Alfred D. Chandler, Jr., *Strategy and Structures, Chapters in the History of the Industrial Enterprise* (Cambridge, Mass.: Harvard University Press, 1962).

29. Jacob Marshak, *Efficient and Viable Organization Forms and Theory of an Efficient Several-Person Firm*, Cowles Foundation Paper No. 150 (New Haven: Yale University, 1960). It would take too much space to give references to all the relevant writings of this author, who is now director of research at the Western Management Science Institute of the University of California at Los Angeles.

30. See J. Aitchison and J. A. Brown, *The Lognormal Distribution with Special Reference to Its Use in Economics* (New York: Cambridge University Press, 1957), and J. H. Gaddum, "Lognormal Distributions," *Nature* (October 20, 1945), p. 463 *ff.*

31. Vilfredo Pareto, *Cours d'économie politique* (Paris, 1897), II, pp. 304 *ff.*

32. Gerald Kingsley Zipf, *National Unity and Disunity* (Bloomington, Ind.: Indiana University Press, 1941), and, above all, *Human Behavior and the Law of Least Effort* (Cambridge, Mass.: Addison Wesley Press, 1949).

33. Benoît Mandelbrot, "New Methods in Statistical Economics," *The Journal of Political Economy*, LXXI:5 (October 1963). This article gives references to other writings by the same author.

34. M. Petruszewicz, "Loi de Pareto et processus Markhovien," *Mathématiques et Sciences Humaines*, No. 3 (April 1963). (This journal performs an important service.) Various models accounting for the distribution are discussed in P.

Thionnet, "Sur la distribution des revenus et les modèles qui s'y rapportent," *Études de Compatibilité Nationale* (Paris: Imprimerie Nationale, April 1960).

35. For an example of this technique, see Yujii Ijiri and H. A. Simon, "Business Firm Growth and Size," *The American Economic Review,* LIV:2 (1964), pp. 77–89.

Index